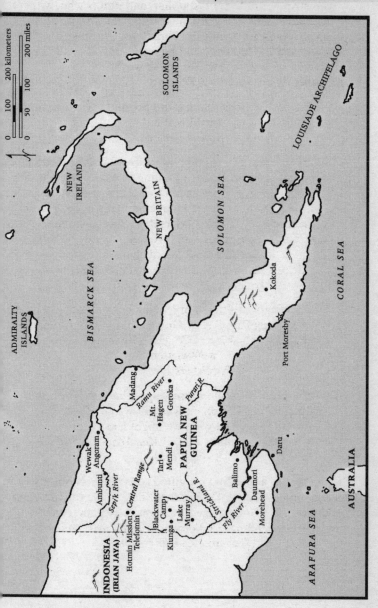

Kira Salak was born in Illinois, USA, in 1971. She has travelled extensively to countries with little or no tourist industry, and was the first person to successfully kayak solo 950km down the Niger River in Mali, from Sego to Timbuktu. Awarded a Writers at Work Fellowship and the AWP/Prague Fellowship award in non-fiction, her work has appeared in *Best New American Voices 2001*, *Best American Travel Writing 2002* and *2003*, *National Geographic Adventure* magazine and a host of literary travel journals. Kira Salak is currently pursuing a PhD in English Literature while she plans her next trip to Mongolia. *Four Corners* is her first book.

Acclaim for *Four Corners*:

'Imagine that you have read every travel book ever written and were then invited to a party with all the authors. Having just finished reading *Four Corners* I can tell you exactly what you'll be thinking when you walk into that room: "Which one is Kira Salak?" '
Brad Newsham, author of *Take Me With You*, shortlisted for WH Smith's Book Award (Travel Writing) 2003

'Kira Salak has written a travel book that transcends the genre. Yes, she has wild adventures, and goes to places that many seasoned war reporters would never dare to go, but she has crafted more than this, a subtle meditation on the escapist nature of "exotic" travel itself. It is, like all the best travel narratives, a resonant interior journey, and offers wisdom for our times'
Edward Marriott, author of *The Lost Tribe*

'Kira Salak brings to us the fresh air that the dark, misunderstood, dripping forests of New Guinea have been lacking from travellers. This is the real thing – not a tale of a tropical island bedevilled by cannibals and fanatical snakes, all inhabiting a mythical Land That Time Forgot, but a passionate head-to-head encounter with her bare hands. Salak undergoes her quest with gusto, and armed with open eyes. What she finds is a steaming jungle collage of eternally hopeful missionaries, forlorn rebel fighters who take on guns

FOUR CORNERS

A Journey into the Heart of Papua New Guinea

Kira Salak

BANTAM BOOKS

LONDON · NEW YORK · TORONTO · SYDNEY · AUCKLAND

FOUR CORNERS
A BANTAM BOOK: 0 553 81550 4

First publication in Great Britain
Originally published in the United States by Counterpoint,
a member of the Perseus Books Group

PRINTING HISTORY
Bantam edition published 2003

1 3 5 7 9 10 8 6 4 2

The author wishes to thank the editors and publishers of
National Geographic Adenture, *Quarterly West* and *Grand Tour: The
Journal of Travel Literature* for encouraging her work by publishing
early versions of some of this material.

Set in 11/12pt Times by
Kestrel Data, Exeter, Devon.

Bantam Books are published by Transworld Publishers,
61–63 Uxbridge Road, London W5 5SA,
a division of The Random House Group Ltd,
in Australia by Random House Australia (Pty) Ltd,
20 Alfred Street, Milsons Point, Sydney, NSW 2061, Australia,
in New Zealand by Random House New Zealand Ltd,
18 Poland Road, Glenfield, Auckland 10, New Zealand
and in South Africa by Random House (Pty) Ltd,
Endulini, 5a Jubilee Road, Parktown 2193, South Africa.

Printed and bound in Great Britain by
Clays Ltd, St Ives plc.

To I.C. – as promised

'The purpose and nature are never clearly revealed. Human behavior is a series of lunges, of which, it is sensed, the direction is inevitable.'

PATRICK WHITE

CONTENTS

Prelude: Four Corners   13
Prologue: July, 1992 – The Road to Tete,
  Mozambique   15

Part One

1 Where Do We Come From? What Are We?
     Where Are We Going?   49
2 Independently, Without Prior Arrangements   65
3 Salvation of the Lost and Sinful   75
4 Barbed Wire, Attack Dogs and Lessons in
     Emergency Response   88
5 Bush Mary   114
6 Damsel in Distress   152
7 The Silent War   179

Part Two

8   Long Way Too Much   233
9   Mozart and the Cockroaches   255
10 Hungarian Delights   274

11 Making Rain   288
12 Rafting the Sepik   311
13 Time Travel   337
14 Hands and Feet   358

Epilogue   370

Four Corners

I'm eleven years old. I'm in that single spot in the United States where I can be in New Mexico, Arizona, Colorado and Utah all at the same time. Why I might want to be, what possible meaning it could ever have, I don't know. But I stand on that brass plate in the middle of a desert off US Highway 160, and a phenomenon occurs. I'm in four places at once – but this is a serious business. Four places at once.

I can become superhuman.

The feeling doesn't last, and with disappointment I step back into New Mexico. The tourist behind me asks where I'm from, and my breath quickens. I stammer out Chicago, aware that my answer may lead to more questions, require more answers, and I am one of those children who is painfully, mortally shy. My mother waits at the end of the line for her turn to stand on the four corners, and I retreat to the desert. She has warned me not to do this, threatening rattlesnakes, tarantulas, scorpions, but all I know is the idea of being in motion. Never stopping. Never allowing the world to catch up.

My mother is yelling to me. I stop. The fear of all those desert creatures rushes back to me. The crunch of pebbles below my feet sounds like a rattlesnake's warning. I scan the dusty ground for giant spiders, scorpions. Glancing behind me, I'm surprised to see how far I've gone. As if across a great ocean, my mother yells to me from her asphalt island. She's angry. Don't I know? The desert, she is trying to tell me, isn't meant to be entered.

July, 1992 – The Road to Tete, Mozambique

It's not true about time 'healing' the wounds left by certain memories; it only dulls them, takes some of the sting away. Dreams are when I realize how thoroughly my mind has grown around a memory, claiming it, absorbing it the way a tree will enfold a bullet shot into it.

Last night I dreamt about Mozambique. My dreams always start out as repeats of the actual memories until the end comes, and I become truly superhuman. I can suddenly jump over people's heads, soar up into the sky and land in four different places at once. No one ever catches me in my dreams. I always get away. No one puts their gummy hands on me.

Then I wake up, my mind lingering in the past. It's July, 1992, again. I'm in south central Africa, in Malawi, trying to hitch a ride to Tete, Mozambique, along a road appropriately named the Bone Yard Stretch.

Blantyre, Malawi. Dr Banda keeps me company. Everywhere I look, a picture of him flutters in the wind. On every street lamp, on every overpass, Dr Banda. Dr Banda. His scathing eyes, the incongruously friendly expression. A formidable man. Except for him, the streets are completely deserted. Only my footsteps give voice to the silence.

I'm twenty years old and my age feels comical. What do I know about anything? And more to the point: what is this place that I've reached now? Two summers working in a factory packaging croutons to get myself dumped off here, in yet another dark, dusty African town. Nowhere to sleep. The towns endlessly coming before me. My feet, as usual, keeping me in motion so I won't panic and stop moving. Stopping is when I question the sanity of it all, and tonight more than any other night, I must keep going.

I head resolutely out of town, my backpack heavy, the sweat like oil upon me. Dr Banda smiles benignly as I approach another of the distant street lamps. I tell the Malawian president that I know about him. So many Malawians have come up to me and secretly told me about their sons or daughters disappearing in the night. I'm American, and so they think there is something I can do. I haven't the guts to tell them otherwise. I have all these people's names – people probably dead now – and I don't know what to do with them. From the banners, Dr Banda's face snickers.

Around me is the Malawi most visitors don't hear about. If there are visitors, they can usually be found in the old resort town of Monkey Bar on Lake Malawi, though Malawi isn't the tourist destination it used to be. The large country of Mozambique with its civil war is an inconvenience for overland tour buses from South Africa and Zimbabwe. Now there's no safe way to get to Malawi except by air or through Zambia, and all I ever hear about is what a corrupt, exhausting pain-in-the-ass Zambia is, all of one's money going for customs officials' bribes.

I spent a few days in Monkey Bay with some South African tourists. It was from them that I first learned of the insanity of Mozambique, woeful Malawi sounding like an Eden by comparison. Think of the worst thing one human being can do to another, I was told, and I'll find it in Mozambique. Worse than anything Dante could have thought up and all of it honest-to-God reality. Babies used for target practice. Little girls kidnapped and made into sex slaves. Torture. Mutilation. Killing sprees. The army, on both sides, composed mostly of adolescents conscripted into one side or the other after their families were butchered. You name it.

And I was only twenty, I reminded myself. I was nearly as old as Mozambique's war. The entire situation there had sounded nearly inconceivable.

The South Africans said they hadn't wanted to get near Mozambique and had flown into Malawi. When I told them I was interested in crossing through the country to Zimbabwe, that I'd heard it was possible to do so along the 'Tete Corridor' – a single road used by convoys of trucks transporting goods from the east of Africa to the south – they shook their heads: not possible. That route was too dangerous now, was always being sabotaged by rebel soldiers. But I had never been more serious in my life. I wanted to try to get across, see that other world.

It was hard for me to understand the idea of a civil war. I'd glimpsed such wars on the news, but the images never seemed to gel in my mind as being *real*, reality. I wanted to see what was actually taking place. And in the process, I would see if I could actually get through such a place. If I could, then maybe I would have proof that I could do anything, that I could change as a person. Maybe I could believe in myself for the first time. I would just try to avoid getting embroiled in the politics of it all; I would stay as neutral as possible, focusing instead on the crossing itself, on the idea of making such a trip on my own.

I headed to the Malawian capital of Lilongwe to try to get the elusive transit visa to cross Mozambique. The South Africans had said I'd never be able to get one, but uncanny luck intervened on my behalf: when hitchhiking in town, I was picked up by a man who claimed to be best friends with the Mozambican ambassador to Malawi. As everything in Africa seemed to depend on who you knew, I received my visa in a miraculous five minutes. Suddenly there was nothing stopping me from crossing the country, except finding someone to take me through.

And so the town of Blantyre now. I search for a truck depot, and the chance of finding someone going across the Tete Corridor. I continue up the highway under Dr Banda's watchful eye and arrive at a lit area, which is filled with parked trucks. As I approach from out of the dark, I must look like an apparition. An Indian manager in an office stops talking mid-sentence. The truck drivers standing near him fall silent. I'm profoundly conscious of being the only woman among them, and they struggle to account for me.

'Yes, Miss. What can I do for you?' the manager asks, with hints of curiosity and alarm in his voice.

'I'm wondering if there are any trucks leaving tonight for Mozambique.'

'You want to go through Mozambique?'

This news is passed on to the rest of the men, and everyone gapes at me and laughs. Why would I want to do such a thing? Has anyone told me that Mozambique is in the middle of a war?

The manager shushes everyone and beckons me to him. 'Please tell me,' he says politely, 'why you would want to do this.'

I can't tell him the real reason. I would sound insane. So I tell him, 'I want to know what's happening there . . . maybe write about the place.'

He takes a deep breath and examines his feet for a moment. 'What is happening there is very bad. Three drivers were ambushed last week. Killed. I think you should know this. Also, forgive me, but it's not a place for a young girl like you. Forgive me. But I think you should reconsider.'

The manager bows his head and looks on with gentle, curious eyes.

I explain that I've set my mind on it already. I want to see Mozambique. I want to know what's happening there.

The other drivers, I notice, have grave faces and are now silent.

The manager sighs. 'I believe you are a brave girl,' he says, 'but this is the wrong decision. Now is a very bad time. But I cannot stop you.' He raises his hands and looks at the night sky. 'If you must go, God willing, you will be safe. My friend will take you to the trucks that may leave tonight. I am sorry to tell you that a group already left for the border. Maybe, though, you will find one or two who were lazy and have not left. You can ask.'

His friend leaves the building and starts walking down a hill. I follow. Soon we arrive in the midst of rows of trucks. Most of them are parked, deserted, but there are a few with their engines being revved, and work being done under the hoods.

'Follow me, Miss,' my guide says. 'There are a few trucks that may leave tonight. We'll ask. Do you have money?'

'Yes, I can pay the driver something.'

'Good. Good.'

We walk past the trucks and my guide makes inquiries. Refusal after refusal.

'Simmias?' my inquirer asks a man seated in a far corner of the lot.

Simmias is a little man, much shorter than my five foot seven, with a plainly sincere and trusting face. He has tiny mahogany-colored eyes hidden beneath the front of a brown pilot's hat, which is too large for him and engulfs his head. I can't help smiling at it and when his quick little eyes register why, he laughs.

'I would take you,' he says, 'but my company forbids carrying passengers. I could get fired.' The crowd of men around me has dispersed. Simmias seems to be my last hope; I see no one else preparing to leave.

'I'll pay you,' I say to him.

'Yes, but the others will see you and tell my boss.' Suddenly he holds up a finger. 'We will ask Jerry. Jerry is my best friend.'

Jerry, a tall man in khaki shorts doing work under the hood of a truck, appears indifferent to all the commotion I've caused.

'Jerry,' Simmias says.

No response.

'Jerry, hello!'

His friend finishes some adjustments and looks slowly

down at us. He doesn't seem the least bit surprised to see me. 'Yes, what is it?' he says to Simmias.

Jerry is somewhere in his mid-twenties, and he's definitely not Malawian. His eyes are dark, his features more pronounced. His cheekbones reign strongly over a wide face with a flat, shapely nose. An attractive man, he seems clearly of Zimbabwean descent.

'Jerry, will you take her through Tete, to Zimbabwe?'

He sighs, irritated, and jumps down from the truck. He rubs his oil-smudged hands together and shakes his head.

'She shouldn't go,' he says to Simmias. 'The fuel injector is broken. There is a chance the truck will break along the way.' And to me, 'There is a chance the truck will break, do you understand?'

'Yeah. But you're still going, right?'

'Yes, yes. This is my job.'

'I still want to go,' I tell him.

Simmias now speaks to Jerry in a tribal language, and I hear the tone of their conversation crescendoing.

'You'll pay me something?' Jerry suddenly says to me.

'Yes.'

'How much?'

'I have eighty kwachas left.' About thirty US dollars – a great deal of money for a Malawian or, I figure, a Zimbabwean.

'But do you have a visa for Mozambique?' He thinks he's got me now.

'Yes. I've got one.'

'Yes . . .'

'Jerry,' Simmias is pleading, 'take her, okay?'

'You know there is a war in Mozambique?' he asks me.

'Yeah.'

'Trucks get attacked, blown up. All the time. I been in two ambushes in the past month. Bullets hit my truck.' He points to the steel frame of his truck, to a scattering of small dents. 'It is real, you know.'

'I know.' But I realize I'm lying – both to him and myself.

He sighs and shakes his head. He doesn't ask me why

I want to go through the country. It doesn't seem to matter. I can tell this is a man who has already learned to avoid the tediousness of asking questions and pondering answers. For him, life has become one great game of getting from one place to another in the quickest time, and with the highest monetary reward. This is the truck driver's game, this is what he's paid for. His life is worth only as much as his wealthy South African boss will pay him to deliver his cargo through Mozambique's war.

'Get in. I will take you through, but if she breaks . . .' He clucks his tongue. 'She could break, you know.'

He opens the passenger door of his truck, and hoists himself inside behind the wheel. He starts clearing away garbage.

'She's really not meant for you,' he says. He points to a sign on the dashboard: LONELY LOVER.

When he starts the engine, it catches roughly. He gets out to do a few last-minute adjustments under the hood. He isn't carrying any cargo in back, and explains that he's anxious to get the truck back to a country with better repair service and cheaper parts than Malawi has: a wasted trip, then, but a necessary one. And if, in this dangerous truck driver's game, Jerry's life is worth as much as the cargo he's carrying, then it has now depreciated in value to almost nil, to the thirty dollars I'll be paying him. He accepts this as a matter of course, jumping into the driver's seat with an eagerness to get started. His only concern, his only reason for pause, is for his truck. 'She is sick,' he says of it, shaking his head.

It's an old truck, dirt matted in the rubber floor covering, the numbers worn off of the gearshift knob. Garbage is still strewn about, and I push some aside with my foot as I lean back in the seat and look in front of me. My eyelids droop. I feel hypnotized by the idling of the engine.

The Lonely Lover climbs up behind the wheel. He looks at me and his stern face releases a faint smile. I realize, as he does, that this is my last chance to change my mind and get out of the truck.

I don't move.

He puts the truck in reverse. 'Ready? We go!'

It is one in the morning, and I sit with Jerry and Simmias outside the truck as they boil flour over a portable gas heater. We're parked on the side of the road behind a long line of trucks, all of us waiting for the border crossing into Mozambique to open in the morning. Most of the other drivers are asleep, but Simmias and Jerry are wide awake and chatting in Chichewa as they prepare our dinner of *mili-mili* – boiled balls of flour filled with tomatoes and chunks of beef.

As we eat, I open my journal and, by the light of the gas flame, begin writing.

'What are you writing?' Jerry asks.

'A journal entry, in case I'm killed tomorrow.'

'Before, they did not kill the white people they ambushed. They were frightened of your embassies.' Jerry slides some dough into his mouth. 'But now they kill everyone. Especially white people.'

'Oh.'

'When I first became a driver, my boss said I must go through Mozambique or not get the job.' Jerry rearranges himself Indian-style. 'That was a few years ago, when they did not have soldiers to escort the trucks. I was young and poor, so I said, "Okay, I will go." I was almost through the country, almost through the Bone Yard Stretch—'

'The first half of the road we travel on tomorrow. The worst part of the road through Mozambique,' Simmias explains as he washes out his plate.

'Yes, the worst. The most dangerous. So anyway, I was almost through, almost into Malawi when *pptt! pptt! pptt!* Ambush! The rebels kill the driver in the truck before me, and they stop my truck and they tell me to get out.'

'You saw a man get killed?' I ask, incredulous.

'Oh, yes,' Simmias says, 'it's no lie.'

'They shot him in the neck,' Jerry says. 'So anyway, I get out and the rebels steal everything from my truck.

They steal the radio and my food, my shoes, my clothes. Everything I have. I only wore underwear, and they wanted to take that too! But they didn't. Then they hold their guns at me and laugh and say they will shoot me. Very funny for them. But the leader, he says, "Run! Run!" He wanted a game. So I run very fast, you know, and they shoot at me until I run into the bushes and they cannot see me anymore.'

'And Jerry was close to Malawi, and he walked the whole night and most of the next day, very frightened.'

'No! I wasn't so frightened!'

Simmias slaps him on the shoulder. 'You were too, my friend.'

'And I crossed the border into Malawi. A week later, my company sent me through again.'

'You should have quit!' I say. 'You were almost killed.'

'Well, I was too smart for them.'

'Doesn't it scare you that the same thing could happen tomorrow?'

'No, I am not scared of death. I been in many ambushes, and I seen many men who were shot. I seen trucks blown off the road, the drivers burned to death.'

'Oh, yes,' Simmias says, his tiny eyes peeping out at me from under the pilot's hat.

'Perhaps you will see it tomorrow and you can write about it in your little book.'

Jerry sighs now, obviously sick of talking, and gorges himself on more *mili-mili*. When I finish writing and close my journal, Jerry turns the flame off. Simmias says good night to me, and we head to the trucks.

I curl up in the front seat of Jerry's truck under my Maasai blanket while Jerry lies on the pallet in the back.

'Good night,' he says. There is no further formality and he is soon asleep.

I'm too exhausted to think about anything and close my eyes. I can't even think about what might happen tomorrow.

As if a moment later, dawn arrives, the stark orange light from the east promising another hot day. My uneasy sleep is shattered by the sounds of revving truck engines. Drivers walk quickly toward the customs house, impatient to get their passports stamped and the paperwork out of the way so they can be one of the first trucks to leave Dr Banda and his country behind. Jerry and I join them.

We have only just entered Mozambique, yet the signs of war are immediately upon us. I can see the front of our snakelike convoy of trucks curl around land-mine craters in the road and dive in and out of potholes. We pass a blown-up jeep or two. An occasional truck.

Jerry has explained to me that the Mozambique National Resistance (MNR), known as Renamo, plants the mines at night for the incoming trucks to hit during the day. If the rebels had the chance to do some work on the roads last evening then someone will die today. That simple.

Jerry pops in a mix tape, and Bob Marley starts singing. '. . . *vibra-tions, oo-oo* . . .'

Marley wails out our open windows. I wonder if there are any rebel soldiers out there who can hear the music and recognize it.

Mozambique seems a scorched country compared to Malawi. I'm reminded vaguely of Arizona. Somewhere hot and dry, with parched soil and scant brush. There was once potential here, though. Jerry said people used to come to this region of the country to vacation. I notice that it's rather hilly by this Bone Yard Stretch, and the mountains' higher elevations are covered with vegetation. They're not very high mountains, but they're appealing enough with their gentle slopes and mix of autumnal shades. Hiking used to be quite popular.

Our truck starts to climb, groaning in a low gear.

'That's where an ambush happened two weeks ago,' Jerry says, pointing to a growth of trees nearby where I see a charred metal truck frame.

I realize that Renamo soldiers could be out there right now, hiding in the brush. The dark shadows under the branches could conceal a machine-gun nest. They could be anywhere, the rebels. They could be right at the bottom of this hill, near that stream that curves so peacefully across the arid landscape.

We reach the bottom of the hill and I see the remains of four more trucks beside the road.

'This part of the road, in Chichewa, means "Makes Many Cry," ' Jerry says.

We pass a few deserted villages. Round mud houses with thatch roofs in disrepair, the mud chinking in the walls having crumbled to reveal gaping holes. What were once small vegetable gardens behind the houses are now tangles of shriveled weeds and debris.

It's strange to see no sign of life here. Having gone across East Africa, I'm used to seeing an abundance of animals. But here in Mozambique there is nothing. No antelope, wildebeest, lions or giraffe. Not even a mangy dog, a scavenging bird. Not even a human being. Nothing.

A few buildings are left behind where there were once villages of some kind. Most of them have been reduced to rubble, the white stucco walls lying in chunks about the yellow grass. The bullet holes that litter the still-standing sections tell of days scourged by shooting matches.

Our convoy travels now on a flat plain. The area within fifty yards of either side of the road is newly burnt. All trees – except the baobabs – have been crudely cut, three-foot-high stumps scattered about the charred terrain.

'Why did they burn everything?' I ask Jerry over the beat of Marley's band.

'This is the best place to ambush trucks, so the soldiers burn everything down. Burn, burn, burn. Now the rebels have nowhere to hide.'

'Then why did they leave the baobabs?'

Jerry looks at them and shrugs. 'I think, maybe, because they are special trees. They take a long time to grow.' He hums loudly to Marley.

'They care about that?'

Jerry shrugs again and turns up the song.

I look at the thick trees with their stubby gray appendages and tough, ringed trunks of smooth bark. They are the only things left to posterity, yet they're of the perfect width to conceal soldiers with their grenade launchers. Is it possible that a people so concerned with killing could be, at the same time, sentimental about their trees? The idea is too strange, too daunting. I listen, as Jerry does, to the Bob Marley beat.

A jeep of government soldiers passes us on the right. Five young men sit inside while a sixth man stands behind a machine gun. The red bandanna he wears around his neck flaps wildly in the wind. They're all almost identical in appearance: tall, emaciated-looking figures with taut faces flashing a hint of perverse delight. Their dark skin glimmers with a film of sweat. Their camouflage uniforms hang loosely on them like shedding snake skin, red berets falling down to their brow. I stare at them, these men ordained my Protectors, the ones guarding our convoy from rebel soldiers. They're mere fledglings to the job of death. Most of them look to be fifteen, sixteen. The oldest seems eighteen. He's the one with a sweaty hand lounging over the stock of the machine gun, and it's he who spots me first.

He points at me. The other soldiers lean on their AK-47s to take a look. Through my open window I hear Portuguese utterances.

Jerry turns his head and sees the jeep keeping pace with his truck. Usually nothing seems to faze him, but here is an exception. His face tightens and he puts on the brakes. The jeep sails past and he makes sure it's long gone before he presses on the accelerator again. Trucks pass on the right now, but he doesn't seem to care.

'One time,' he says suddenly, turning down his music, 'I was crossing on this road, and there was an ambush. The soldiers with us shot back at the Renamo soldiers. *Pptt! Pptt! Pptt!* Then it stopped. Very quiet. The rebels were killed and some soldiers and drivers went to collect the dead bodies. When they saw the bodies,' Jerry laughs hysterically, 'when they saw the bodies they saw that the dead were government soldiers. The soldiers had shot their friends!'

'I don't understand. Was it a mistake? What, were they traitors? Deserters?'

'Oh no,' Jerry laughs. 'There is no difference. They are both, you see. During the day they fight for the government. At night they take off their uniforms and join Renamo.'

'I still don't understand. Isn't there loyalty or anything?'

'You are not meant to understand things in this country. There is no loyalty, no rules. If the soldiers are hungry, they ambush a truck, kill the driver, steal his food and his money. Then they say Renamo did it. Or,' he adjusts his mirror so he can see Simmias behind him, 'they just join Renamo because the killing is easier. No pretending.'

'Chaotic.'

'Yes.' He looks at me with impatience. 'Of course.'

Jerry goes on to say that every once in a while, a bus full of Mozambican civilians will attempt a crossing down the Bone Yard Stretch. They leave from the city of Tete – controlled by President Joaquim Chissano's government soldiers – and make an exodus through Renamo's domain. Perhaps they'll migrate further south into their country or, more likely, they'll illegally enter Malawi or Zimbabwe as refugees. But the idea is just to escape. They'll risk everything not to become a victim of Renamo. They've seen or heard of the torture, the massacres: innocent villagers burned alive, asphyxiated, maimed, gang-raped, gunned down by bored soldiers taking potshots.

These refugees fleeing in their buses know, of course, what kind of a chance they're taking. Completely unprotected, their single crammed bus rumbles down the gutted road with heavy black exhaust marking the passage as blatantly as would a bellowing loudspeaker. I picture them in my mind, see them as some sick animal left behind by the herd, prey to the whims of the hunger-driven predators.

I'm now looking at the result of their being discovered. I'm looking at a land-mine crater easily four feet deep. What's left of the bus – some singed metal bits and an axle – is scattered about in the surrounding grass. Shards of window glass cover the asphalt and reflect the sunlight like glitter. Sun-bleached clothing flutters in the breeze. The bodies are gone, but a book lies open, its pages flipping back and forth as if moved by invisible hands.

'Here last week,' Jerry explains, 'nineteen people died.'

I shudder and put my backpack up against the window as if it could protect me from rebel fire, exploding mines – whatever. But I put it down again. The hell with it. If I get shot I get shot. I'm starting to understand how Jerry can do this job for a living.

I look at the bits of clothing: those people had almost made it. Bob Marley finishes his song and the tape turns over. Silence. I feel, strangely, just as I felt when I visited Auschwitz. A heavy nausea for the human race. Yet here, in the Bone Yard Stretch, in the midst of such an inescapably horrible reality, I begin to feel a profound change coming over me. I'm surprised at how suddenly it occurs – not in days, months or years, as one might think, but in a single moment. Suddenly, *now*, it happens: I unwittingly grow up. My innocence abandons me, and I'm left only with a fear of the world that I know to be irrevocable. Mozambique greets me soberly. I wonder what the hell I'm doing here. What self-centered fool-hardiness led me here? It's as if I just woke from a dream, and I want to tell Jerry to turn around, take us back to Malawi before we go any further. I made a terrible mistake. I'm not ready for a war.

But I say nothing. Some Kenyan music starts – lively chords and jovial whoops of Swahili. I roll my window up and lean my head against it, my sweatshirt a pillow. Our truck's wheels plummet down and out of the crater and we leave the wreckage behind. Jerry takes a swig of orange drink and starts tapping his fingers on the dashboard to the beat of the music.

'This place really doesn't scare you?' I ask him.

'No, no. People fall dead going to the toilet. I do not ask when my turn will come. I do not care.'

'Fate. You believe that if it's meant to happen, it will.'

Jerry looks at me and shakes his head. 'You are funny,' he says. 'You sit with me in a broken truck, on the road to Tete, in the middle of land controlled by Renamo, and you talk about death. You are a funny girl. Do you know where you are, Kira?'

It's the first time he's used my name and I sit up.

'I know where I am,' I say. But I have never felt more lost. I have only the truck and its rough, coughing hum of momentum to orient me.

I watch a truck pass us, roaring by in a race to the front of the convoy. Jerry scoffs as a second and third truck pass. Embarrassed, he explains that if his truck were in full-working order he wouldn't keep losing his place like this.

I start to understand that the truck drivers have made crossing Mozambique into a macabre game of machismo, the object of which is to be the first truck in the convoy to reach Zimbabwe. Jerry tells me he's been first five times already. *Five* times – a distinction not to be taken lightly as the first truck in the convoy usually discovers any newly planted mines.

'I have a reputation now,' Jerry says.

'What reputation?'

'They say my luck is very good.'

The city of Tete. The end of the Bone Yard Stretch.

I'm halfway to Zimbabwe and smile, having gotten through what I think is the toughest part of the journey. The side of the tape with Bob Marley's pleasant reggae beat is playing again, as though to congratulate us.

'Are we safe now?' I ask Jerry.

'No. There are still ambushes, but not as many. We still

need to go with a convoy or Renamo will – *pppttt* – kill us easy. Easy, if they are by the road.'

But I'm less concerned because life has returned to the landscape. To my right is the Zambezi River flowing from Zimbabwe, and I see a few women about to start their washing. They walk along the mud-covered banks, baskets balanced on their heads. They're the first women I've seen since entering Mozambique, and the lacka-daisical way they go about their work has me confused: I wonder where the war has gone.

The bridge over the Zambezi has been blown up and repaired so many times that it can only take one truck at a time. Our convoy idles in a long, single-file lane, await-ing passage. Some local peddlers try to sell the drivers their wares as we wait, and items are passed in and out of truck windows.

Jerry inspects a yellow baby shirt handed up to him and asks the price. What interest he, the Lonely Lover, could have in a baby shirt, I'm not sure, but the man points to the shirt Jerry's wearing – a green cotton one – and gestures that he'd like to swap.

'Ha! This is fine quality.' Jerry pinches his shirt and speaks to the man in English, aware that he doesn't understand. 'This was bought in Johannesburg. Jo-han-nes-burg. Ha! Stupid man. South Af-ri-ca.'

Jerry tosses the baby shirt out the window. The man catches it, babbles in Portuguese, and moves on. In the truck's mirror I see Simmias behind us, buying the baby shirt for his little girl back home.

It is now almost our turn to cross the Zambezi. The truck before us is halfway across the bridge and as soon as it exits on the other side, Jerry starts to roll forward, pressing on the gas. I watch the river pass below, shrunk to half its normal size from a drought that has struck much of south central Africa. I remind myself that these same gray, dismal waters once flowed down the mighty Victoria Falls.

We enter downtown Tete now, which looks to all appearances like a typical African city with its gray and white stucco buildings and high-rises and grid work of streets. Yet, strangely, no one is out on those streets, and there are no cars. Some stores advertise different services or products – groceries, auto repair, Coca-Cola – but they're all closed, and appear to have been closed for some time, the storefronts guarded by padlocked iron shutters. Graffiti mars the sides of buildings. Scrawny dogs wander and sniff about garbage piles. It's possible to believe that the city of Tete was, at some point, a thriving place, but now everything looks unkempt or abandoned, weeds sprouting from the grime covering the roads. Tete reminds me of one of those Armageddon cites in some sci-fi movie. Abandoned. Left to the vermin.

'We will leave Tete, now,' Jerry is saying.

'Good.'

The engine lurches and the hand of the tachometer flickers. Jerry downshifts, but the engine gains no more power.

'Shit. The fuel injector.'

We're creeping along now. I watch the back of the truck we've been following sail away from us down the road. The trucks behind us start passing on the right. One. Then another. Another. *Oh, God, three more . . . four more . . .* Two jeeps of government soldiers zoom past, the men inside looking back at me. When Jerry pulls over onto the side of the road, a couple of passing trucks honk at us in pity.

Simmias, of course, is still directly behind us, and he pulls over, too. Jerry stares at the tachometer as though he can fix the problem with his gaze. I bite my lower lip and remain silent. Outside is a wasteland of rocky soil. The baobabs are gone, and the sun is oppressively hot. It must be easily over 100 degrees, and there is no wind. Sweat runs into my eyes, burning them.

Simmias pokes his little head through Jerry's open window. For such intense heat, he still wears that pilot's hat.

'Hi,' he says to me, smiling.

Jerry frowns at him. 'Fuel injector. What did I say to you?'

They speak in Chichewa for a moment, and Jerry gets out of the truck. He opens the hood and examines the engine, shaking his head. More trucks roar by with honks of condolence. These passing trucks are getting fewer, I notice. The convoy must be almost past us.

I've been so concerned about the trucks leaving us behind that I don't notice we've got visitors. A jeep of government soldiers has parked behind our truck, and some soldiers are walking toward Jerry and Simmias. One man sees me in the passenger seat and whoops, pointing excitedly. The others come by to see what he's pointing at, and their excitement is evident in their eyes and laughs. They taunt me in Portuguese, and one soldier cups his hands at his chest and makes obscene gestures.

I crouch down in my seat and lock the door, remembering what Jerry had told me about their dual loyalties, their brutality. From my backpack, I pull out my Swiss Army knife and open it to the largest blade. Little comfort, though: each soldier carries an AK-47 over his shoulder. I stick the knife into the pocket of my jeans, and watch with relief as Jerry and Simmias walk up to them. Jerry speaks some fractured Portuguese, smiling as though there's nothing wrong.

But Jerry never smiles.

From their gestures, the soldiers are determined to know whether Jerry realizes that he has a young white woman in his truck – as if I were Jerry's property, as if he might consider loaning me out. Jerry slams down the hood. He puts his fingers to his mouth to tell them that we've stopped to eat lunch. That's all. When one of the soldiers points to me again, Jerry says 'American,' waving me aside, blatantly directing them toward their jeep. To my surprise and relief, they leave.

Jerry walks over and climbs into the truck. When he sees my fright, he sighs and shakes his head. 'They are animals,' he says. He pulls out his bag of flour and gas stove, saying only, 'We will eat lunch now and I will think what to do about my truck.'

The convoy has completely left us now. A few stragglers, delayed for whatever reason, grind up the road toward us. They also have no way of catching up with the 'herd' and so park to make lunch with us: strength in numbers. We are nine trucks now and have no jeep escort to protect us (if, of course, we *would* get protection from such soldiers). I unlock the door and hop down onto the dusty soil of Mozambique as if into a pool of murky water, the depth of which is beyond my ability to comprehend. This is the first time in my life that I've set foot in this country, excitement the last emotion I'm feeling. I hate the idea of leaving the truck. I see a single, rather bushy shrub and head to it. I hope it's not my fate to be blown up while I take a piss.

There must be a village close by because, just as I finish, a congregation of young boys gather on a nearby slope. One of the drivers making *mili-mili* chucks a stone at them and they scatter, only to return again with hesitant steps, their eyes following our actions.

The drivers ignore them, talking in Chichewa or Shona while they prepare the porridge and pour themselves cups of water from huge plastic jugs.

The boys, I notice, wear nothing but strips of filthy rags. They're skinny, and the younger ones all have swollen bellies that they touch lightly – almost tenderly – right above the belly button. They're dirt-smeared, their eyebrows gray with dust, and they squint at us in the sunlight with crusty mouths held open.

Another driver throws a stone at them and the pack disperses, regrouping at a safer distance.

'They *steal*,' the driver says to me after he's thrown another stone. 'They grab at you – *grab grab grab!* Then you look and everything is gone.'

'They're starving.'

'Yes, Miss, but in another year most of them will be given a gun and they will hide out and wait for me to pass in my truck!'

He throws a handful of rocks at them now, but they're too far away for any of his missiles to hit.

'Humph!' The driver digs a hand into the large ball of dough Simmias has removed from the flame. The others dive in, but not before my little friend has removed a large portion for me and placed it in a separate plate with some mashed tomatoes.

I eat it all, not wanting to waste any in a country like this. Simmias makes another batch for the drivers, while the boys look on with longing. I pity them, not so much because of what they endure now, but because of tomorrow, of what this war will do to them when they're old enough to be given a gun. I don't want to believe that what he said is true, that they're destined only for war and killing. Yet, I'm aware that a good part of the world is preoccupied in the same way. Angola, East Timor, Guatemala . . . It feels strange for me to be here in their country, in the midst of their chaos, because I'm only an observer. I can always leave them behind, return to three meals a day, air-conditioning, clean clothes. Safety, sanity.

And they cannot.

The meal ends quickly, and Simmias is left with a plastic plate of leftover porridge and a few chunks of meat. Jerry takes the plate from his friend and, amid the other drivers' protestations, marches out to the skittish group of boys. He stands at the top of the slope. Hand resting impatiently on his hip, he extends the plate. One of the braver boys drifts toward him and, with a ravenous lurch, grabs the baseball-sized ball of dough and struggles to shove it in his mouth before the other boys can get to him. Too late. The others reach him, and they pull at the dough between his lips. The smaller boys grab for any morsels still left on the plate, practically ripping it from Jerry's hand. Food flies everywhere. The boys scramble for the scraps in the dirt, scratching, punching, clawing each other aside.

Jerry calmly watches it all, seeming to care only when the plate may be taken from him. Finally, he yanks it away and heads back toward us. The drivers, long since bored with the spectacle, are busy washing their hands.

Simmias takes the plate from Jerry and rinses it off.

'Let's go,' Jerry says to me as he hoists the bag of flour to his shoulder and hands me the gas heater. 'The sun will soon start to leave, and my truck, she is very sick now. If Renamo is out there, we may die tonight.'

I want to believe that this is more of his machismo. 'But is the truck as bad as—'

'She is bad. She can only drive very slow.'

I suggest, if the situation is so grave, we leave his truck behind altogether, go with Simmias to the border.

He scoffs, glares at me. 'I will not give my truck to Renamo.'

I bow my head, chastised.

'But we must all go now. It is safer to travel in a group. We cannot wait anymore because the sun is going. I need you to watch the right side of the road. I will watch the left.'

'Watch for what?' I ask him.

He sighs impatiently. 'Anything that moves.'

I stop him before I climb into the truck. 'Jerry, how bad is it?'

'You are a funny girl,' he says.

It's only Simmias and us now. We've been doing a pitiful twenty kilometers an hour. Without a military escort for protection, we're as much a pair of sitting ducks as that busload of refugees blown up a week ago. The other trucks of our small pack all waved goodbye to us more than an hour before, when our speed started to drop. They were anxious to reach the border and live to see Zimbabwe the next day.

'If Renamo is by the road, we're dead,' Jerry says, speaking in an unusually low tone. He squints from one side of the road to the other as though reading small print.

I study every thick growth of vegetation, trying to

discern soldiers-in-waiting. What they would look like –
or even what I'm supposed to be looking for – is unclear.
My heartbeat is loud, my senses acute. I'm conscious of
the adrenaline rushing through my body like a thick sap,
and I would give anything to be safely at the border right
now.

I keep scolding myself for being here, doing this. *This is
for real, no joke. You're in the middle of Mozambique, in
the middle of a war, in the middle of country controlled by
rebels, in a faulty truck that could completely go at any
moment. There is absolutely* no *form of military protection
and the sun's going down.*

I nod. I know. But beyond all this is the part that hurts
the most: there is no waking from this nightmare.

I glance at the tachometer, and I will the truck to pick
up speed. Simmias, in his blue-striped truck, is pacing
us on the right, his little eyes frisking the countryside.
Occasionally, he looks steadily at Jerry and they nod at
each other: best friends – literally – to the death.

But perhaps some kind god has more in mind for
us in life because in the distance are the mountains of
Zimbabwe. Beautiful wonderful Zimbabwe. I smile because it is so close, and my ordeal, I think, is over.

Then our truck dies.

One thing you don't want to do in Mozambique is stop.
Not ever, for any reason. We have already stopped once,
and Jerry is wary about doing it again. Simmias has
stopped with us and has been trying to get Jerry to
abandon his truck. This is a futile business, though,
because Jerry doesn't want to leave 'her' behind. He's
fond of the broken old thing, and so am I: though it's
been like riding a lame horse, we've gotten this far. We're
only a few miles from the border, and Jerry hopes to fix it
and get it across.

The alternative, Jerry explains, is to leave it behind for
Renamo or the government soldiers to find that evening,
or perhaps the next morning. They'll take it, of course.
Or, if they can't get it working, they'll pick it apart. Steal

his spare, the parts under the hood – everything worth any bit of money.

'They are animals,' he says. It is a familiar refrain.

Simmias doesn't seem to hear him because he points down the road. From the direction of the border, we see a distant vehicle approaching.

'The animals are coming,' Jerry announces, not moving.

Simmias grabs my hand. 'Quickly,' he says, his English disintegrating in his frenzy. 'Your rucksack, take, take! Bring to my truck!'

I follow his orders in a panic, Jerry still standing in a state of indecision by the side of his truck. From the small size of the vehicle coming toward us, and from the speed, it appears to be a jeep of government soldiers. Jerry isn't ready to surrender to them. He stands with his hands clenched, glaring with obvious disdain for Mozambique and its war.

Simmias hurries me to his truck, and I sit on his pallet in back. With a composure that surprises me, as if someone else has taken over my actions, I find myself shoving my passport and money pouch down the front of my jeans. It's hot, but I throw on a black pullover and stuff my journal into the front pocket. There's spare money and traveler's checks in my backpack that I've forgotten about. Quickly, I take them out of their various hiding places and shove them down my hiking boots.

Simmias starts his engine and squints outside. I can hear the vehicle pulling up beside us.

'Not Renamo,' he says. 'Government soldiers.' He motions with his hand for me to get down, and I press myself into the corner, to hide.

Simmias has his hand on the gearstick knob. The truck is idling fiercely. Yet we don't leave: not without Jerry.

It's dim in back, and I feel as if I'm watching a play from behind the scenes. I try to assure myself that I won't have to participate, that Mozambique is someone else's show. I lose this feeling of immunity when I hear voices outside and Simmias abruptly leaves the truck.

The minutes pass. I hear arguing, but know better than to make an appearance. I wait, listening to my heart thumping away. With my black pullover on, the heat is overwhelming.

The passenger-side door suddenly opens and Jerry swings himself inside.

'They want me to leave my truck. They want to take us to the border,' he snarls, dumping some things beside me.

Given the circumstances, this seems like a good thing. 'Are we going to do that?' I ask.

'You are a very silly girl. They won't take us to the border.'

I look at him in silence. My hands have started to shake and I order myself to be calm. 'What do we do?'

Jerry sighs and glances outside. 'I am thinking. Don't leave this truck.'

The truck door slams. More waiting. More snatches of conversation drifting in from outside. The driver's-side door opens now and I think it's Jerry again. Then I see the red beret and a dark, sweaty, excited face. When it sees me, it smiles broadly, white teeth beaming.

'American?' it asks. This young man can't erase the smile from his face. Something is extraordinarily funny or ironic to him.

It occurs to me that I've seen this face before: it's one of the government soldiers who had earlier passed us when we were eating lunch.

Now the moronic-looking soldier, still smiling, reaches back for me. I feel his damp, eager fingers on my wrist and strike them away. His smile breaks into a wide grin. He reaches for me again. I punch him away.

'Get the fuck away from me!'

He reaches, I punch. Again and again. I wonder how long this game is going to go on. The soldier, though he looks directly at me, doesn't seem to see me or to know what's happening. Such vacuous eyes, and that shit-eating grin.

Another soldier climbs into the passenger seat. He is older, maybe in his mid-twenties, and looks angry and impatient as his eyes settle on me. I have also seen this face before, recognize that one eyeball lolling off to the side, sickly and invaded by a brown patch of infection. I sense he is the leader, if indeed there is such a thing in this ragtag army. But a dream now, surely not reality: his rifle trained on me and my life sitting before me. That it is such a minuscule life, so easily done away with, shocks me.

The rifle goes down. This man's hand is gummy and strong on my arm as it pulls me from the back of the truck. I try to wrench away, and succeed, only to be promptly grabbed again and reprimanded in Portuguese. My stubborn actions amaze me, for we never really know how we will act when faced with a real threat. We can speculate. We can be certain we'll remain calm or scream, will fight with vigor or curl up helplessly. But when it comes down to it, there is no way to know until it happens. And then it is simply too late.

And now I discover myself punching and squealing at this man who won't let go of my arm. He grabs me by the hair, and so does his still-smiling friend, and I know only that I must get their goddamn hands off of me. Nothing in the world matters but freeing myself from them. My hand pushes at the face of the moronic boy and he stops smiling and lets go of me. The other pulls harder on my hair, and the pain is intense. I'm certain my scalp will be ripped from my head, and as I reach out to strike him, the moronic boy grabs my arm. Again, the gun in my face. My body is shaking uncontrollably. I cry out, and discover myself calling for Jerry over and over again. I sound like some wretched creature torn from its mother. To my amazement, Jerry responds from outside the truck. He is pleading with them to let me go.

They do. They let me go.

'Come out,' Jerry says to me. 'Don't make them angry.'

I wait till the soldiers leave the truck then slowly get out, a certain buoyancy to my movements from the adrenaline rushing through me. Jerry stands near me while I get down, though the soldiers surround us now.

Simmias is some distance away, kneeling on the ground, pleading with the soldiers who nudge him with their feet. I suddenly understand how I have endangered Jerry and Simmias by traveling with them. If only I could take back the events of the past two days! If only I could put myself back in Malawi when I was making this stupid, selfish decision to cross Mozambique, and decide not to do it. Why didn't I realize the added danger my presence might cause? The soldiers knew I was traveling in a broken truck, and they knew we fell behind the others in the convoy. I wonder if there is anything I can do now – but I see that it's too late. Much too late.

Jerry's eyes are focused on some point down the road. 'Listen,' he says to me. 'These soldiers, they want to do something with you, do you understand?'

I don't understand. I don't want to understand.

One of the soldiers, a boy scarcely older than fifteen, harshly reprimands Jerry for talking, but Jerry ignores him. 'They say they will take you to the border, to a rest house. But this is a lie.'

'Just me? Where are they going to take me?'

Jerry's eyes are still locked on some point in the distance. 'Listen to me – when it is dark, *run*. We are close to the border.'

I feel weak all of a sudden, physically sick from this news.

'Where are they going to take me?' I ask him again.

He shakes his head slowly. 'I don't know.'

The building is crumbling, reeks of piss. It's empty but for the bench where I've been sitting for the past half hour, watching two young boys playing soccer with baobab pods in the dusty yard out front. But watching isn't the right word. My eyes refuse to focus on anything. I'm numb, and can't seem to move. It is a strained kind of numbness, though, as if I were on the verge of snapping.

Though we left the main road, we're near the border. I know that much. Jerry and Simmias were left behind, and I've not seen them since. They were trying to convince the soldiers to let them go to the border. Maybe they succeeded. I don't know. I hope they succeeded. As I was being driven away, I saw Jerry standing next to Simmias. Jerry was flashing phony smiles, and I noticed that the soldiers' rifles were shouldered. I suspect the soldiers were just interested in me.

The soldiers refuse to let me leave this building. Someone has brought beer for them, and they are – for the moment, at least – busy getting drunk outside on the veranda. When they need a diversion, which is often, they come inside to bother the American girl. These diversions have gotten predictable, and take one of two forms.

They may try to hit me on the head with various objects. They've thrown everything from plastic water bottles to stones, though they prefer baobab pods – hard, yellow-skinned objects the size of a tennis ball, which often shatter on the wall above me and shower me with seeds. They've hit me twice already, to the accompaniment of hysterical, wheezing laughter.

The second diversion is to walk up to me and demonstrate what they intend to do with me. The drunker the man, the worse the demonstrations. Knives imitating copulation. Putrid breath as the leader with the sickly eye stands an inch from my face and asks me lewd questions in a smattering of bad English or reaches for me. My legs are clamped together till the muscles strain. As stupid and terrifying as these games are, I know what's supposed to happen when they're over.

Strange: they don't do anything with me yet. Just taunt. But it can't go on like this much longer. I don't know if they're waiting for someone – another leader, maybe – or are drinking away any hesitation. They've probably never had a foreign woman in their possession before, and perhaps they're nervous. Not nervous about raping someone – God, no. But repercussions. Maybe they fear some kind of political outcry, something they haven't anticipated. I don't know.

What I do know is that I'm pretty close to Zimbabwe.

All of this beer had to come from somewhere, after all, and when they brought me here I could see the mountains of Zimbabwe in the distance. It's nearly dark outside, and I know I have to run. Still, new soldiers and even some plain-clothed Mozambican men, seem to be coming all the time, and they swarm around the building. Inside, I know I'm the main attraction, that a back room is being cleared out for me.

I can't wait much longer. I struggle for the necessary courage, all the while keeping the blank expression on my face. When they nudge me, I move like a rag doll. I want to bore them, make them think I'm lifeless though I watch everything now. I watch soldiers going into a small toilet room across from me to take a piss. When one of them suddenly throws a beer bottle at me, I dodge my head just in time and it misses. Beer splatters on me, glass litters the floor, and another sharp smell is added to the stench of the room.

A perfect moment is not going to come, I tell myself. *Now. Right now*.

It takes all of the willpower I have, but I get up.

'Toilet,' I say to the looks of surprise. I point at the toilet. 'Toilet,' I repeat. My hands are shaking wildly and I press them against me. I wonder if they can hear my heart beating, it's so loud in my chest. I'm terrified that they can somehow sense what I'm about to do and will stop me before I can even try.

But just as I had hoped, the soldier with the sickly eye waves me permission from where he lies on the veranda outside.

I walk to the toilet and close the flimsy wooden door behind me. There is a small, grimy window in front of me. Through it, all is blackness but for a single light far off in the night. A lone light that seems to be in the direction of the border.

I feel this drive in me now, so strong, so ready for anything. I haven't a plan, but a plan seems unnecessary. All I need to do – all that matters – is getting past the soldiers hanging around the front of this building. I don't doubt myself at all after that. I know how hard I'll run.

I turn around, push open the door. I head slowly across the room, as if returning to the bench. The soldiers speak to me in Portuguese and try to get my attention by pssting me as if I were a dog. To my left is the way out of the building. I turn as if to face the soldiers, then, in a rush, I run as hard as I possibly can.

I'm out of the building! I run past men on the veranda, certain my heavy steps will cause the whole structure to cave in. *Faster, faster, faster!* I'm on the ground now. Soldiers are getting up, but too slowly. I'm leaving them behind. Only the dark ground before me. I tell myself not to trip over anything. *Watch where you're going, keep up the speed.*

Here is what all of those years of competitive running were for. Here is where it all matters. I run toward that distant light, barely able to see anything else. Behind me, shouts. The voice in my head starts to get cocky. *You can run faster than them! Keep up the speed.* I feel as if I'm running in the State meet again, listening to that inner voice which is like a drill sergeant's urging me to the win. The only thing I'm scared of now are their guns, of a bullet in my back. Yet, I haven't heard a shot. This gives me hope – I must not be a target. I must have eluded them. Each move of my legs feels mechanical, like a piston moving, and the sounds of my pursuers start to fade. I don't hear shouts anymore. Nothing but my own heavy breaths and the thudding of my hiking boots on the ground. The money shoved down my socks pricks my feet and wads under my heels.

Now I slow down, but only a little. I have to pace myself. I keep running toward that distant light. As my eyes adjust to the dark, the stars above seem abnormally bright. I glance over my shoulder for signs of pursuers. No one. Just scraggly bushes and a dull moon. I know the night has a new meaning for me now. I grew up with the requisite tales of bogeymen and ghosts, but those tales dim by comparison to the darkened landscape before me, and bushes that might not be bushes at all, rocks that might be anything but. I could be running straight toward a rifle aimed at me, a return to that stinking house. Is there even an American embassy in this wretched country? No one knows where I am. (Such a sinking feeling now.) No one at all. If I died here, no one would ever know.

At last, I decide to stop. That once distant light is close, shining dimly by a few buildings in the distance. The border crossing? Or am I already in Zimbabwe? I'm afraid of going any further, of being seen or heard by someone in the night, and decide to wait out the dawn to try to figure out where I am.

I see a large bush nearby, and settle down beneath it. I'm exhausted and spend my time trying to discern the causes for the myriad sounds about me. When it at last seems as if my mind is making them up, I rest my head on the ground, ready to give up. I look above me. To watch a night spread out in constellations, moving in an ordered pace across the sky, is to learn the nature of loneliness. I measure the progress of time by tracking the stars through the tangled branches of the bush that hides me. Nothing in the world could make the evening pass faster. I know this. Yet I try to convince myself that time can get away from me, mercifully pulling the stars farther than they should go. A slight wind rattles the brittle leaves of the bush. A bird sweeps by. Now, for the first time, the tears. They wash over my face, down my chin, staining the dirt beneath me. I ask myself: is this what you were looking for? Are you glad you came, Little Girl?

Are you glad you came?

I see that I was looking for a journey that wouldn't require any responsibility on my part. A journey that wouldn't require me to become invested in the horrible reality of the situation and the people around me: Jerry's and Simmias's safety, the cruelty of a country ravaged by civil war, the politics of the situation and the way my own incongruous presence complicated that picture. In short,

I didn't expect there to be any ramifications to such a self-indulgent, foolish trip across the Bone Yard Stretch.

And, to top it off, I haven't become anyone new. And if I'm any different – and I know I am – it's not in the way I might have hoped. Instead, provided I can somehow get to Zimbabwe, I must live with the guilt and terror of this entire experience.

It's impossible to sleep, though I feel utterly exhausted. The questions stay with me, mock me, as the eastern horizon grows into clarity, revealing my ghosts and monsters of the night to be bushes, termite mounds, rocky earth. The questions stay as I get up to see the road to Tete surprisingly close to me. The electric light is still on in the distance, marking the border post into Zimbabwe. Rows of parked trucks, having arrived too late and stuck in Mozambique for the night, sit in silence before the border, their drivers asleep inside. The trucks, I know, are my way out. As I cautiously approach them, I recognize two: one without cargo in back, the other with a telltale blue stripe across it. And now I see my two friends. I smile and start to run. The sun is reaching out, gaining the momentum of day.

Part One

CHAPTER ONE

Where Do We Come From?
What Are We? Where Are We Going?

Only a few years after escaping Mozambique, I left for Papua New Guinea. This trip began in paradise. In Tahiti. It was one week before the French nuclear tests on the Mururoa atoll, one week before protestors' riots and looting ripped apart the Tahitian capital, Papeete. I saw none of that coming. I had never been to a more peaceful place.

I was staying in a youth hostel, and it wasn't long before a grubby group of us invaded the Hyatt Regency Hotel, occupying the terrace restaurant and securing seats overlooking the sea. We wanted to improve on our view. We wanted beer nuts and cocktails at eight dollars a shot, and the feeling of life being as close to perfect as it could ever be.

It came close that night. A magnificent South Pacific sunset graced our efforts. Gilded waves, a blazing sky containing every shade of red imaginable. We gaped at the west, our eyes never leaving it as we talked lazily about many things. Why Americans never travel anywhere. Why Germans always do. Didn't Marlon Brando have an island somewhere around there? Didn't his daughter kill herself? We all looked over at the dreadlocked Brit who asked this last question and admonished him with our gazes: inappropriate subject. We would not tolerate such questions. Not now. Not in front of such perfection.

Every day in Tahiti ended with sentimental perfection, as if it were always the last day before the end of the world. Beauty was ostentatious there. The air reeked of tiare and orange blossoms like a land wearing too much perfume; walking the streets meant treading on flowers shed like autumnal leaves. I wondered absently when I'd be dropped to earth again, a mortal. Too soon, surely. And I wasn't yet prepared for the sobering jolt.

The quietest of the group, I was surprised when the others joined me in silence. To the west, the night was taking over, creating an edge to the colors and slowly blowing out the scene. Mauve. Dark maroon. Slowly, slowly. The sky and sea joining. A slice of moon asserting itself. The sounds of insects. A cooler ocean breeze.

And night.

Something akin to disappointment overtook us. The beers and cocktails became much too expensive for us. The Hyatt Regency Hotel too stuffy. We counted out our loose change, piled it on the table, and left to the relief of the hotel staff.

Heading to the youth hostel with everyone in the back of an old truck, I felt like one of Tahiti's *tupapau* – ghosts – which people believed wandered endlessly and could only be persuaded to rest by lighting a kerosene lamp in the night. I was already feeling anxious to leave Tahiti. Inexplicably, I always needed to be somewhere else. I'd left behind so much this time. Graduate school, my teaching job, my chance at having some savings. A boyfriend who loved me and whom I might have allowed myself to love back.

The stars above, for all of the truck's speed, didn't seem to move. The wind lashed our hair back, sent our clothes beating upon us. Tahiti and its people appeared in glimpses of light: an old man walking beneath a street lamp, a pale ocean, a mother on her front stoop calling to a child.

I looked at the young people around me. Most of them had been in Tahiti for months, glorying like Fletcher Christian's mutineers in how successfully they had evaded the rest of the world and its responsibilities. They lived, as I did, out of a backpack. They spent their nights getting Polynesian tattoos and drinking beer around bonfires on the sand, a society of merry vagabonds. I was always tentative about joining them, sitting on the fringe of the circle of light like one of H. G. Wells's morlocks. I liked to watch them, wondering what happened when paradise officially became one's home. Did the escapes stop then? Did one live a charmed life? For their lives, these happy people's, indeed seemed charmed.

I'd found that the most paradisiacal places in the world only distracted me for a few blessed days. It was like having an out-of-body experience: I stepped away from myself and my past, and resided in turquoise waters and white sands, pretending I wouldn't ever have to return to anything. Rest and relaxation, people called it. I called it hope.

My favorite artist, Paul Gauguin, never did return home. He had decided to exile himself in French Polynesia. Ironically, the South Pacific nearly killed him with its beauty: it had no interest in accommodating sour moods with dull, gray days or cold nights. Often on the verge of suicide, Gauguin was forced to greet the daily mockery of a blooming, verdant land always busily engaged in cycles of rebirth. Such a paradise was then, as it is now, a place where only the most important, the most fundamental questions could be asked. Gauguin asked them in one of his masterpieces, a painting that – had he not botched a suicide attempt – would have been his last:

> *D'où venons-nous? Que sommes-nous? Où allons-nous?*
> Where Do We Come From? What Are We? Where Are We Going?

In the youth hostel that night, Coco was telling me how nice the bodies of young women are. So soft, he said. So firm. He smeared coconut oil on my back, them warmed his hands over a kerosene lamp. He told me he could give Tahitian massages all day to young women like me, and I believed him because he was a lonely man. His wife had been living in the United States for the past two years, and he had the dazed, frazzled look of a middle-aged man who has kept company with ghosts.

Coco owned the hostel, dividing his time between running it and seducing the female clientele. He talked openly about some of his past 'friends': a young Swiss woman whom he'd hired to make airport runs for him, a Danish woman, a number of French girls. But never an American, he announced, as if I were already on his list. He said he liked foreign women because of their variety, and claimed he could expect different responses from each of them when he gave them massages.

'And what are Americans like?' I asked.

'Nervous.'

I laughed. 'Am I nervous?'

'Your whole back is stiff. You don't like to be touched down here.' He grazed my thighs with the back of his hand.

'My boyfriend used to touch me there all the time.'

'A lucky man,' he said in French. 'And where is this boyfriend now?'

I saw James again, his kind, determined smile. The play of desire always in his eyes.

'*Au revoir.*' I cut the air with my hand. 'Good-bye.'

Coco tskked. 'Not so lucky then, *n'est-ce pas?*'

I changed the subject. Did Coco just give massages? Nothing else? I wanted him to know that I wasn't looking for anything else.

Only massages. He told me about his Swiss 'friend' again. She would come back late from the airport and couldn't go to sleep without one of his massages. They were that good.

'A wizard,' I said in French, smirking, and then his hands were on my back, smearing the coconut oil in. When his hand ran up my thighs, I said, 'Only a massage.'

He chuckled. 'You Americans.'

52

I looked out the window of Coco's room. We were near the beach and the sound of the surf reminded me of where I was, though I felt as if I could have been anywhere. Somtimes – particularly at night – all places blended into each other and I became disoriented. These were the times when I panicked and made sure my room's doors and windows were locked, and I slept with a light on. Or, if I was in a hostel in some country somewhere, I'd roll over to look at the sleeping forms of the other people. I'd listen to their breathing, the easy rhythms, waiting for the air to smell as it should again. Like Zanzibar, perhaps, thick, dank, sweet. Like Nepal, Bangladesh. The beating of a fan overhead, maybe. Or rain pounding through the trees. The world returning, telling me where I was again.

Coco brought me back this time. When he got up to prepare more oil for my massage, I watched him. He was not just big but colossal, a giant. Long, thick arms. Heavy Polynesian cheekbones. His whole body bristling as he poured oil in his hands and worked them over the top of a small kerosene lamp.

This was his specialty, he explained. These massages. He'd learned from his father. His father had learned from his father before him. It was an art. A gift. Learning how to move the hands just right. Maintaining balance with each motion, the body a canvas.

Coco dripped more coconut oil on me and his hands again arrived hot from the kerosene lamp to knead my skin. My eyes stayed focused on the lamp's fluttering shadow on the window's curtain. The surf rushed, retreated into the room's silence. Coco became a ghost: I felt only his hands rolling and pressing. Whatever it was he was doing, it became another kind of perfection. A forbidden one. A fantastic one.

He asked how long I planned to stay in Tahiti.

'Not long,' I said. 'This is a stopover. I'm going to Papua New Guinea.'

'You're going there on holiday?'

I felt the press of his fingers on my thighs. 'No,' I said.

'What will you do there?'

'I don't know yet.'

He tskked. 'I hear it's not safe.'

I turned over and looked at him. 'Yeah. Well, no place is. No place on earth.'

He turned me back around. 'Here it is safe.'

But I wasn't convinced of that, either. I didn't *feel* safe, even within the confines of his four walls, with his strong hands on me.

Coco's hands moved up to my shoulders, massaged the back of my neck.

'Your neck is very stiff.'

'I know.'

He pressed hard into the tight muscles. I winced and started to protest.

'Shh,' he said. He said it softly, drawing out the sound, kneading my shoulders, my back. Again, his fingers ran down my thighs. I rolled over, anxious.

'I think you should stop.'

He considered me. 'Does it feel good, what I'm doing?'

I looked away.

He rested a hand on my leg and told me to watch what he was doing. The fingers smoothed across my skin in a single, deliberate movement. 'A Tahitian massage is very special. It's about touch.'

I sighed, and shut my eyes. Coco started to tell me his theory about me. He said I don't let many people touch me. His fingers traveled up my back. He said that I've probably never been in love.

Outside, the other backpackers at the hostel were gathered around a bonfire on the sand and I could hear them laughing.

'I think I scare you,' he said.

It hadn't occurred to me that I was scared.

'You're scared of me,' he said, 'because I'm touching you like this. Shall I stop?'

Part of me didn't want him to stop. Part of me wanted to be in someone else's care. This was such a rare feeling – I was used to traveling the world alone, taking care of myself. No matter what, I needed to be able to take care of myself. Growing up, I had learned to rely on no one.

Yet, maybe I could deliver myself over to him, if only for a night. Though he was a stranger, I wanted to tell him how his paradise of Tahiti scared me more than his touch. I didn't trust the perfection of it. Such free and benevolent beauty surely came with a price. How to pay for this reward of sunsets and surf, and the numbing smell of hibiscus and tiare? How is it that I had won this all without effort? I felt as if I were being drugged and deceived, and that it would all be taken away in a second. I didn't know how to enjoy it fast enough, if I even deserved to enjoy it at all.

My nakedness suddenly felt like a veil around me. Coco sat on the corner of the bed, studying me. I was shivering, and threw my shirt on, getting up. Coco attentively watched me, smiling.

'*Tu as peur*,' he said. 'I scare you.'

I heard more laughs from outside, around the bonfire. I went to the door and told him I had to go.

This man knew me: 'You always go, *non*?'

I always needed to be gone.

It was as a kid that I first got the idea that the world I wanted, and couldn't seem to find, lay elsewhere. It was just a matter of getting there, somehow. Of having the strength and determination to find it.

In my family, strength and determination meant everything. Independence and resiliency were virtues my parents cultivated at all costs. They'd had no tolerance of any behavior that might be thought to show weakness or vulnerability. No physical fragility allowed, no sacrificing anything to others, no outward expressions of love. Ours wasn't a hugging, touching family. We were like a family of strangers inhabiting the same space, crossing paths, yet always convinced of our inherent aloneness. My parents rarely celebrated holidays, as if the mere act of celebrating, of sharing anything together, was too foreign and frightening a prospect. Consequently, there weren't birthday or graduation parties. Virtually no outings. With the exception of a trip out West, vacations were almost always too expensive; amusement parks, a waste of time. I was taught that the families who did those kinds of activities were just the ridiculous toadies of popular culture. We were supposed to be different.

Instead, my father would take me to the firing range. I'd been eleven when I'd fired my first gun. A Walther P-38. I liked it; it had a nice kick. I remember standing in the booth, a lanky blonde-haired girl in pigtails and glasses, with the P-38 aimed at the figure target at the other end of the room.

'Between the eyes,' my father said from behind me. I could barely hold up the gun with both hands. 'Steady, and get 'im between the eyes.'

I got him. Twice. Between the eyes. The third bullet grazed the imaginary shoulder. My father, ecstatic, went to the booth next door to tell the two men standing there that his daughter could shoot better than the boys. His enthusiasm told me that here, finally, was something I was good at. Finally.

Not that I was bad at everything else. Rather, I was an over-achiever in the classic sense: A's throughout elementary school; excellent in sports; studious and polite, almost to a fault. But all of this seemed to pale beside my brother, Marc, who was two years older and had a genius IQ of 158, excelling at just about everything. If I was good at something, Marc was inevitably better – or so I was led to believe by my family and friends. My parents decided to put my brother in private school from the second grade on. (I, on the other hand, would stay in public school.) After all, Marc was the beneficiary of my family's most important expectations – he was to be carefully, meticulously groomed for the Ivy League. We were a lower-middle-class family, my mother a waitress, but my parents took out a second mortgage on the house to pay for his 'rich man's education' at the private schools. Marc was going to a New England boarding school, by God. And he went. To one of the most prestigious ones, out in Connecticut. He later ended up at Cornell. All according to plan.

As a kid, I never stopped feeling like the consolation prize contestants win on game shows; something people don't really need but are still required to graciously accept. This feeling made me try all the harder for the recognition that would never come. If one academic achievement wasn't enough, well, maybe the next one would work. Or the next. Maybe I would finally be noticed for something. I soon started to think that the problem lay in *who* I was. If I were only smarter, more talented or creative, I could stand ground against my brother, and my parents would send me on to private school, too, and have the same expectations for me. Then it occurred to me that if *I* changed, became someone else altogether, I might be able to fix everything.

I'd been writing stories since I was six years old, and I saw in my writing my first chance to escape and become someone else, someone better. When I was nine, I put together a file box filled with scribbled notes describing scenes and places in the world. It was a special box – no one could get near it because inside were my adventures. It contained lengthy descriptions of who I'd become for the day, and I could constantly reinvent myself. I'd turn into a soldier or explorer, a medicine woman or empress, possessing the fantastic strengths and abilities of each of these roles so that it was disappointing to return to my real self. In my imaginary adventures, I was in full control of my life. I was able to plan what characters I'd encounter, what journeys I'd have, what marvels I'd accomplish. Sometimes the places I chose never existed, were fantasy lands like something out of a Tolkien novel. More often, they were from the past. I lived in a nondescript suburb of Chicago that offered little in the way of adventure, but I was always reading *National Geographic* and watching PBS documentaries. At school, I carried around a notebook in which I wrote the scenes of adventures so I could playact them by myself at home.

My summers were spent in heady excitement over where my make-believe would take me next. One day I might be in the Great Plains, the next day Mesopotamia, the Andes . . . New Guinea.

New Guinea was, by far, my favorite place. It was a land of ferocious headhunters (whom I always managed to befriend) and jungles full of man-eating crocodiles and tribes of people who built huts in the trees and lived on jungle fruit, insects, wild boar. Even back then, though, New Guinea had seemed foreboding. It always sat on the very edge of my imagination, both fascinating and ominous, like a mysterious temple I was forbidden to enter. If I could get through the jungles of my imaginary New Guinea, I'd reason, I could do anything.

These imaginary journeys soon took the place of the company of other people, as I avoided nearly everyone: I had, simply, a debilitating shyness. It was due in large part to an increasing lack of self-confidence, a feeling that anything that came out of my mouth was worthless and unimportant; there was nothing I could say or do that would impress anyone. The shyness got worse as I grew older – the anxiety and tightness in my chest, the fear of condemning myself through words. Conversation itself seemed a strange, laborious ritual with rules that constantly eluded me. I was terrified of stuttering out something stupid or, worse, incoherent. Gradually, I just gave up and withdrew from people. If put in their company, I became mute. Silence meant safety. It meant anonymity. No one could get near me.

It had been those early file-box stories that introduced me to the idea of *actually* making some arduous journey, miraculously becoming someone else by the end of it. As a kid, I knew that my extreme shyness made me different somehow, an oddity, like someone who had a mysterious medical condition the doctors couldn't treat. My peers at school, not understanding the reasons for my avoiding them, attacked and ridiculed me. After a particularly bad year of junior high school, my mother had to put me in a new school, but by that time the damage had been done.

Not only did I hardly talk to anyone, but I could find no convincing reason why I should. My file box and its stories became more important than ever now. I could become anyone I wanted, and I could always leave for a different world. A better world.

When I turned thirteen, my parents sent me as a scholarship/work-study student to a boarding school in Wisconsin, where it was hoped I would 'come out of my shell.' But life at Wayland Academy was regimented and uneventful, and did little to help. I found myself waking up each day wondering what I could possibly do that would mean anything. I felt like a carnival horse going around and around, futilely bobbing up and down to the same old music, never destined to arrive anywhere. Never destined to stop. Except for weekends, every hour of every day was allotted for something: chapel, classes, dining hall, study hall, sports. Sports were mandatory. I said I liked to run, and was put on the cross-country team.

Sometimes our lives are chosen for us, and we have about as much control over the matter as we do the situation we're born into. If I had hoped for a new identity, a way beyond the silence and the self-loathing, I hadn't intended on running to be my way out. Running was a strange, unwanted gift. My body, quite unexpectedly, won races for me. It won the Conference meet. Went on to win the State meet. When my coach told me I was one of the top-twenty high school runners in the country, I felt as if I'd stumbled upon an identity I couldn't refund. Suddenly there was talk of national competition, the Olympics. Colleges wrote promising full scholarships – all I had to do was run for them. I had gone from being a sort of phantom sitting at the table in the corner of the dining hall, to the Runner noticed by everyone, particularly my parents. My father drove up to Wisconsin to attend my running meets, video camera in hand. My mother showed off newspaper clippings to her friends in which a young girl in braces smiles reluctantly from a photo, the headline above reading, 'Wayland Harrier Wins State.'

The pressure became incredible, the demands of the new identity stifling. The file-box stories from my childhood seemed silly and worthless now. I couldn't go to any of those places; my life didn't feel my own anymore. When I woke up, I relinquished my days to the expectations of the people who now noticed and relied on me. I lived for parents, coaches, teachers, college sports recruiters with their whispers about the Olympics. I lived to beat record times, to beat other people – to always win, no matter what. To not win a race was to risk returning to the person I'd been before, and this became a terrifying incentive to keep going.

Yet, I began to hate what I had become. Trapped in all the unwanted expectations, I had dreams of my legs suddenly breaking. I contemplated running into cars, falling off cliffs – whatever, as long as I had an excuse to never run again. After setting the state record in the mile, I went to my dormitory room, locked the door and tried desperately to break my legs with a piece of pipe. That they wouldn't break, that they refused to respond at all to my blows, didn't discourage me. If I persevered, pretended I was, say, a Green Beret from one of my childhood adventures who could ignore the pain, maybe I'd get lucky. Maybe a bone would fracture. Something. And then I could stop running. It'd be over.

Nothing broke. My legs were bruised, but the pain had been too great: I'd been too much of a coward. Desperate and suicidal now, I decided to just quit. It was the hardest thing I'd ever done, worse than running in the most demanding of the races, worse than the specter of my actually losing a race. To this day I don't know where I got the courage to make that decision. The audacity of it! I felt as if I'd let down the entire world. All of the people pleased with the Runner I had become – parents, mentors, relatives – wanted to know what I would do with myself now. No more free rides to college. No more guarantees. Many prominent people in school, whose opinion I trusted implicitly, warned me that life only offered one shot at such glory. Surely nothing I could do in the future would match what I had given up.

I ended up seeing a psychologist over the decision. It took an entire year of his ministrations before I was able to stop hearing everyone else's disappointment. I kept telling him what I'd secretly been telling myself ever since I was a kid: I wanted to be a writer. He suggested I tell my parents this, get it out in the open. I did. Predictably, they didn't understand. Writing? But what was the point? Could I ever have a future in that? To them, writing was a path with few – if any – guarantees, while running would offer me full college scholarships, newspaper write-ups, national competition, maybe even a chance at the Olympics. I saw that they had wanted the ease and convenience of living vicariously through my running successes, while there was no glory to be found in scribbling out stories. Writing was merely a 'hobby,' a quaint occupation that I stubbornly insisted upon pursuing. That I could ever be good at such a thing, that I could ever make any money or a career come of it, was utterly inconceivable to them. They were convinced that my true calling, my only calling, was running, so writing was seen as a tragic waste of energy and time. What they didn't know, though, was that I did it as a kind of survival, as a way to keep going. It was not something I could suddenly stop doing at a moment's notice. It was not something that I could ever give up.

Yet, though I still wrote constantly, I rejected that as an ambition for myself and began looking elsewhere for some vision of my worth. Who would I become if not the Runner? Already, I had reverted to the quiet girl I'd been before, skittish around people, feeling as if I had no discernible place in the world. I started to wonder whether change was truly possible for me, or if it was already too late.

It was in this way that I first discovered traveling. When nineteen and deciding to get away to study abroad in the Netherlands, I realized that all I had to do was get on a plane. It would take me to an entirely different world where none of the same old rules applied anymore, and where no one knew me. Suddenly, I wasn't required to do anything for anyone. Rather, *I* had exclusive control over my life; I could avoid the scrutinizing eyes of the past and re-create myself. I started to save up money and, the first chance I got, went to Egypt by myself. Here, suddenly, were the fantastic lands of my childhood. I greeted a world of dust and diesel fumes, calls to prayer piercing the walls and ancient tombs, rattling thoughts with the idea of something greater than oneself, something invincible and wrathful, yet kind. *Insh'a allah*. God willing. Your life was His, and you turned it over to Him five times a day, on the prayer rugs facing Mecca.

Trapped for years in my silence and its solitude, I had suddenly been given this new world. Wisdom seemed to be lying everywhere: in those dark, foreboding chambers beneath the tombs of Saqqarah; in the elderly women cloaked in chadors, wandering the beaches of al-Ghurdaqah, Bur Safajah. If only I could figure out what it was all trying to tell me. Who was I? Where was it that I belonged?

I slept in the dingiest of places in Cairo – rooms covered with dust where men's eyes flickered behind peepholes in the walls and shadows crept under the door. Where was my husband? The eyes flitted as I got up, pulled on a skirt, braided my hair. I imagined them struggling to keep me in view as I moved about the room. My whole life I'd felt anonymous, but here, finally, it ended. I could be absolutely anyone now. Traveling could allow me to be reborn.

I left Tahiti behind, still hearing Coco's words, *You always go, non?* The plane rose and I watched the shores of French Polynesia fade to a spread of blue ocean. The fragrance of Tahiti seemed to linger on my skin, in my hair, like a memory that couldn't be washed away.

A flight attendant handed me an Air New Zealand survey. One of the questions asked: 'How do you generally prefer to travel?'

I smiled to myself as I checked the box 'Independently, without prior arrangements.' A lifetime summed up.

I began to look forward to Papua New Guinea; it was one of the most unfamiliar and daunting places I could think of choosing for a journey. In particular, it had a vast, uninhabited jungle that would be so indifferent to my presence that it could consume me without a trace. I would go way into that jungle and get myself out again. It would be hard. It would be the ultimate test. I knew that Papua New Guinea had a reputation for being especially dangerous, overrun with gangs of hoodlums and terrorized by violence. So here again was the challenge: *Get yourself out of the place.* I would have to toughen up like never before. No fear. I would be forced to have confidence in myself, and to trust in my capabilities. I would need to become someone new, altogether, an entirely different kind of person. A fighter.

I tried to imagine what the country would look like, and recalled the photos from *National Geographic* and other magazines showing a jungle so thick it resembled the entrails of a giant beast, vines winding about primordial trees. Here, *here*, was the place for accomplishing something, for transforming.

And who knows? Maybe through the process I would emerge in some new wild and fantastic place like one of the lands of my childhood imagination. It might be a place similar to what Gauguin had found when he left Tahiti in 1901, fleeing to the remote Marquesas Islands, where he'd written that 'poetry wells up of itself, and one has only to drift into dreaming . . .' I imagined some similar untouched and sacred land, an entry into a true paradise that would offer the kind of rest and peace that I would never want to leave.

Down below, Tahiti's perfect illusion was succumbing to the chaos that had started just as I left. French authorities seized Greenpeace's ship, *Rainbow Warrior*, arrested the crew, and went on with their first of five nuclear tests on the Mururoa atoll. Papeete's idyllic harbor, its quaint oceanfront stores, became the scene of riots. A state of emergency was declared. The airport was firebombed. Looters destroyed and ransacked shops and businesses until French forces were called in to restore order. Through it all, I knew only one thing: the sunsets would look the same, as aloof and splendid as always.

CHAPTER TWO

Independently, Without Prior Arrangements

Cairns, Australia. I sit at a café table, sipping from my third glass of Fosters. The beer does little to calm my nerves. Tomorrow morning I'll be flying to Papua New Guinea, and if even a shred of what I've heard about the place is true, I've got reason to be nervous. The country's reputation for violence has been backed up by every Aussie I've talked to. Port Moresby, the capital, ranks among the most dangerous cities in the world.

Add to these facts the difficulty of altogether abandoning the familiar – the difficulty of abandoning it on my *own*. No more of the safety and luxury that a place like Australia offers. I can only hope I'll be strong enough this trip, that I'll have what it takes, whatever 'it' might be.

But maybe if I can get a vague plan going, I can waylay the anxiety. I take out my map of Papua New Guinea and smooth it down on the table, my beer bottle putting a wet ring in the middle of the Coral Sea. The map shows a marvelous mass of jungle without roads or railroads. One big landmass with tiny circles to mark the occasional village – lone circles a hundred miles from each other, circles in the midst of mountain ranges, circles hidden in swamps. Many of the circles don't have a name. I try to imagine reaching the circles. Surely it can be done. Rivers branch into streams, which branch into creeks and swamps, all of which one could conceivably cover by canoe. And, for those lonely circles in the mountains, one merely has to walk.

Drunk – or nearly – I see that PNG has two main rivers: the Fly River in the south, and the Sepik River in the north. In between them is the Highlands, a 14,000-foot-high backbone that traverses the island of New Guinea. British explorer Ivan Champion had been the first European to cross PNG by going up the Fly, over the Highlands, and down the Sepik in 1927. Why not try doing the same thing? Does it make any difference that I'm a woman, wanting to do it alone? *Should* it make any difference?

Of course none of the New Guinea explorers were women. Men were always the ones surveying the new terrain, figuring out convenient routes from one valley to another. The jungle had been informally declared off-limits for women: it was considered too hot and danger-ous; it had an annoying habit of muddying up clothes, sweating up bodies. And women were supposed to be too frail to go climbing up mountains by themselves, too squeamish to tolerate the assorted jungle creatures. Men in the adventure stories were always intentionally leaving their women behind – burdensome, awkward charges – only to discover, paradoxically, that they were the reason to return home. I'm not ready to buy any of it, though. I want all the mud, sweat, bugs, toil. *Worse*, if possible. I haven't a single romantic notion in my head about this trip: I know it's going to be the hardest thing I've done yet.

I remember when I was a kid. Some girls have dreams of becoming a model, a hairdresser. I always wanted to become a Green Beret. I didn't know if a woman could join the Special Forces – I didn't know much about any of that – but a Green Beret was what I wanted to be. I was attracted to the physical and mental demands, the rigors of a warrior's life. I read all these books on the Special Forces, imagining myself in their hallowed ranks. I'd be the quiet, dedicated soldier, doing what I was told, exerting myself, proving that I could take it and survive and be the best soldier I could. New Guinea, in this sense, feels like the test come at last. My chance to prove that I've got what it takes.

But like it or not, my femaleness acts as a constant reminder that I'm stepping into an arena where, even today, women aren't often allowed – and perhaps for good reason? It's hard to get cocky about any trip when I know that I carry along an additional liability most men can hardly fathom: the omnipresent possibility of rape. Sometimes I wonder where women might go, or what they might do, were it not for this fear holding them back. Yet, at the same time, I don't want to become immobilized by obsessing about it. If I didn't take my chances, I probably wouldn't go anywhere.

But this had better be a good adventure, for all I'm sacrificing for it. I spent my past two summers in a factory, packaging bread – six days a week, nine to ten hours a day – for the money I have for this trip, so it's money I don't easily part with. Every six dollars I spend equals one hour of my life pissed away endlessly packaging hamburger buns and croutons. I could have bought a decent used car, a good computer for my troubles; instead, I chose a trip to Papua New Guinea. I wonder whether I've made a huge mistake, naively anticipating a trip that's simply too outrageous or impossible. Regardless, I'm going. I *have* to go. I want to see what I'm capable of.

I drink down half my beer and study my map again, wondering about the logistics of my trip. Where there are rivers, there are boats or canoes. All I have to do is get myself into one. And as for the Highlands, with its hiking trails, I just have to walk.

I feel satisfied. The world has receded into something pleasing and plausible: I have a plan. I fold up my map and see a man eyeing me from a table nearby. He so intently examines me that I'm wondering if he's some figure from my childhood. That I don't recognize him – and should – unnerves me.

He gets up and walks over.

'I saw you with a map of Papua New Guinea,' he says, eyes grave, his glass of whiskey-on-the-rocks threatening to spill. If I'm drunk, he's much drunker.

He's in his early thirties, has dark, intense blue eyes, a high forehead, and an undisciplined head of blond hair that flies upward over sharply receding hairlines. He looks exactly like one of those busts of Beethoven.

He drops a hand on the chair across from mine, introducing himself as Chris. I motion to the seat across from me.

'So are you going to Papua New Guinea?' he asks with an accent I can't quite pinpoint. It's American with a tinge of something exotic.

I nod.

'So am I. How many countries have you been to?'

I imagine them before me like a collection of bottle caps.

'I don't know.'

'How many do you think?'

I laugh. 'I really haven't counted.'

'I bet you travel a lot.'

Do I have an oddly placed mole? Some telltale sign? 'I like to travel,' I say, 'whenever I can save up enough cash.'

He nods with the utmost seriousness. I might have just mentioned something tragic. He takes a sip of his whiskey. His eyes focus on a single spot on the table. Suddenly, he calls the waiter over and orders us another round.

'Have you been to Africa?' he asks.

'Yes.'

He nods gravely, his hand tapping nervously on the table. 'What countries?'

Reluctantly, I list them. I feel as if I'm giving the names of some valuable baseball cards I've managed to collect. He looks more and more morose. He listens, shaking his head, and it's only when I mention Madagascar that he gazes at me.

'What was that like?' He leans forward with such

interest that he doesn't see the waiter put down my beer and another whiskey for him.

'Well, if you need to buy secondhand syringes, that's the place to go. But if you can get to the rain forest – or what's left of it – it's pretty incredible.'

I might have just told him something confidential. He leans closer to me. 'I want to go there.'

I shrug and pick up the beer he's ordered for me, taking a sip. 'Thanks,' I say, motioning to it.

But he's looking fixedly at some point off in the distance.

'I'm trying to find a place,' he says at last, 'where there are women who won't love me for my money.'

I take another sip of beer. 'You're pretty rich, then?'

'Oh, yes.' He winces.

'And this is a bad thing?'

'Yes.'

I smile. 'You could get rid of the money. I'll take some off your hands.'

'I'm trying to find a woman who can love me for myself. I'm going to go to as many countries as I can.' Serious eyes. Desperate voice.

'Why don't you go to a place where they've never heard of money?'

Chris takes a quick sip of whiskey and nods, sitting up.

'Papua New Guinea's not a bad bet. Go way into the place. Way into the interior.'

He waits patiently for me to continue.

'Some places there, the only wealth anyone cares about are dog-tooth necklaces and pigs.'

'Yes?'

'They have no need for money. No stores to spend it in.'

He nods, his eyes gazing profoundly into his whiskey glass.

'I was also thinking Thailand,' he says at last.

'Yeah, Thailand. Thailand might work.' I shrug. No use arguing with him.

He doesn't say anything for a long moment.

'I'm from Florida and Germany,' he says finally. 'Those are bad places to find a woman.'

I nod in commiseration.

'I was engaged to a woman from Düsseldorf. But I found out she just cared about my money. When I stopped buying her things, she left me.'

'Hmm,' I say.

'I haven't met anyone in Florida. I live in a house in Palm Beach when I'm not traveling, and that's a terrible place to meet a woman . . . Where else have you gone? Any places to recommend?'

I offer Malawi, Tanzania.

'AIDS,' he says with a wave of his hand.

'Well . . . what about Israel?'

'My parents are German.'

'So? I don't understand.'

He just looks off cryptically.

I hold up my hands in defeat. 'Have you thought of just not telling anyone that you're rich?'

He does a characteristic European sputter of the lips. 'They know,' he says in irritation. 'They find out. I don't have a job, you know.'

'Oh.'

'And if I take them to my house in Palm Beach . . .'

'Yeah. Difficult, huh?' I sigh and take a big gulp of beer. 'Incidentally, I'm just curious, what makes you think that all the women you meet only care about your money?'

He looks at me intently.

'Because some women – thank God – have enough self-respect to want to make their own money.'

'Yes?' he says softly. He runs a hand through his hair. 'Where do I find them?'

The beer is making the street in front of me quiver and I can almost believe that this bizarre, Beethoven-like man is an alcohol-induced illusion.

'Well, there's one right here, believe it or not,' I say to him. 'And I hope to God I'm not the last of my kind.'

He gives me an impatient, incredulous glance. 'I'm going to look in Papua New Guinea.'

'Maybe I'll see you there.'

He finishes his drink in one gulp and promptly gets up. He leans against the back of the chair, his body lopsided. 'And why are *you* going there?' he asks. His intense eyes seem to suspect me of something.

I smile at him. We aren't so unlike each other. Both of us certain that contentment is something that can be stumbled upon like some misplaced object. If only we look far enough. If only we don't give up.

'Ask me when you see me again,' I say to him. 'World this small, we're bound to run into each other.'

'Small world? Is it?' He releases his grip on the chair and gapes at a whiskey stain on the front of his shirt. 'My God,' he says, pawing at it.

Stumbling away, he pays the waiter not only for our drinks, but for everything I've ordered this afternoon. I want to thank him but he's already vanishing down the Cairns street, a lanky, dejected figure who appears to be counting sidewalk cracks.

It's later. Almost night. I'm watching some lousy movie in a theater in Cairns, and I suddenly can't breathe. A scene in the film has triggered the attack, and my heart is running a marathon in my chest. I have the irrational certainty that I'm being pursued, am on the verge of capture. The situation is desperate – I have to leave the movie theater at once.

I slam into the knees of people seated in my way as I get out of the row. The images on the movie screen – a man has just been killed – help flash me a view of the way out of the theater. I run, gasping, crying, through the bright lobby and into the balmy heat of a Cairns dusk. I see an empty bench in the city's central square, and go to it because it seems the most open spot anywhere. I need to see the sky above me, to have nothing around me but an open view of the world from all sides.

I sit with my head between my knees, taking deep

71

breaths. I know it'll be a while before I feel any better. What's important is that I don't try to force myself. A nearby street musician pipes out a tune on his flute, something quick and airy, and I concentrate on his music. A little girl walking past looks over her shoulder at me until her mother promptly yanks her to eyes-front.

After what seems a long time, I sit up and look around. Night-time now. The street lamps lit, the lackadaisical town alive with tourists. People's conversations ricochet about, the night somehow making them sound especially intimate.

Everything, I see, is the same as it was before. In less than twelve hours I'll be on the plane heading to New Guinea. I'll be doing it again, going blindly to some place. It is the realization of this fact, and the accompanying fear that I've been denying for weeks, which has just blindsided me, forcing me to pay attention finally.

I think about the trip I took four years earlier, to Mozambique. I never put that place behind me – I don't know how to get over it. If there's some magic elixir that allows one to forget, I haven't been given it. Mozambique stays. The images of a dusty Africa with its boy soldiers. An Africa without women – what had they done with them? – and gutted buildings and scorched terrain. Images from a place sixteen years deep into civil war.

The question of why I went there is the one question I always avoid. I haven't discussed it with anyone, and I don't like to think about it. Yet I must think about it tonight, because tomorrow I fly off to a new place and I don't want this issue to remain unanswered any longer, to overwhelm me when I least expect it – as it has tonight. I need to ask myself why, when I could have just stuck to an itinerary of backpacking around East Africa, I chose to go to Mozambique during its war . . . barely getting out of the place.

It occurs to me that I didn't really think about my safety when I made plans to cross through the country, and I certainly didn't understand my motivations. Rather, my crossing Mozambique's war zone had felt almost imaginary in nature, undisturbed by thoughts of risk or negative consequence. It was as if I were a disembodied character in a story, going through fictional motions. Getting out in the end was a guarantee I never questioned. Incredibly, I had somehow convinced myself that nothing could go wrong and that I couldn't actually get hurt. Only years later did the painful epiphany come, when I realized that I had risked my life – had, in fact, come quite close to being violently raped and killed – in an attempt to finally accomplish something 'extraordinary' that would get me noticed.

I glance at a tourist couple walking slowly along the lighted boulevard, hand in hand. Above them, the palm trees wave and rustle in the breeze. Everything is as it should be. Over there now: kids run from their parents to peek excitedly through the window of an ice cream store. Across from me: young German men laugh and josh each other in a language I wish I could understand but never learned. I breathe in the sweetness of the tropical air and close my eyes.

And here it comes, the knowledge that I cared so little about my life. Always have, ever since I was young and hiding from the world, hating myself. Ever since I was accused of chucking away a life, a future with my running. Mozambique happened because I was willing to bargain with my life. It was the sink-or-swim philosophy of someone desperately trapped in herself.

Funny, too. I had thought there might be some wisdom for me in such a frightening place – so many war veterans have claimed that they had to come close to dying before they discovered what it meant to live. *I* wanted to know what it meant to live. I would demand an answer. Like a petulant child, I would go straight to the principal's office with my demands, and I wasn't even afraid of being reprimanded. It was as if I had become someone else altogether, someone who thought herself fearless, even superhuman.

And what about this time around? Am I going to Papua New Guinea for the same reasons? Do I consider myself as equally immune to the violence and tragedy?

I shudder at the thought. I won't be able to leave tomorrow if the answer is yes. So it must be no – a fervent *no*. This impending trip isn't a death wish but a *life* wish. A way to learn how to move on from my past and reinvent myself. I'm no longer trying to prove anything to anyone. Hell – no one but the boyfriend I left behind knows where I am and what I'm prepared to do. That, in itself, should say a lot.

And how *could* these two trips be the same? I know about reality now. I know that Mozambique can exist anywhere, in its various manifestations. All the death and disease. The barbarity. Why would I be seeking any of that? I wish only that I could be like a member of tonight's crowd in the movie theater, unperturbed by the brutality on the screen. If only I could watch those movies again, convinced that such events are fiction, and that the world is actually much kinder, more gracious, than it really is.

But tonight's panic attack reminds me again of that Mozambique trip gone horribly wrong, and of the world I had found out there.

Getting up quickly, I go to a crowded café to order a beer.

CHAPTER THREE

Salvation of the Lost and Sinful

My plane takes me farther and farther away from Australia and the familiar. This flight feels like an unsettling metaphor for my life – I am sealed inside the plane; there is the rush of the plane's departure and the inability to get off. But I find myself wanting to know more. I want to know what will happen to me, where I'll land, whether I'll like it there. The destination is the most nerve-wracking part. Destinations don't tell you anything. They sit in mystery.

I remember how Papua New Guinea was one of the countries I used to dream about as a kid. It's still a place that is considered one of the last true frontiers. An 'untouched' place. Explorer Ivan Champion had described the parts of Papua New Guinea he had seen in 1927 as the Promised Land. And now, as I sit in the plane taking me there, the country feels just as glorious and mysterious to me as it did when I was a child. Just as full of hope.

The people sitting next to me smile nervously at me. They are John and Patricia Wilson. Missionaries. We had barely left the ground in Cairns before they wanted to know if I was a Christian, a 'friend of God.' Our plane ride together is only for an hour's time, and I wonder (and fear) how much attempted proselytizing can be accomplished in that time.

Like me, the Wilsons are in their mid-twenties. They have the rolling-O accent of the northern Midwest.

Milwaukee, maybe. Minneapolis. Patricia's white skirt and pink blouse are so heavily starched she might be wearing a kind of battle gear, yet she strikes me as an unlikely and delicate crusader with her strong scents of strawberry Bonnie Bell lip balm and baby powder. She mentioned she'd never been to Papua New Guinea before, and I wonder whether she knows where she's going or what she's getting herself into; I wonder the same about myself. We are, in that sense, one and the same creature.

I never gave them an answer about their 'friend of God' question, and have considered trying to ignore them for the rest of the flight. While I don't want to lie to them, I know they'll have a field day if I tell the truth. I'm not a Christian. Have never been a Christian. I frankly don't know much about the whole matter, aside from the fact that it has something to do with Christmas and Easter each year. I've considered labeling myself as 'spiritual' instead. One of those who would like to believe in things that can't quite be named. After all, someone or something must have allowed me to make it safely out of Mozambique. Yet the Wilsons might consider it blasphemy if I said that I think the Buddhists and Hindus got it right: we have the capacity to reach the God within ourselves.

I pull out my safety card and study the picures of how to put on an oxygen mask.

Funny – my parents raised me as a strict, Ayn Rand-ian atheist. Even my name, Kira, was a tribute to the heroine of Rand's novel *We the Living*. My parents didn't just think there was no God, but actively preached their belief to the religious people they came across. We didn't have an altar to Jesus or the Virgin Mary in our house; rather, we had an altar to Ayn Rand, Goddess of Individual Liberty and the Virtues of Selfishness. Beside a framed photo of her were autographed first editions of *Atlas Shrugged, Anthem* and *The Fountainhead*. I grew up reading these books before I even knew what any of it meant. I was taught to believe that the 'In God We

Trust' on money was a religious conspiracy to abolish the separation of church and state. I was taught that spiritual people were gullible and foolish, wallowing in weakness. Not needing God enabled one to bravely face the world. Not needing God was the key to raising the human being to its highest level, restoring free thought and initiative to the world. I was taught, in short, that Ayn Rand *should* have been God, had God ever really existed.

Now, though, I see how that philosophy served as a rationale for the stilted, distant relationships in my family, and a justification for my parents' painful pasts. It became an excuse for the feelings of loneliness and alienation my family members felt toward each other and the world. When I entered graduate school and discovered the words of the Buddha, Epictetus, Joseph Campbell and others, I realized the existence of love, acceptance and bliss. I started to see fundamental problems in Rand's objectivist philosophy, and I parted ways with my family's vision of a world in which everyone is unashamedly out for him or herself. I became spiritual. I became, in my father's words, 'a goddamn Democrat.' I tried volunteer work and found to my great surprise that altruism – a four-letter word in Randian circles, connoting actions motivated purely by guilt and obligation – provides one of the highest joys there is.

John leans toward me with a reserved sort of smile on his face, as if its sincere expression depends on my upcoming answer about religious affiliation. I notice that he, too, is impeccably dressed in a starched white shirt and paisley tie, his brown hair black from sweat. Just looking at him makes me uncomfortably hot. His nose keeps beading with sweat, and he repeatedly swipes at it with a tissue.

He asks me again: 'So are you a Christian?'

'No,' I say, and look out the window. I can see the Pacific Ocean down below, and a faint brown hue in it that is the Great Barrier Reef.

'May I ask for your thoughts on religion?' Patricia asks.

'My thoughts on religion.'

'Your feelings on religion. On why Christ doesn't play a role in your life.'

I'm reminded of the big role that Christ plays in Papua New Guinea. Nearly 40 percent of the indigenous population are Catholics or Lutherans. Another 28 percent are of some other Christian denomination. Not bad for a country virtually unexplored up through the second half of the twentieth century. A hearty 34 percent, however, still follow animistic beliefs and are the missionary's mainstay, inspiring such offenses as 'Operation Mobilization' and 'Operation Tribal Evangelism.'

My feelings on religion . . . John and Patricia look on in heavy silence. When it becomes obvious that I don't want to say anything, John says, 'We're just wondering, that's all. Just your thoughts?'

'I really like Eastern religion,' I tell him. 'I read a lot about Taoism, Hinduism, Buddhism, Shintoism. I really like the *Upanishads* and the *Teachings of the Buddha*. No offense, but I never had any great interest in the Bible. I've read parts of it, but I didn't get very far.'

'May I ask why not?'

Reluctantly, so reluctantly, I explain that I have a problem with the idea of everyone being born sinful.

'So you have trouble accepting the idea of original sin?'

I nod. 'I don't want to accept it.'

Patricia wants to know why. I shrug and look out the window to see if the sight has changed yet. It hasn't: the green strip of Queensland cut off by the plane's belly; ocean as far to the right as my eye can see. 'I went to this one place,' I tell her. 'Little boys with guns. That kind of thing. Changed my perspective on a lot of things.'

'Where was that?'

Why should it matter where it was? Anyhow, I don't want to get into it.

Patricia pats her throat. John reaches inside his bag and pulls out a small pamphlet. On its green cover are the words: 'How to Know God.' He hands it to me.

'Why don't you read this,' he says.

I hate when missionaries hand me their literature. As if

they know exactly what I need. Maybe if John were someone like Mother Teresa, I'd accept the literature, read the literature, feel grateful for his attentions, feel as if he were in the position to actually teach me something. But John and Patricia aren't saints; in fact, they don't strike me as being any wiser than the next person, which makes their handing out of literature smack of annoying self-rightousness.

'Can I ask you something?' I say to John.

'Of course.'

'Have you found peace of mind yet, salvation from life's suffering?'

John and Patricia glance at each other. 'We have peace of mind,' John says, 'when we place our trust in God's care.'

'But all the time?' I ask. 'Now, for instance?'

He looks at me, is about to say something and stops. Finally: 'Not always, no. We all have to battle temptation.'

'Then we're both in the same place,' I tell him. 'On the same road. You know?'

But not being Christian – or even baptized – I probably couldn't convince them.

John pulls out another copy of the pamphlet and leans across Patricia's lap to point out a quotation from the text: 'God is a just judge, and God is angry with the wicked every day.' John taps the quote.

I nod politely. The quote does nothing for me. I have seen no evidence of an angry God, and have no guarantee of any kind of justice. I recall the life of the Buddha instead. Of a pampered prince taking chariot rides into the world of old age, sickness, death. Of mendicant wanderings. Asceticism. Dazed, starving days waiting for the world to reveal the reason for suffering, and the way to elusive truth.

John sits back. Patricia fluffs her bangs out and watches as the flight attendant pushes the beverage cart up to our row. For them, everything in the world can be adequately explained by consulting their New Testament. For all I know, maybe they're on to something. Wouldn't it be nice, a book to act as panacea like my parents' *Atlas Shrugged?* I flip through the pamphlet, then drop it in my backpack. Pulling out my map of PNG, I study all the dashes – the walking trails – leading off into the jungle.

After we've been served our drinks, Patricia unbuckles her seat belt and turns to me: 'So what brings you to Papua New Guinea?'

'I really want to see the place,' I say.

'Are you a student, doing research?' her husband asks.

I squeeze my can of Coke and shake my head. 'I was a student. I decided to take a break from grad school.'

'And come to Papua New Guinea?' John's leaning forward with interest now. 'If you don't mind my asking, what do you plan on doing there?'

I explain how I want to get from the south to the north of the country via the major rivers.

'An expedition?' John suggests.

I laugh. Nothing so dramatic. 'Actually, I have no idea what I'm going to be doing. I'm just going to wing it as I go.'

'That's a little dangerous.'

'I don't know. Maybe.'

'Are you traveling alone?'

I nod.

'Always travel alone?'

I nod again and wait. I know what's coming.

'I highly recommend you get yourself a group to travel with. Or at least a male companion.'

I've heard this before. I first heard it when I was nineteen and backpacking around Egypt by myself. And I'd heard it just the other day, during my stopover in Cairns, where several people offered their own versions of Papua New Guinea's notorious violence, followed by the advice: too dangerous; don't go by yourself. Which is why I am going. By myself. The only rule I try to follow religiously in life is not to listen to most people.

I ask the Wilsons about themselves. John explains that they're from Minnesota, the Minneapolis–St Paul area.

They have degrees in missionary studies. Patricia describes the classes she's taken: cross-cultural communication, evangelism methods, anthropology, Bible studies. And – mysteriously – a course called 'freedom and obligation.'

'We're so excited,' Patricia says. She reaches for her husband's hand. 'God has sent us to Papua New Guinea. There is so much of His work to be done.'

I shift awkwardly: this is a language I neither speak nor understand.

Her husband nods, but with more vigor. 'A lot of work. This is my second time to the country, my wife's first.'

'What kind of work are you doing?'

'Salvation of the lost and sinful,' John says. The words sound so foreign that I half-expect his serious expression to break into a smile: just kidding, just a joke. John soberly continues. 'We teach believers the technique of personal witnessing. We're also working with child evangelism. Teaching English as a second language is one of our new ministries so we can better share Christian literature and the Gospel. There is definitely a lot of His work to be done.'

I'm not sure of the appropriate response. Do I congratulate them? Should I say, 'Well, I hope you successfully complete His work, and change some lost and sinful ways'? Actually, I picture myself poised at a starting line with John and Patricia and every other PNG missionary, waiting for a gun to go off. Can I visit the traditional tribes, get a glimpse of their cultures before John and Patricia get their hands on them?

I wish they'd answered by saying that they're going to New Guinea to 'help the poor' or to 'give free medical care.' Something practical, even admirable. Yet their answer spoke only of indoctrination, of compassion at a price.

I turn my attention back to my map. They look at the section spread out on my tray and shake their heads. 'It's a big country, isn't it?' John says.

'Huge.'

But I want him to know just how huge. Perhaps he'll

get discouraged by all the 'work' there is and decide to leave people alone.

'Too huge,' I say.

John isn't fazed. 'I think you should read that pamphlet I gave you.'

Obviously there is only one version of the truth – their own. I know he considers me one of his lost and sinful. It seems a convenient, arbitrary verdict, as easily applied to a rapist or murderer as to a person like me. Yet, is he any less lost? Is he any more moral? But I'm in no mood to argue. John and Patricia have already made their judgement. I am, as of right now, damned – along with all those other unknowns in PNG who await their arrival.

Well, if I'm damned that would explain a lot, though Buddhists would say I'm stuck with the karma of a past existence's negative actions. I like to do this: explain my life through humanity's myriad theories. If only I knew which one was accurate. If only I could unconditionally believe something. I know I have become the product of my parents' upbringing, nothing in the world seeming to smack of truth. Nothing holding any sort of legitimacy. I was taught to doubt everything, to apply a cynical ear to all I hear. Nothing feels quite honest or real to me. I fold up my map and settle down, nose against the window, looking at the spread of blue below that is the Pacific Ocean.

To the north, just appearing, a greenish land reaches into the sea. I'm seeing my first hazy glimpse of the island of New Guinea. Here's the place on which the Western world, up until recently, had taken only cautious steps. In 1526, during the height of the East Indies spice trade, the Portuguese governor of the Moluccas, Jorge de Meneses, first landed on the northwestern tip of the island and gave it the name 'Ilhas dos Papuas,' 'Papua' coming from the Malaysian term 'orang papuwah,' or 'fuzzy-haired man.' After that, however, the old sailing ships usually passed New Guinea by. Too many mariners brought back stories of ferocious, man-eating men, and a foreboding, malarial jungle that seemed to go on forever. Better to avoid the island altogether. Better to seek more hospitable and profitable places.

I wish I could have been there with de Meneses, though, or some of those other intrepid adventurers who were the first Westerners to glimpse this fantastic world. They wouldn't have wanted to take a woman. I would have had to plead with them, or stow myself away until the ship left port. Something. Whatever it took. But I swear I would have gone.

I glance at John and Patricia, realizing that missionaries have become the explorers now. Ironic: those with the greatest aversion to the traditional ways and beliefs of indigenous people should be the ones to first discover these isolated and fascinating peoples. But it's always been that way. Long before anyone really cared about New Guinea, the missionaries set up lonely outposts on the coast. Those not done in by malaria or typhoid, dengue or giardiasis, occasionally braved inland trips up the rivers. Many were killed – even eaten – for their audacity, but by the nineteenth century indigenous coastal populations had become used to a foreign presence. This, of course, helped allow the Dutch, British and Germans to move in, and the western half of New Guinea officially went to the Dutch and the mighty Dutch East Indies trading empire in 1828. By 1884, the British and Germans split the eastern half of the island, which would eventually end up as present-day Papua New Guinea.

But, as is typical with colonial grabbing and wrestling, boundaries were notoriously troublesome for New Guinea: a straight line going up and down, left to right, divided the diverse tribes according to the obscure ethics of latitude and longitude. It was a problem the peoples of New Guinea would never quite overcome. Those tribes unlucky enough to be stuck in the Dutch half when it was turned over to Indonesia in 1963 found their land seized, their villages razed, and their people slaughtered by two of the greatest butchers of the twentieth century: Sukarno and his successor, Suharto. The British and German division, which became independent Papua New Guinea in 1975, resulted in two separate national languages and unending political and tribal strife. So much for the age of exploration.

Yet from the air, I can see nothing of politics, of discontent. I like that fact, the way a simple plane ride can give the illusion of a world free from chaos, from John's 'original sin.' People could be starving, killing each other down below, but from 10,000 feet, who knows the difference?

Our plane finally edges down over a pleasant green land of small houses with corrugated iron roofs, a colorful patchwork of rusty brown squares dotting green hills. I don't see a jungle, or anything resembling a jungle. Port Moresby erupts from a small peninsula and sprawls for miles in all directions. It's a town of roughly 180,000 people, but is so spread out it gives the appearance of a larger place. A place without an end.

Our plane glides over the airport's runway, hovers for a few seconds and lands with a sobering thud.

'Welcome to Papua New Guinea,' John says to me.

And what was Papua New Guinea an hour ago? Only a strange-sounding name on a map. Papua New Guinea. It lives, it breathes with relevance now. Suddenly, quite unexpectedly, it exists.

When I walk down from the plane to the tarmac, I don't expect my first steps on Papua New Guinea to be solid. I expect to step right through as if I'm in a dreamland. I might then decide it's time to wake up. I'll be back in grad school. I'll still have my job, my boyfriend and my savings, and this entire trip will be forgotten.

But the ground firmly supports me.

As I walk to the airport arrivals hall, I stare at the arid, dusty hills surrounding the airport. The land resembles the plains of East Africa: low dirt hills covered with scrub brush and acacias. The people themselves, said to be related to Australia's aborigines, aren't much taller than me with my height of 5'7". Compared to some of the women, I feel like a giant.

The heat arrives now. It's a heavy, debilitating heat, which suggests the existence of a jungle I haven't yet seen. As we all enter the customs building, the heat follows us inside, spread about by a few lethargic overhead fans. On the drab airport walls, I see nothing advertising PNG as a tourist destination. No suggestions of itineraries or must-see attractions. During my Air Nuigini flight there had been nothing, either. It occurs to me that the idea of being a tourist in PNG is, perhaps, a bit naive. I know of a few tour companies, though. They mostly haul tourists a short way up the Sepik River to the village of Tambunun, which has consequently discovered the lucrative business of chintzy tribal art. But few tourists seem to go beyond Tambunun. Great parts of the country have barely a cursory mention from those beloved sages at Lonely Planet, whom many trust as the ultimate authority on places worth visiting.

However, there are two things that Papua New Guinea *is* famous for among expatriates: its scuba diving and violence. Often you can't have one without the other, and even private vessels out at sea will be overrun by hoodlums, those on board robbed, beaten, killed. A small price to pay, apparently, for what many diving enthusiasts consider the best reefs in the world.

I don't dive, though. In fact, I only really enjoy oceans when I don't have to be in them, and so assume I have only the violence to look forward to.

Waiting by the luggage belt, I see that I'm the only one arriving with a backpack. There are a lot of Australian businessmen, however – expatriates who probably help run the mines or coffee plantations; a large expatriate population remained even after PNG gained its independence from Australia in 1975. The ones in the airport are now wiping at the sweat gathering on their foreheads, circles of perspiration showing under each arm. They have the tops of their shirts unbuttoned in resignation to the heat, their faces set in what seems a universal look of dismay. Perhaps the luggage isn't coming quickly enough. Or perhaps they'd have rather stayed in Australia indefinitely. There's excitement, though, from the PNG nationals. They gather their bags of Australian goodies, smiling, obviously happy to be returning home.

When I finally make it outside the airport, I watch the expats on my flight being whisked away into waiting cars. Patricia and John Wilson (looking a little overwhelmed) are greeted by a smiling Papua New Guinean man in a suit and tie who ushers them into a white Toyota van and on to their new lives.

I'm not in any hurry. I want to acclimatize to the country, get a whiff of what's considered normal. I change some dollars into PNG kina, and walk outside again to join the crowds of barefoot men in holey shorts and T-shirts who apparently have nowhere to go and nothing to do, either. We all stand just out of the sun beneath the front awning of the airport arrivals hall, watching the front parking lot of the airport. After a while, I discover that there's nothing happening in the front parking lot. A helpful little voice in my head suggests that I try to find some place to sleep for the night, and I desert their ranks. Only their eyes respond, a quick flicker of acknowledgement.

I cross the parking lot. Beat-up cars speed by, releasing clouds of foul exhaust. The heat from an overhead sun makes my face feel on fire, and creates a world in which everyone moves slowly, heads bowed. I don't know where I'm going. PMVs – Public Motor Vehicles, which are nothing more than sorry-looking Toyota vans – are the only form of public transport in the country, and I figure a PMV stop must be nearby. Following a path beside a road, I kick up dust as I walk and my legs are getting covered in it. It's important not to leave the path, as brush on either side doubles as a latrine. Blood-like betel nut (or *buai*) juice splotches litter the dirt below, as do bleaching newspaper, banana peels, rotting garbage. Strangely, I welcome this change. Pristine cleanliness and order are gone. Here, at last, is that other reality that I've not seen since being in East Africa.

No more façades. Papua New Guinea feels like the real thing.

Some women have gathered on a road nearby and chat pleasantly in Pidgin. They wear colorful yet simple handmade skirts and *meri blouses* – flared shirts printed with pictures of flowers or slices of bright color. Their clothing is made of thin cotton, straight off the bolt and unpretentious. In such heat, fashion becomes practical and functional, with less demand placed on appearance. I can appreciate that. Whenever it comes to clothing, I have only one means of judging it: can I climb a tree in it?

When I ask them for directions to the nearest PMV stop, the women eagerly walk me over, their plastic flip-flops kicking up dust. These are the 'rude, inhospitable' people I was warned about by an old PNG expat couple on holiday in Cairns. Everybody has an opinion. The women stay with me and we chat about school, America. They suggest I try staying at the YWCA and when I agree, they put me on the right PMV heading there. Their teeth stained red from years of chewing betel nuts, they smile and wave good-bye.

This is a place that either frightens or excites utterly. And, so far, Papua New Guinea suits me better than any place I've ever known.

CHAPTER FOUR

Barbed Wire, Attack Dogs
and Lessons in Emergency Response

Barbed wire. Everywhere. It's only my second day in Port
Moresby, and I've never seen so much of it in one place.
From the sheer varieties available, one must need a
fashion sense to choose it. There's your basic barbed
wire: single strands going up tree trunks and around the
roofs of people's houses. There's also coiled barbed wire,
pickets of barbed wire. Barbed-wire doors and gates. A
traditional, multistrand variety tops chain-link fences.

I've also seen ingenious imitations of barbed wire,
though their efficacy is arguable. People cement broken
glass onto the tops of brick walls. Or use sharp pieces
of metal instead of glass. Or bamboo instead of metal.
I've seen one family with a smorgasbord of scrap metal
cemented onto their wall like some postmodern vision of
security. The point is: don't go without some kind of
protection. Ever.

I suddenly feel crazy for coming here. All everyone
ever talks about is how dangerous Port Moresby is. I want
to simply dismiss these rumors and accuse people of
exaggeration, yet I have no way of explaining the city's
skewed sense of outdoor decoration, or the newspaper
I hold which tells me that security is the fastest-
growing business in the country. Port Moresby itself
boasts some *fifty* companies in operation. I'm even more
interested in the national daily – instead of an Arts or
Living section, it carries a supplement called the 'Security

Review,' detailing the very latest in high-tech protection for homes and businesses. There are tips on how to keep your guard dog properly nourished. There are advertisements for close-circuit television, perimeter fence detection, weapon detection systems, mobile patrols. Have a new security guard and don't know how to outfit him? Look no further than the Bismil company with its 'complete range of security accessories and overalls.' Wondering what brand of pet food to feed your attack dog? Pedigree's half-page ad recommends their Pal Meaty Bites brand, the 'working dog formula.'

On a PMV taking me out of the downtown area called Town, I turn to an amiable-looking Air Nuigini flight attendant sitting next to me and ask him if Port Moresby is expecting an invasion.

'Invasion, Miss?' He blinks several times and looks at me, perplexed.

'The barbed wire.' I point out the window. 'It's everywhere.'

'Oh, yes.' He sits back, relieved that he understands. 'For those rascal boys.'

I've heard a lot about these 'rascal boys.' The name isn't to be associated with the 'Little Rascals' of the old black-and-white comedies; there is nothing endearing about Port Moresby's rascals. They're a PNG phenomenon and the reason why Port Moresby is one of the most violent cities in the world. The rascals are generally young men who come to Port Moresby from all over the country. They leave behind tribal homelands to converge in the big towns with the hopes of discovering an El Dorado of wealth and Western goods. Many of them are uneducated, and their hope for a better life entails wild expectations. Maybe they'll be able to have their own house with electricity, running water, a color TV. And what about a car? Surely a car! A few have never seen a car before, but they've heard about them and they know they're important. Of course, it takes a great deal of money for such things, but in Port Moresby everyone knows there is plenty of money.

This attitude about Western material goods reflects

earlier times when Western explorers started to make first contact with remote New Guinea tribes. The local people found the airplanes and other strange objects so otherworldly that they could only explain them as being gifts from the gods. Aptly named 'cargo cults' formed to pay homage to the strange and inexplicable bounty from the gods. But people soon started to wonder why the white men had gotten all the gifts. Outraged individuals came forward to explain that the fantastic objects were from the Spiritland, and that the irreverent white men had actually swiped the gifts before any local people could get their hands on them. And so it was only natural, in a tribal culture used to sharing everything, to want to take back some of the gifts.

The cargo cult attitude still isn't dead in PNG, and while most young men now understand the idea of 'Made in Hong Kong,' collecting one's fair share remains a popular idea. And so they leave their tiny Sepik River villages or Highlands town for the streets of Port Moresby. When the wealth doesn't come as planned, and they find themselves living in shantytowns or on the streets, they get drunk, join gangs, go after anyone better off. And so Port Moresby rests bleary-eyed and vigilant behind its barbed-wire defenses, awaiting the next rascal offensive.

Which is a shame, really, because Moresby, as the locals call it, is an attractive place. It doesn't have the neglect and tragedy of, say, Tete, Mozambique, in the midst of a protracted civil war. It doesn't have the congested, dusty confusion of Jakarta, or the weariness of ex-Communist Warsaw. Close to the equator, Moresby has lively turquoise waters in its bay. It has coral reefs and yachts at sea, palm trees, pleasant beaches and the blooming flowers of the tropics. Moresby has never been bombed, has never been overrun by rebel soldiers, never razed. The British built Moresby as a capital for their foothold on the island, and not even the Japanese army, with all of its samurai-inspired perseverance, could lick it during World War II.

The flight attendant sitting next to me shakes his head with regret as he tells me about Moresby. His city, he seems to be saying, could have been such a special place. Now it isn't uncommon for schools to shut down because the teachers have been robbed or raped. And there is little that the average citizens can do to protect themselves short of buying more barbed wire and praying to forestall the inevitable. Because it's never a question of if, but when. Everyone has a story. Everyone has met the rascals.

I have been wandering around Moresby for some time and am lost. It's too dangerous to be getting lost here. I know that. Yet, sometimes I don't keep track of where I am. My feet take me places, while the past so contains me that I could be anywhere. Walking forward is enough. The movement is all.

I am still back in Kenya, on the beach near Malindi. I can see the special sand that looks afire in the sun. To my left, the ocean. There is the Maasai man in full warrior regalia of breechcloth and beaded sash, hair slicked back with red ochre, walking far ahead of me. He never looks behind him, never sees that I'm following. With each step he stabs the sand with his spear, and I follow the circular impressions, being careful to fill his footprints with mine. The sand beneath my feet looks gold. An entire beach of gold.

I come back to myself. Some young men have taken notice of me and point me out to their friends. I must look confident now, as if I know where I'm going. But I never know where I'm going. I'm momentarily surprised by the glaring brightness of this sun, a drier heat, the rotting fragrance of the tropics. I'm in a part of Moresby that consists of long streets going past clusters of ramshackle corrugated-iron houses. The humidity gives the air a heavy, sickly sweet smell, picking up the odors of backyard fires and decaying garbage lying in patches of weedy growth. Chickens and dogs, remaining at a cautious distance from me, scavenge along the road.

Children play or wander. The people here are too poor to afford barbed wire or fences and so look especially vulnerable. I doubt they have anything to steal, though. Even their clothes are threadbare, the colors faded from years of hand-washing and drying in the sun.

I stop and can feel the fear rising in me. It constricts my stomach and shoots adrenaline through my body. Whenever I allow myself to stop, I begin to assess the people around me, try to judge their potential to inflict harm. If the world wants to hurt me, it can and will. I know that much. Doesn't matter where I am. I see glimpses of Mozambique, those stubborn memories that have since removed all gloss from the world. The stark African landscapes. The terror of night. I start walking again with more certainty, more clarity. At least I know I will put up a fight.

Up ahead, I see a sign by the side of the road. A store of some kind? I speed up until I can make out what it says:

Coffins made and sold here
Babies to Adults
Open 7 days

Its message is written in red paint, which runs down the wood like horror-movie script. I remember the missionary couple on the plane from Cairns, and the question they'd asked me: *So you have trouble accepting the idea of original sin?*

I make my way through the macabre front yard, in which crude coffins of various sizes are on display, approaching a corrugated-iron garage where a man is busily at work. The owner? His T-shirt, soaked with sweat, clings to his back as he fits boards together and nails them. Large sheets of plywood stand beside him, awaiting measurements. Business is obviously booming.

'May I help you, Miss?' he asks.

He removes a tiny notebook from his front pocket, picking up a pencil from his workbench. Strange: for a moment, I'm actually embarrassed that no one I know has died. He wipes sweat from his face and waits patiently.

'Actually, I'm lost,' I say. I explain how I got here, and where the YWCA is located in the part of Moresby called Boroko.

He surveys the road out front. An assistant is loading a small coffin into the back of a beat-up pickup truck, and they speak in rapid Pidgin. The volume of their voices sounds hopeful.

'Too dangerous to wait for a PMV,' the owner says to me at last. 'It is late. My friend will take you to Boroko.'

I thank him and hop into the cab. The assistant gets in, and the ancient truck pulls out, sputtering up a hill. The little coffin rattles loudly in back as we go over bumps. I ask the driver who it's for.

'Boy. Killed.'

'Killed!'

'Oh, yes.'

'How? By rascals?'

'Rascal boys.' He nods and mutters to himself.

'Why did they kill a little boy?'

'That is a question for God.'

The driver downshifts. Toyotas, a couple of Mercedeses, zip past us – most with white drivers behind the wheel, a glaring reminder of PNG's recent colonial past. We near the top of an area called Three Mile Hill and down below I see a spread of houses obscured by barbed-wire fences, claiming perches on some of the most lucrative property in Moresby. These are mostly the expatriate houses, overlooking the sea to the west. I wonder how much of the ocean can be seen, though, through all the fences and security trappings: video motion detectors, surveillance cameras, electronic sensors, patrolling security guards with attack dogs. It seems an insane way to live.

The coffin maker's assistant at last reaches the YWCA and drops me off. The YWCA building might be a military training center, it's so well secured. It sits strategically on a hill, its grounds surrounded by and heavily fortified with a high chain-link fence topped with the requisite barbed wire. A security guard sits near the front gate. When he looks at me stoically, I'm afraid I'll be required to utter a password. Instead, he merely nods and opens the gate when I approach. His eyes flit about suspiciously as I enter. When the gate is closed behind me, I feel officially initiated into the realms of the paranoid.

Turns out I've just missed the YWCA's latest encounter with rascals. A couple of weeks earlier, a whole truckload of them descended upon the compound. They had guns; the security guard didn't. (I've been told that, incredibly, security guards in Moresby aren't allowed to be armed – they have to rely on walkie-talkies to alert police.) The very same man who had just let me in was beaten and tied up, and the rascals invaded the main building. They rounded up all of the women from their rooms. Everything of any value was seized and loaded into their truck parked out front. One of the women had gotten to a phone and called the police, but they didn't come until a few hours later: she'd made the mistake of mentioning that the rascals were armed.

Rascals are unique in that they don't just rob people – they love excessive violence. In the case of the YWCA, the women thank God that nothing 'especially terrible' happened to them, though the actual details of their experience are grim enough: several women had been beaten; one had a hatchet held to her throat; another had the barrel of a gun shoved in her mouth until she'd gone into shock. No more details were forthcoming, though I suspect it had been worse. I know only that the entire event traumatized the small population of the YWCA, and they have a great deal of trouble sleeping at night.

None of this bodes well for me. I want to get out of chaotic Moresby and find the Papua New Guinea I saw as a child in the PBS documentaries: steaming jungles, isolated villages, colorfully bedecked tribesmen. I want to find Ivan Champion's New Guinea, his 'Promised Land.' Port Moresby reminds me of the world of my nightmares, where, ever since getting out of Mozambique, I've been pursued night after night by one shady group after another. Like a cartoon character with nine lives, I always narrowly escaped capture, always waking myself up on the verge of being caught. But Moresby is a place that feels claustrophobic and inescapable; there is nowhere to run but further indoors, behind more barbed wire and locked doors.

In the YWCA's meeting hall, I spread out my map of PNG and consider my trip after getting away from Port Moresby. I'll go way into the mass of jungle and swamps. The whole country, the whole world, can't be like Moresby. There has to be a certain point when it all changes and the world reverts back to some earlier innocence and respect for life. There has to be a place where no one's ever heard of barbed wire or AK-47s, rascals or attack dogs.

But maybe I'm being completely naive now?

The women in the YWCA start to gather around me and my map. They politely inquire where I'm going, and I try to explain that I want to get from the south to the north of the country via the rivers. To my surprise, none of them doubt I can make the trip. No one advises me against it, and my gender is never referred to. Instead, these young women with their tattooed faces lean down beside me and point fingers at the map. They tell me fantastic stories of the jungles I'll find here, the people I'll meet there. They know. They have *wantok* – family – just where I'm going, and they say I can buy a canoe, paddle to all sorts of places, see all sorts of fascinating cultures and never get my fill of it. They've lived in those places. They know. And they say there's no place like Papua New Guinea on this earth.

Suddenly, I'm showered with addresses of wantoks. In PNG, who you know means absolutely everything. It can make the difference between something being possible or not. It can get me into a place, or out of one. Connections. Wantoks. They're my ticket through the country.

The word 'wantok' comes from the English 'one talk,' and literally means someone who speaks the same language, comes from the same tribe or extended family. In a country with over 700 distinct tribes, the idea of a wantok is a powerful one as it describes who's a member of the tribe and who's an outsider. The women at the YWCA seem to use the word loosely, applying it to nearly anyone with whom they have some kind of connection. Friends become wantoks. Old co-workers. Friends of a friend. In the case of Mrs Hassengut, who runs the YWCA, she seems to know church people in every nook of the country, and they become wantoks. But regardless of whom one includes in the category, the wantok system is invaluable: it ensures that, when traveling, one will never go without food, shelter and assistance. It ensures survival.

The YWCA women tell me that the rules of the wantok system are simple. All I have to do is approach their friends in the villages. I'll then be invited – me, a complete stranger – into their houses, their huts, their lives. I'll get immediate access to their hospitality. They'll give me food, will help me along in my journey as best they can. My obligation in return is to offer a gift of money or canned food – whatever – as long as I reciprocate the generosity somehow. This is the Melanesian way, coming from New Guinea's deep roots. One never takes without making an offering in return. To do so not only is bad manners but upsets the mores of the tribe: how can a person function solely off of greed? What kind of person forgets how to give in return?

I'm starting to appreciate having wantoks of my own here in the YWCA, and I feel as if I belong to some kind of extended family now. Strange: my own family doesn't even know where I am – I could be anywhere in the world. When I was in Mozambique, thinking I was going to die, I remember realizing that no one on earth knew about my predicament; if I died, I would be leaving life anonymously. Now, though, the women call me 'sista,' sister in Pidgin. They've adopted me into their fold, and their wantoks exist like a support network around the country, able to keep tabs on me and to help, if necessary.

The women invite me to dinner, and for hours I field their questions about America.

'Do you speak Canadian?' one young woman asks me.

'Is America a small country?' asks another.

Their questions tell me that, thankfully, this country is still remarkably innocent.

Payday.

All that keeps the drunken mob of rascals away from us in the YWCA is a fifteen-foot-high chain-link fence. On the top of the fence runs a coil of barbed wire, rusty, sagging in spots as if it has lost confidence. *I've* lost confidence. I wonder if the fence is there to keep them out or me in. And I wonder if a certain tenacious man will discover a weak spot in the structure and lead an entire exodus of rascals into the YWCA compound. It happened only two weeks before. It could happen again. Maybe, even, tonight.

On the other side of the fence, it is anarchy. In the darkness beyond the floodlights of the YWCA compound, the crowd of rowdy young men throw beer bottles and yell obscenities at each other. Some policemen have come to try to disperse them, and when their batons hit the heads of the ruffians I hear a hollow *clonk*. Batons make a different sound on the bodies of the men, a kind of dull, meaty sound followed by a screech. The moment after a young man is hit, he looks dazed and strangely helpless, like a confused child. But there are always more to replace him. More *clonks*, more sounds of breaking bottles on asphalt. More jeers and swearing and fights to add to the insanity.

These fortnightly paydays have long stopped being a bizarre spectacle for the women at the YWCA. They're used to the clockwork chaos every two weeks. When workers receive their paychecks, Moresby enters a state of emergency. Employees get drunk. Rascals rape and steal. These are the nights when security guards earn their money, and when all people who value their life and possessions lock themselves up in their houses and don't come out for anything.

The YWCA women try to apologize for the chaos outside, telling me that tonight is an especially bad pay-day night. We all gather in the meeting hall, ostensibly for bible study. While the women sit quietly with their bibles, I pull out *Tender Is the Night*. But like them, I can only pretend to read. Outside there are noises by the fence that we can't account for. It's like living out those child-hood fears of ghosts wandering the hall. Every noise sets us on edge. We think we hear footsteps, a fence clatter-ing. One of the women races over to the window and peeks out through the curtains. Are they coming? Are the rascals coming?

A communal sigh. Nothing. No one.

To help distract us, one woman prepares a snack of fried bananas, and I answer questions about America until we hear a rumbling outside. A truck! Outside the front gate! Everyone jumps to the windows. What does it want? A couple of bolder women tiptoe to the door and step outside. Word is given, is relayed to the rest of us: it's okay, no rascals.

It is the rumbling of trucks by the front gate that especially scares: that's how they come. Criminals by the truckload armed with M-16s or AK-47s like the bad guys in the insanely popular Rambo movies. Whenever there's a rumbling – and there are frequent rumblings – the YWCA matron, now stationed by the window, pulls aside the curtain and peers out. At one point, a woman's jubilant laugh from outside sounds like a scream. We all jump up. Where to go? What to do? We all contemplate how to preserve our lives.

I decide to go to bed early. In my small room on the second floor, with the floodlight streaming in through the window, I invent an escape plan. My passport and traveler's checks need to be kept in easy reach beside my bed so I can fling them behind the wardrobe. My journal and notes go under the bed. I must keep the window open and unlocked so that – if necessary – I can easily push out the screen. Of course everything depends on where they come from. If they head down the hallway, or come from the back entrance . . . But it occurs to me that there is nowhere to run to. It is absolutely impossible to feel safe here.

Outside, some young men speed by in cars, howling and chiding the YWCA security guard as they pass. I can't go to sleep. I've got to leave Port Moresby. Get the hell out of here.

Payday is over, thank God. All of the chaos will wait for another two weeks, and the morning is quiet, uneventful. Birds sing feebly by the debris left on the streets. I head to the docks, wanting to try to get myself stowed away on some rubber ship or supply vessel bound for the Fly River and the interior of New Guinea. I don't much care how I manage this or with whom, as long as I can leave soon. The first step of my plan is to simply ask the captain of a ship if I can go along. The women at the YWCA explained to me that Western insurance companies have somehow made their way to the jungles of Papua New Guinea, prohibiting any extra passengers from getting on board ships. So I'll have to find not just the captain of a ship, but a person willing to break the rules.

The docks of Port Moresby are a busy place. Businesses go about their affairs of dropping off cargo, checking receipts, loading ships. The air smells heavily of diesel fumes and rotting fish, a combination so thick I can almost swallow it.

I decide to try to do everything the legal way. I head to the offices of the Steamships Shipping Company. These are the people who have all but monopolized commercial trade in PNG, and use the Fly River as a kind of super-highway, delivering goods to the interior towns of Kiunga and Tabubil – towns that exist because of the lucrative operations of one of the world's largest gold and copper mines, Ok Tedi. Though the PNG government is a fellow shareholder in the mine, the Australian company BHP runs everything, reaping enormous profits.

I reach the administrative building and decide to see if the Big Boss himself will see me. This is my 'experiment': I really don't expect to get permission. But who knows? He could always stick me on board with the cargo. I climb up a flight of stairs to the Steamships main office, remembering something my mother once told me that has made it possible for me to humiliate myself with strangers ever since: 'You'll never see the person again.'

I walk inside and ask a manager if I can speak to the boss.

'On what business?'

'Shipping business.'

He gives me a quizzical glance, but permission is granted. I'm ushered into the office of a large Australian expat who clearly exhibits his power and authority through the excessive use of an air conditioner. The office feels like a meat locker. Covered in goose bumps, I sit down in front of his desk and come straight to the point. Does his company take passengers up the Fly River?

He lights a cigarette and studies me with an empty expression. His red face is heavily wrinkled, and cigarette smoke streams from his nostrils.

'Why do you want to go *there*?' he asks.

That is The Question, of course. The one my ex-boyfriend asked me just before I left on my trip. Why do you want to go there? What do you want to do there?

I tell him the story I have ready: 'I need to do work for my graduate thesis. I want to cross the country from south to north and see the tribes along the way and take notes on how they live.' I look him straight in the eye.

'How old are you?' he asks.

'Twenty-four.'

He takes another long drag on his cigarette. The expression on his face doesn't change. Even with the ice-box temperature in the office, the wisps of graying blond hair on his forehead look damp from sweat.

100

'Do your parents know where you are?' he asks, smirking.

'No.'

He leans forward, readjusts himself in the chair. 'They don't?'

I shrug. I don't want to play his game. 'As far as the work I'm doing,' I say, 'it'd be ideal to go by ship up the Fly River. That would be a perfect way to head into the interior.'

Our eyes meet. I want him to know I'm serious.

He looks at me incredulously before glancing at the papers on his desk. 'Well, I can't help you,' he says. 'We can't take passengers. Cargo only. None of the ships take passengers for insurance reasons.'

'Any exceptions?'

He sighs and mashes out his cigarette, glaring at me. 'No exceptions. No one will take you.'

'You're sure?'

He gets up and walks to the door. 'It's been jolly,' he says, opening it. 'I've got work to do.'

I leave the Steamships' office, pausing outside the door to figure out my next move. Do I go to any other offices, make a fool of myself again? A young man is heading toward me from across the street. I ready myself for some kind of annoying come-on.

'Hi. I'm Thomas,' he says when he reaches me. He speaks perfect, Australian-accented English. 'I'm a manager for Steamships.'

I can well believe he's the manager of something, he looks so unusually well-dressed in his crisp white shirt and tie. He can't be older than twenty-seven, has light-brown skin, hazel eyes, and the strong, fit body of an athlete. We shake hands. I tell him my problem, how I've been trying to get on one of the ships leaving for the Fly. How *difficult* it's been so far.

'I can arrange it,' he says. 'Come to my office.'

His arm confidently around my shoulders, he leads me away. He's a smooth one, all right. A very attractive man

101

who obviously knows it. If he'd grown up in the Hollywood Hills he might have become a Calvin Klein model, an actor – his looks are that good. Here in PNG, he has to content himself with the position (though a coveted one) of Steamships manager.

'Didn't I talk to you last week?' he asks me as we walk. 'Sue, is it?'

I roll my eyes. 'You're thinking of someone else,' I say.

'No, I have a very good memory. It's something with an "A".'

I give him my name, spell it for him.

'But I know I met you last week.' Thomas stops us in the middle of the street. A car is coming but he doesn't appear to notice it. 'It was here. Last week.'

'Maybe it was my sister,' I offer.

'You have a sister?'

'No.'

Thomas looks confused for a moment. But only a moment. Suddenly his face bursts into a smile and he wags his finger at me. 'You're being difficult,' he says.

We start walking again. His office is in a loft above a cargo-loading area, but instead of going up there, he directs me to various workers. Arm snugly about my waist now, he starts to introduce me to each of the men as if we were old buddies. I smile briefly and give them little nods. Barely into these introductions, I pry Thomas's hand loose and give it back to him. The men laugh and chide him in Pidgin, but he isn't fazed: as I walk up the wooden staircase to his office, he follows, hand on the small of my back. His secretary eyes us wearily as we walk by, as if Thomas is often in the habit of bringing women into his office. What he doesn't seem to realize, though, is that I'm on to him. Or, perhaps realizing it, he doesn't care. When his eyes and nose crinkle up with laughter, it's hard for me not to be taken by him. Surely he knows his effect on people. At any rate, he knows his effect on me. He laughs quite a bit, and it's so pleasing to watch that I don't try to deter him.

I sit down. He turns on the air conditioner to its highest level and hands me a Coke.

'My Dad's Australian,' he says all of a sudden. 'He's living there now.'

I nod. 'Australia's a nice place.'

'I've been twice to Australia to visit my cousins.'

He explains that his mother is a Highlands woman. His Australian father never married her – in fact, rarely sees Thomas or his mother anymore – but Thomas's father works for Steamships, and got Thomas his prestigious managerial position. Now, Thomas can send money home to 'Mum' each month.

We start to talk about how I'm supposed to get myself on a cargo vessel. I remind him that it's illegal, and that the big boss said no.

Thomas gives me one of his seductive laughs and waves my comment aside. 'Doesn't matter,' he says. '*I'm* the boss here.'

From the nonchalant way Thomas talks, it seems to be a matter of just getting me on board undetected. He explains that the captain is in charge after the ship leaves the port, and then issues of legality are overlooked. Thomas, knowing all of the captains personally, will ask for a favor. A ship is apparently leaving for the Fly River in a few days, and he'll arrange a place for me. All I have to do is arrive at the docks after dark and get on. Easy.

'Me and some mates are going out for some beers tonight. Why don't you come?' He walks over and sits down on the arm of my chair.

'Am I supposed to be doing something in return for your help?' I ask. 'You should tell me now, for the record.'

He acts shocked. 'I don't expect anything.'

I get up. I tell him I'll call him.

'Do you have a boyfriend in America?' he asks as I head to the door.

'Would it make any difference to you if I said I did?'

'No.'

We laugh.

Only my first day in PNG, and I can now add it to my list of countries where I've been asked the Boyfriend Question. There isn't a country in the world where the question hasn't come up at least once. In some countries (like Egypt), I'd been asked it about a million times to the accompaniment of marriage proposals. Right now I could be wearing a veil as mistress of a sea shell shop on the Red Sea. Men and women's travel experiences are undoubtedly different. I feel as if I can never, ever get away from my gender when I travel alone. Sometimes this isn't a bad thing. In some cultures, men feel obliged to assist a woman, and I've been able to go places and do things that a male traveler would have a lot of trouble finagling. Take Thomas, for example: if I were a man, he probably wouldn't have approached me at all. But then again, is Thomas such a good thing? I'm not sure.

I tell him that I have a very jealous fiancé waiting for me back home – he has a black belt in karate and can break five boards with his hand. He's also a medical student. At Harvard. And has climbed to the top of Mount Everest. Twice.

I stop my lying because while Thomas seems to believe me, he's not especially impressed.

'But does he play rugby?' he asks, crossing his arms.

'No,' I say.

'What kind of man is he, then?'

I shrug. Maybe he has a point.

I catch a van back to the YWCA, taking a backseat next to the window. I put my sunglasses on to conveniently block out the world, easing myself into a space where my thoughts can run. My conversation with Thomas has unleashed thoughts of James. He's the actual 'boyfriend back home' whom I had stopped seeing just before this trip, and whom I knew I was starting to fall in love with – though I refused to indulge in the feelings. He had always been big on psychology, suggesting that I intentionally avoid dating men who can offer me what I need. He used to theorize that the idea of my loving someone was 'too frightening.' And he was probably right. It actually feels easier to go off alone into some New Guinea jungle than to undergo the hazardous journey of getting close to another, loving another. Which isn't to say that I don't want to do it, but the idea does indeed terrify me.

I used to always approach the men I dated as if I were hoping they'd hire me; I was careful to give them everything I thought they might be looking for. I was a good listener, a supportive friend, a passionate lover. Inevitably, though, I would feel miserable and alone with them. None of those men knew anything about me. I didn't trust them with my memories; I didn't believe they, or anyone, could offer me the opportunity for the safety or happiness I so secretly and desperately needed. Instead, I became the quintessential Good Thing that delivered and delivered, requiring no reciprocal effort on their part. It was a role I was used to – that of caretaker, of stranger.

Then James came along. I remember his caresses and soft words, the way he encompassed me with a single gaze: *I will take care of you.* And the joy and terror of such an idea! At what price would his ministrations come? And worse still: what if I got used to being taken care of, and he suddenly stopped? What then? I would be on my own again, but this time I would know what I was missing.

I lean further into the corner of the PMV, further into myself. An image comes, overriding my thoughts. It clouds out the scenes of a bustling downtown Moresby, obscures the hot, choking smells of diesel exhaust. As is usual, it comes more in the form of feelings. A smattering of image and emotion from a childhood so successfully forgotten that it exists more as a blot of gray space, a drift of years without substance. A mirage. I cannot go back to those years with any degree of exactness or certitude. As if I were once again standing on the Four Corners, I find myself everywhere and nowhere at once, existing out of time.

It is an image of my trying to hug my brother good-bye

before he went away to college. My parents are marveling over the novelty of this, while my brother smirks and guards himself with crossed arms. My brother chides me for needing to indulge in such a 'pleasantry.' When will I learn? Expressing love is nothing but a character flaw, a weakness that requires swift reprimand and correction.

Our PMV travels by the ocean now. I watch sunlit waves reaching and receding across Moresby's empty beaches. A yacht bobs in the distance, its sails slapping in the wind. I wonder if James would like it here, find any of this beautiful. He called this trip 'an escape.' He had warned me against it, perhaps because his pride was piqued. He wanted to know what I was looking for that he couldn't give me.

My problem is that I always want guarantees. About him. About me. About changing myself. And yet there are none. Everything's a risk. This PMV ride through dangerous Port Moresby – yet another risk.

Our van passes buildings encircled with the ubiquitous barbed wire. We skirt Town proper and head up Three Mile Hill toward Boroko. I realize that our van could break down. Rascals could get on and rob us. We could crash.

Absolutely no guarantees.

Sunday is a very important day at the YWCA. All of the women, without exception, go to church, and they've asked me to come along. They want me to 'find Jesus' with them. I don't dare tell them about my Ayn Rand upbringing and agree to try out a genuine Papua New Guinean Baptist service in the morning, with a second helping at a Methodist church in the evening. I've only been to church once in my life, when I had to stay at a neighbor's house; I'm actually more familiar with Hare Krishna protocol from my days of interviewing devotees for articles in college.

Ursula, a large woman with a blue tribal tattoo in the middle of her forehead like a Hindu *tikka* dot, is taking me to the Baptist service. She's the only Papua New

Guinean woman I've met who has actually been to the States. And not just to the States but to the University of Arizona, Tucson – where I went to graduate school. Too coincidental for us to bear, we dazzle the other YWCA women with stories about Mount Lemmon and saguaro cacti.

I have no appropriate clothes to wear, so Ursula loans me one of her old, white cotton sundresses that's too small for her. She ties it in at the waist and gives me a pair of white dress shoes. I sit down on her bed so she can do my hair. Laboriously curling it, she puts it up with a pink ribbon. Feeling self-consciously female and dainty, I head into the hallway to look at myself in the mirror. With terror, I greet the Pollyanna I've become.

'*My God*,' I mumble. Perhaps I ought to go trick-or-treating.

I never dress up when I travel. Instead, I make it a point to dress as the local people do. In Papua New Guinea, I bought a couple of those simple skirts they were selling in the market for a dollar each – they're just a piece of printed flower material sewn with an elastic waistband. Appearing in one of these along with a T-shirt and sandals, I wouldn't impress anyone, but in some places, if you're a woman traveling alone, you don't *want* to look good. You want to look downright unattractive if you can manage it.

Today, though, is different. Ursula and I are catcalled during nearly every stage of our trip to the Baptist church across town – proof positive that being dainty has its drawbacks. She shoves her way past the pssting men on the PMV, her hand firmly in mine as I take clunky baby steps in her dress shoes, trying to keep up. Already, I have blisters; high heels are surely a masochistic invention. The dress itself gives me a strange anxiety I've all but forgotten about: I find myself guarding my legs, nervous of possible thigh exposure.

We make it to the service just in time. I'm surprised to discover it's being held in a convention hall in one of the most elegant hotels in town. Leaving the *buai*-stained, diesel-reeking streets of Moresby for such air-conditioned opulence – complete with jumbo swimming pool – could be an incentive in itself for joining the Moresby Baptist Church.

Officiating at the service is an African-American man from Norfolk, Virginia, named Tony. He's surprisingly young, in his late twenties, and my thoughts are turning very carnal. Very attractive, Tony has a smile that clearly captivates and invigorates his audience. People walk up to him in droves, greeting him, slapping him on the back, joshing him. The idea, it seems to me, is simply to be *near* Tony, however it can be managed.

I take a seat next to Ursula in the front row. As we wait, I leaf through her New Testament. Nearly every page has extensive marginal notes. The text is so thoroughly highlighted it reminds me of my old high school history textbooks. I flip it open to James 1:2–4, to some sentences that had escaped the highlighter:

> Consider it pure joy, my brothers, whenever you face trials of many kinds, because you know that the testing of your faith develops perseverance. Perseverance must finish its work so that you may be mature and complete, not lacking anything.

It is a universal wisdom that could have come as easily from the mouth of the Buddha, or Mohammed, or Krishna. It speaks to everyone, infidel and saint. I wonder, though, how one knows when the perseverance is over? How does one know when it's time to go home, 'mature and complete, not lacking anything'?

The service is a lively one, like something out of Harlem. It's a pageant of movement and sound and clapping hands, with Tony's every word being uh-huhed and amen-ed. Whenever he says something like, 'I'd like to turn to Acts 2:17,' people in the audience pipe in, 'You do it, Tony!' or 'Yes, amen.' I'm struck by Tony's uncanny charisma. He could probably send armies jumping to their deaths at his command.

After the sermon, we all head to the beach for an afternoon picnic and volleyball game. I gratefully peel off the dress and put on some shorts and a T-shirt. Tony greets me on the beach. He introduces me to a thin, muscular man reclining in the grass near the volleyball net. The man, he explains, was a sprinter who was at the 1984 Olympics in Los Angeles. An Olympic star! The man, I notice, is partially paralyzed. Tony explains that shortly after his return from LA, several rascals beat him up. Only recently has he been able to walk, and he will never run again.

'Jesus!' I say – a bit too loudly, I fear, for members of the congregation.

The man nods. 'It's very dangerous here,' he says. The Olympic star picks up his leg as if it were a dead weight and dangles it for me.

We start our volleyball game. Making a dash for the other team's first serve, I try to spike the ball and break it open. I've broken it in half, actually, and it lies limply on the ground. We all gather around, pondering it. It isn't an official volleyball, is more like a cheap, dime-store version, but they don't have another ball and so we can't play anymore. A couple of men make friendly jokes about how strong I must be, but I feel really bad about it. I should have played differently. No spikes or anything like that. I should have played like some goddamn Pollyanna.

It's Monday, and I meet Thomas at his office. He says he wants to buy me lunch and struts over to a brand-new Land Rover being guarded by one of the dockworkers.

'I have good news for you,' he says in a singing voice, opening the passenger-side door for me.

'What's that? I can leave on the ship?'

'Tonight. Tonight you will go!'

I let loose a hesitant smile. 'You're sure?'

'Kira, Kira . . .' He gives me one of his hurt expressions. 'Don't you trust me?'

'Not really.'

He pretends to pout and starts the car. The Land

Rover is fully equipped, must have cost a fortune in a country where the average person is lucky to make $800 a year.

'Is this yours?' I ask, tapping the dashboard.

'Yes, of course.'

Thomas starts driving it with the reckless indifference of someone who hasn't paid a dime for it. The car roars down the city streets as if he were going after a Formula One title, pedestrians diving out of the way as we speed by.

We zoom past a crowd of young men waiting for a bus. Thomas nearly hits a couple of them and I look behind us for casualties. When he stops at a Shell gas station, I consider getting out of the car, just completely abandoning this whole ship idea.

He comes back with some ready-made sandwiches and cans of Coke. He piles these in my lap and starts the car again.

'Lunch?' I ask.

He nods and pulls out, zooming into the traffic.

'I need to go back to the YWCA soon,' I tell him.

'No worries. Let's go to my dad's house to eat.'

His dad's house is in the elite area of Moresby, on the hill overlooking the sea. As we drive up the narrow streets, little kids recognize Thomas and his Land Rover and go running off at the sight of us, announcing to the whole world that Thomas has a *wait meri* – white woman – in his car. Now, instead of going at his usual break-neck speed, Thomas creeps along the streets. He honks at the kids, at any people he meets along the way. He wants the whole neighborhood to see us together, and I can't stop myself from frowning.

We finally turn into a driveway. Thomas unlocks a perimeter gate (topped with the ubiquitous barbed wire), then an inner gate before we can get anywhere near his house. Ironically, the house doesn't look worth the effort of robbery. For one thing, it's not very big. Mold streaks the whitewashed walls. Waist-high weeds grow all over the yard, yellow fronds dangling from neglected palm trees. Everywhere, ancient dog turds sit in petrified piles in the sun.

We head into the house. The inside isn't much better than the outside. It's a two-bedroom house, furnished with some dingy teakwood chests and wicker chairs, giant spider webs stretching across the ceiling. The place smells of mildew, and the gray carpet looks as if a few thousand people have spilled whiskey on it.

I bat a spider off the wicker sofa and sit down. Thomas is busy in the kitchen putting our sandwiches on plates and opening the Cokes. He's singing some song, has taken his tie off and unbuttoned the top of his shirt.

'Where's Dad?' I ask.

'Dad? Oh, he's not here now.'

'When's he coming back?'

'I don't know.'

'I get it,' I say, feeling like a dupe.

Thomas finishes preparing our sandwiches and hands me a plate. Some past food is solidified on the edge of the plate, and I pick at it with a fingernail. He sits next to me on the sofa, his thigh touching mine. *Here we go*. I scoot away from him and keep our conversation on the ship I'm supposed to get on tonight. Thomas says he'll have to call me this evening, around six when he gets the final word. He has to be careful, though. Figure out the best time to sneak me on.

'So I'm definitely going tonight?' I ask.

'Of course.'

I quickly finish my sandwich and Coke. Getting up, I tell Thomas I have to go back to the YWCA.

'Will you look at my photo album, first?' he asks.

I sigh. I see no way out. Reluctantly, I accept the album. He quickly turns the pages for me. Glimpses of him as a boy, standing behind his white Aussie cousins at the zoo in Sydney. Glimpses of Mum. Of Dad. More cousins. More aunties. Suddenly Thomas turns the pages slowly: adult pictures of him as a rugby player, as a swimmer in tight Speedos.

The pages run out and Thomas tosses the album down.

111

I get up and go to the door. I tell him that I have to leave now, get back to the YWCA—

His body is up against me, and he's kissing me. His hands are on my breasts.

I shove him back. I'm not scared of him. Not him. I don't find him threatening, just annoying. So I have to have sex with him in order to get on the ship? I glare at him, pushing him away from me.

I leave the house. Going to the Land Rover, I sit in the passenger seat, wondering if Thomas's behavior had something to do with the fact that I'm a Western woman and am supposed to be 'easy.' I experienced the same thing in Egypt, men assuming I was like the loose, big-breasted blonde flirting unabashedly with the hero of some American B-action flick playing during a bus ride from the Red Sea.

Thomas runs over. He gives me an embarrassed look as he gets behind the wheel.

'Sorry. I couldn't help myself,' he says. 'You're so beautiful.'

I groan, rolling my eyes. 'Just take me back.'

We go back. In silence.

Thomas drops me off in front of the YWCA, saying, 'I'll call you about the ship,' but I know he won't call. I've been much too naive. I know this is the last I'll see of him, and that the ship idea is officially dead.

I decide I will fly to the island of Daru tomorrow, an island at the mouth of the Fly River. It isn't how I'd wanted to begin my trip, but at least the journey will be starting already.

The YWCA women throw me a farewell party. We exchange addresses, and I tell them that whenever I get back to America, I'll write. I don't know when – or even if – I'll be home again, though. I don't know anything, the uncertainty and anxiety beginning now on the eve of my flight.

I return to my room, to the sight of the YWCA cat sitting before my door. As soon as it sees me, it starts purring loudly and bumps its scabby body against my legs. Actually, it doesn't belong to anyone, is the most disgusting-looking creature I've ever seen, half its fur gone, its ear swollen from mosquito bites, its nose scratched raw. Scrawny and starving, it should have died a long time ago. That it hasn't died, that it's lived somehow, against all odds, impresses the hell out of me.

I've been feeding it scraps of meat, bought it corned beef hash and chicken. It ate the chicken – bones, tendons and all – so that not a morsel remained. Within a day, the animal settled itself outside the door to my room, waiting for my returns from Town. The other women in the YWCA tried to shoo it outside, but it always came back in through the window and returned to the spot outside my door, staying there all day. The women thought I was crazy for encouraging it with food until Ursula said, 'It is God's creature,' and that settled the matter. Now they call it 'Kira's cat.' And I suppose it is mine. In a way. Or, at least, for one more night.

As this is our last night together, I pick up its skinny little body and bring it inside my room. I open my first-aid bag and dab alcohol on its nose. I clean its sores and put antibiotic ointment on them. I know no one will take care of it after I'm gone, and I'm starting to feel guilty. I wonder how long it'll wait outside my door, how many times the women will have to shoo it away before it understands that I'm not coming back and that its luck has run out.

I give it a hug, petting its scabby head. 'You were born in the wrong place at the wrong time, my friend.'

More ecstatic purring.

CHAPTER FIVE

Bush Mary

The man who's supposed to be taking me up the Fly River has a disturbing way of stopping mid-sentence to hack up prodigious amounts of blood-colored phlegm. His name is Phillip and he is a formidable chain smoker and betel nut chewer. I don't have a good feeling about this man, but I've been in Daru a week already and Phillip is the only person to come forward with a dinghy and a reasonable price. He's the one. Phillip will take me up the Fly.

Our mode of transportation is a sorry-looking skiff with a simple outboard motor and several red plastic petrol jugs. The most indispensable of the boat's gear are several empty tin cans ('Meat Spaghetti' the labels still read), which float in the water in the bottom of the hull. These, I'm told, are for bailing out the boat as it leaks. Apparently it leaks a lot.

It's hard to gauge exactly when we might be ready to go. Though Phillip told me two days ago that he's ready to leave at any time, several days have passed. Wanting to finalize our agreement and leave as soon as possible, I give him a deposit of money and accompany him to the docks while he goes to 'buy supplies.' He tells me that this means, more than anything else, cigarettes. If he doesn't buy any food, I'm hoping that he'll at least be able to advise me on what supplies I ought to get for us. I have no idea what tribes we'll encounter and whether they'll have food to share or trade. And according to my map, there are large, uninhabited distances to cover. The length of the trip, itself, is uncertain. I don't know what I'll find out there, and whether some place will be so appealing that I'll want to stay. And of course, there are dangers I can't possibly predict. I've told Phillip that I'd like to get from Daru to the source of the Fly, up near the town of Kiunga – however long it takes.

I'm not sure Phillip knows what to make of me, this lone white woman wanting to go up the Fly River for no discernible reason. I think he suspects me of being dishonest by not revealing the purpose of my trip, as if I were acting under secret orders. But I can't tell people the real reason I'm trying to get up this river because it would sound like pure lunacy. I picture myself explaining it all to Phillip: 'I'm trying to find out what I'm capable of. I want to go as far into the unknown as I can, have you dump me off somewhere, and see if I can get out again.' He'd probably just look at me and spit, shrugging his shoulders. Crazy foreigner.

I watch Phillip head toward the roofed area that is Daru Island's little market. He makes slow progress because he encounters friend after friend whom he tells about our upcoming trip. From the excitement of his various conversations and the laughing glances thrown my way, I realize I'm a novelty. I wonder if I made a mistake by signing him on and not waiting even longer for someone a little more professional to – hopefully – come along.

Not that Daru offers many options, making my finding of Phillip seem like a stroke of good luck. A small island, Daru has only a modest population. There are a few stores, a single, incredibly overpriced hotel, the tiny market and a shed that houses the island's only bank. Conveniently situated near the mouth of the Fly River, Daru has a reputation for being friendly and pleasant. It was one of the first places in PNG where the missionaries were able to comfortably settle down without fear of being speared or clubbed to death. Daru and its Kiwai people have been subjected to foreign visitors since the latter half of the nineteenth century, an offical missionary settlement being founded in 1887, which, considering the first exploration of the vast PNG Highlands in the 1930's, is early on the PNG time line. Along with a fear of God, the Victorian missionaries left behind an old church, some now enormous mango trees, and a slow-moving, orderly existence. Only the strong wind from the ocean ruffles the tranquility of Daru, gushing forth to tangle palm tree fronds and send dust and debris into the stilt houses. When people aren't sweeping the dust back out, they can be seen chatting the afternoon away. Life is lazy and uneventful, as if everyone were pleasantly marooned. I seem to be the only one intent on getting out of the place.

As Phillip returns with his smokes and a newspaper full of the narcotic *buai* concoction – betel nuts, mustard pods and a little paper pouch filled with coral lime powder – I wonder whether Phillip has any more addictions I can fund. He grins at me, an unsettling sight as his front teeth were all knocked out, I was told, during a brawl. His tongue creeps out over his gums like an extra appendage he can't control, something with a mind of its own, something predatory.

'So let's leave today,' I say. 'What do you think?'

'Yes, yes, yes.' He breaks the fat end of a yellow betel nut with his incisor, stripping the coconut-like hull away and crunching up the walnut-sized nut in his cheek. 'Tonight, tomorrow. I don't know.'

I smile. 'How about today?'

He licks one of the green mustard pods and dips it into the bag of lime powder, then puts the whole thing in his mouth and starts to chew. Slowly, he examines the sky. 'Today is no good. Maybe rain.'

'Tomorrow morning, then.'

He shrugs, spitting a blood-red missile onto a seashell near his foot. 'Maybe,' he says.

'Maybe?'

'I have big preparation.' He hacks and hacks again, spits, then wipes his mouth and lights a cigarette. 'We need driver and mechanic.' He counts the two men on his fingers for me. 'Driver . . . mechanic.'

Before I gave him the money, just the two of us were supposed to go. I was afraid of this, that as soon as I gave him any cash he'd start to change our agreement. 'I thought you are able to do all that by yourself,' I say.

'But I am Captain.'

I'm confused. Is there such a thing as the Captain of a skiff? My knowledge of nautical matters comes out of *Moby Dick*. How many men are required, after all, to run a rowboat with an outboard? I study the beach for a moment, sure I'm being played. Two boys with blond, sun-bleached hair dive into the waves. The sun shines weakly through a thick layer of cloud, the gray ocean slapping the shore.

'We hadn't agreed to two extra people,' I tell him.

'No worries. I pay them.' He spits into an incoming wave.

PNG isn't a country like Japan or Singapore where you can probably trust most people. The idea of being alone in a dinghy with a group of men I've never met before, all of my possessions on me, no recourse if anything should happen, has me more than a little anxious. I'm not going on a day trip to the local botanical gardens, after all. I don't know where I'm going.

I tell Phillip that I haven't agreed to anyone except him, and that I don't want a bunch of other people coming along for the ride. His tongue creeps up out of his mouth and slides along his lips.

He takes a long drag on his cigarette, then drops it and crushes it out. 'These men are necessary,' he says.

Our conversation has attracted a bevy of onlookers, and we're now surrounded by at least twenty people. Phillip feels compelled to translate our conversation into Motu for them, which gives everyone some comic relief. One of the onlookers asks me, in English, how much I'm paying Phillip. When I tell him, and he translates, the crowd laughs and men come up to slap Phillip on the back.

For PNG, our monetary agreement is quite an exorbitant amount: the average Papua New Guinean is lucky to make $800 a year, and Phillip is getting nearly that much up front. Half of it is to go for petrol to get us a few hundred miles up the Fly River. The rest is a payment to him. My plan is to travel from village to village, where I'll trade money or goods with the local people for a night's lodging and provisions for the next day's travel. Aside from cigarettes and betel nuts, Phillip won't have to spend his money on anything. He's just to take me wherever I want to go, assuming we can get there somehow. I'm told that the native language will completely change every fifty miles or so along the course of the river, and Phillip supposedly knows bits of each tongue. So, too, Phillip will act as translator.

I ask Phillip if he can have his 'big preparation' handled by the next morning so we – only he and I – can leave. His eyes, watery and red from the *buai*, stare at me.

He nods. 'Of course,' he says.

I return to where I've been staying for the past week – with the Reverend Anna Bisai up at the old Methodist church. She's a friend, a wantok, of one of the women back at the YWCA, which is how I got the invitation to stay in her house. Anna has lordly control over Daru, overseeing every aspect of life here, including my plans to go up the Fly. People quake at her approach and I'm going to talk to her tonight, am counting on her to put the fear of God into Phillip so we can leave tomorrow.

In her fifties, caretaker of the old Methodist settlement and the first female minister ordained in the Pacific, Reverend Anna has done more for international women's rights than most people will ever know, having fought a notoriously stubborn and patriarchal system for her ordination. Significantly, she was chosen as a PNG representative to the Beijing Women's Conference and doesn't let anyone forget that she shook Hillary Clinton's hand. Everyone in Daru town is terrified of her. Her formidable presence can often be seen surveying the streets of Town with a frown of disapproval. Reverend Anna might have been Napoleon in a past life but is now in such need of troops to command and battles to wage that she's taken up the cause of the mango trees on the church property. These are under constant attack from passing boys who try to knock the unripe fruit down with stones. I often see Anna striding from one end of the long church property to the other, yelling at the boys in a piercing voice, 'I am very *very* angry about this!'

She is very angry about many things, not least of which the immorality that she believes is slowly leaking into Daru and corrupting everyone. Reverend Anna possesses an uncanny kind of X-ray vision when it comes to morality. She'd gone out of her way to meet Phillip once, briefly, after finding out he'd agreed to take me up the Fly. Her report was typically brief and to the point: 'This is a *very* bad man.' She says Phillip isn't a Kiwai Islander like everyone else on Daru. He's an Outsider, and so not to be trusted. But when it comes to Reverend Anna, I never know how seriously I should take her. She calls almost everyone 'very bad.' Getting in her good favor requires a gargantuan effort, and that I've somehow managed to do it (she's very generous with me, sharing meals and letting me stay in her house as long as I like) has me miffed. I suspect it was the raking. To help her out, I'd spent four days raking grass with other church workers. There was so much of the grass that by the last day I was convinced that raking should become an Olympic sport. During this time, Anna – the re-incarnated Napoleon – stood in the shade of one of the mango trees and supervised our efforts, nodding with stoic approval at my many blisters. I can't help admiring Reverend Anna. She knows how to extract blind devotion like a Lawrence of Arabia, and I've certainly become one of the most loyal grass-rakers there ever was.

This evening, as we sit on the veranda of her house watching the sun go down, I tell her that I'm pretty sure I'll be leaving with Phillip the next morning.

'Don't you believe it,' she says.

'But today he bought supplies. Tomorrow, I told him, I want to leave.'

'That man is always telling lies. I think you are a nice girl,' Reverend Anna says, pointing a pencil at me, 'so you don't know a bad man when you see one. He is no good.'

I want to tell her that I have a pretty good idea that Phillip isn't a saint, but I'm not looking for a saint. All I want is a boat and someone with nothing better to do than head way up the Fly River into the swamps and jungles. I was in Daru a week before Phillip even turned up. No one else wants to take me up the Fly. Everyone seems to think I'm crazy for even *suggesting* the idea. What the hell is to be found up the Fly? Nothing but swamps and, as an expat I'd met in Town put it, 'those really backward tribes.' Why would I want to go there? I must be some kind of crazy foreigner.

But I don't tell Reverend Anna anything. I don't tell her that, in many ways, I'm starting to lose my perspective on things. It's been happening quite a lot lately, like a strange kind of amnesia. I feel as if I've forgotten who I am, that someone or something else is in charge of me. I walk around with an out-of-body feeling, only the shudder of my steps telling me I'm occupying a body. I don't know what it means, exactly. Maybe I *am* going crazy? Or maybe I'm just exhausted by everything – PNG, myself, my life? The farther my plans seem to progress and the closer to the interior of New Guinea I get, the more disoriented I feel. A certain kind of momentum consumes me now, pressing me on regardless of risk. So am I actually going through with this? But I must. Stopping would mean failure, giving up on myself, succumbing to a fear of the future, the unknown.

As a girl I was taught not to be scared of anything. I remember being thirteen and patrolling my empty house with my father's loaded Glock, looking for the source of a strange noise I'd heard. The idea was to confront the fear, to greet it on its own terms. But Mozambique taught me that there are some kinds of fear you can't get rid of, and I find myself terrified by the evil in the world, by what it'll come up with next. I want to find a place where the nightmares stop, where my heart doesn't do sprints in my chest, leaving me awake and shaking in the middle of the night. I keep wondering whether this trip will be the salvation I seek – or some kind of undoing, a worsening of what had started in Africa only a few years ago.

Reverend Anna goes inside as soon as the sun sets. I head down the stairs of the veranda and sit in the grass. Daru's lawn is littered with sensitive plants that snap their leaves shut in an instant if I brush against them: plants that remind me that they're alive – in case I forgot. I'm always forgetting. I sit down on the lawn and it recoils, curls up, closes itself off so quickly that I nearly apologize.

In the distance, a family living on the church grounds is having a barbecue. The family's little boy, six-year-old Winta ('Ween-ta' – Winter in Pidgin) spots me and heads over immediately. He's always wearing shorts, his little body drowning in a huge pair of cowboy boots, which come up to his thighs.

'Hello, Kira!' he yells. 'Dem ghostmens every place dis night, so I come to protect you!'

'Ghostmen?' I say. 'Thank you for warning me.'

'Tonight we're having a big fish barbecue, but no turtle meat. I like turtle meat best, but Dad didn't catch dem turtles today. Just fishes.'

He takes a huge breath. To say Winta is outgoing is an understatement. He's one of the most friendly, talkative kids I've ever met, charming everyone he comes in contact with including, even, Reverend Anna. But he isn't just talkative in a little kid kind of way. Winta can easily out-talk a grown-up, and he definitely out-talks me.

'Winta, if you see a ghostman, will you tell me?' I ask.

'Of course. I will protect you!' He points to one of the mango trees. 'Look, a ghostmen!'

I look. I see nothing.

'Dem ghostmens, all over! You give me your hand.' He

picks up my hand and holds it, shaking his head. 'You 'fraid of dem ghostmens?'

'Not unless I see them,' I say, not very convincingly.

In the distance, the barbecue lets off bright red sparks, which swirl into the night like souls departing for the stars.

'Dem ghostmens, all over! You look!' Winta points at the trees, at the whole of the night sky over Daru, which is, to him, the entire world. 'You see dem?' he asks.

I look all over. I look really hard. Winta is standing with his back straight, heels together, like a soldier waiting for an answer.

'They're everywhere,' I say finally.

'What I just tell you. Dem's ghostmens are all over!'

And maybe they are. What do I know?

'Why you sitting here tonight? *Natnats* coming. Dey bite you all over. No good, dem *natnats*. Why you sitting here?'

'I just like to sit here.'

'Why?'

Kids – they always want to know why all the time. 'It's pretty out. When the stars come out. Don't you think?'

He's reaching into his pocket. 'Look at my shell,' he says. He takes a shell out of his pocket. It's just an ordinary clam shell. He rubs it with his shirt, spits on it and rubs it again. 'Touch it,' he says.

I touch it.

'Do you feel it?'

'Feel what?'

'Magic feeling.'

I hold it, wondering what a 'magic feeling' would feel like. In all of those children's books, only the kids are able to experience the other worlds, the magic. What happens when we grow up? Where do we put our awe?

I hold the shell to my ear. 'Wow!' I say. 'I can hear stuff.'

'Dat's right. You keep it. It's my present to you.'

'It's too special, Winta. You need it.'

'Okay.' He simply puts it back in his pocket and pulls me up by the hand. 'We got a big fish barbecue. Come with me.'

'You'll protect me from the ghostmen?' I ask, pausing.

'Yes! I already tell you.'

'Well, okay then,' I say. 'Let's go.'

Reverend Anna is right. The next day Phillip isn't ready and Anna, fed up, decides to take full responsibility of Phillip's negligence and deal with it herself.

'You're leaving today,' she assures me. 'I am very angry about this.'

We're sitting on her veranda eating breakfast, and she yells for her thirteen-year-old daughter, Leena. A shadow of a girl appears at the door and gazes timidly at us.

'I want you to do this for me,' Anna says to her. 'I want you to find this humbug Phillip and tell him to come here. Tell him I am *very* angry.'

Leena nods and goes to get her sandals on. In the next minute, she's heading off across the church grounds toward the docks.

I watch her go. Leena isn't Reverend Anna's real daughter, but in Papua New Guinea it's not uncommon to pass on children: a culturally acceptable way to deal with unwanted children and with none of the Western red tape associated with adoption. As Anna had explained to me my first night in Daru, she adopted Leena because she needed someone to 'keep her company and look after the house.' The details are sketchy, but apparently Leena was the product of a fling between a woman Anna knows and a deadbeat Australian petrol worker who now occasionally visits Anna when he comes ashore. I picture his visits: the girl busily making him fried chicken and bananas, having no idea that the lanky Aussie man is responsible for her own lanky height, light skin and hazel eyes. Neither he nor Anna bother to tell Leena the truth. For that matter, Leena doesn't know who her real mother is, either. Still, Reverend Anna loves Leena in her practical, no-nonsense way. They complement each other. Anna lordly and outspoken, Leena rarely uttering a whispered word.

A half hour later, Leena returns alone, and I can see from her dejected look that she wasn't successful. Anna stands up, seething.

'I will find him.' She points to me. 'Come with me.'

I get up and put my shoes on, and we head to the docks together.

Reverend Anna stays on the lookout for Phillip as we walk along the main road through town. People selling *buai* on pieces of dirty plastic gape at us as we pass. Women with bundles of bananas on their shoulders stop to watch us go by. We must be a strange-looking pair: Anna with her determined walk and me, striding to keep up with her.

In town, Anna asks around. It seems as if Phillip's Big Preparation for our trip is still under way and he can't be located. Frowning, Anna leads me to the Minister of Transportation's office and we take the cringing minister along in tow, just in case we need some kind of authority.

Back at the docks, Reverend Anna calls over the first two men she sees and conscripts them to our cause.

'I want you to do this for me,' she says to them. 'Find this Phillip who owns the dinghy. I want you to bring him here.'

The men nod quickly, nervously hugging their arms. They know who we're talking about (apparently everyone does), but they hesitate, seeming to have a mortal fear of not finding him. They begin by asking everyone to help out. Boys go running in different directions. Dogs bound away. Chickens dash for cover. And then, miraculously, Phillip appears.

'Uh-huh,' Reverend Anna says as he approaches us from the end of the market, biting the husk off a betel nut.

The Minister of Transportation smiles in relief.

'This man is no good,' Anna says to me. 'No good.'

Phillip takes his time reaching us, busily putting the betel nut ingredients into his mouth. When he finally stops in front of us, he smiles broadly at Anna and says hello.

'Don't smile at me like that,' she says to him. 'You told this girl you were leaving this morning, and you were telling lies.'

A crowd starts to gather around us.

'I need more money,' he says to me. 'I need spark plugs and more petrol.'

The Minister of Transportation has received his cue. He argues with Phillip in a tribal language until the shameless eavesdroppers get into action. Apparently Phillip had miscalculated the distance from Daru into the interior of the Fly River region, and he'll need more petrol money. It also appears as if his driver and mechanic – absolutely indispensable passengers, he insists – won't go anywhere without money for cigarettes.

To say I'm dismayed is to put it mildly. He wants a hundred dollars more in *kina*, and I want to tell him to just forget it, that I'm not his dupe, but he's already spent my deposit money and I won't be able to get it back. And anyway, who's to say whether the next man who turns up with a dinghy won't be just as bad? Or won't cost just as much? Or more?

Reverend Anna is about to sail into Phillip with her most terrifying motherly rebuke. I can see her eyes glaring, her mouth tightening. Phillip takes a step back, preparing himself for an explosion. He's saved, however, by the Minister of Transportation, who assures her that Phillip's new and final asking price is actually reasonable. Anna takes his word for it, relaxing. She's as ignorant about matters of dinghies and petrol as I am, it turns out.

Though I'm not happy about it, I agree to give Phillip the extra money if we can leave today, this morning. Immediately. He agrees, taking the bills I hold out. Reverend Anna, watching him walk off, tells me that I'm not to go handing out more money to Phillip *for any reason*. If this issue comes up again – and I fear it will – I'm to tag her name onto my refusal, for emphasis.

We leave at noon. The boat is crowded: Phillip has *four* indispensable passengers now, in addition to himself. But too late to just forget the whole thing. He has my money. The boat is loaded with his petrol, beer and cigarettes, and the various imperishable food items I bought in town. We're ready to shove off, to finally start.

Reverend Anna stands on the dock, her hands on her hips. Phillip starts the outboard. 'Don't give him any more money,' are her parting words to me, yelled across the frothy gray waves as the boat lurches away.

Our boat careens over the ocean waves, the bow slapping against them and spraying water onto us. The waves are so large that it seems something of a miracle that our tiny vessel hasn't overturned. The sun shows itself at intervals, sending a glitter of light across the gray water. In the distance, getting closer, a dim, uninterrupted spread of jungle meets the ocean – an unnerving barrier of green.

Phillip lights a cigarette, spitting. 'Is this your first time in my country?' he asks.

'Yes.'

He laughs and spits again, then delivers my answer to the other men in the boat. They chuckle and speak in a tribal language for a while.

'They want to know, do you have a husband?' Phillip asks.

I shake my head and look out at the water.

More talk in their language. One man makes jeers and obscene gestures.

'He wants to know,' Phillip says, 'do you want a husband?' Squeals of laughter. 'Because he wants to be your husband. He says he will be a good husband. He will make good love to you.'

I roll my eyes and say nothing. I can't allow them the pleasure of getting a rise out of me. I can't show fear. Yet here I am, alone with them in this boat, and they're already making lewd jokes. If they were to try anything – and who's stopping them? – there is no one who could help me. I am completely on my own.

I size up each of the men. They're wiry and muscular, but no one is bigger than me. Reminds me how I always used to get in fights with boys as a kid. I had a furious temper as well as a favorite wrestling move – a 'full nelson' – which was a kind of two-handed headlock that could render a person helpless. I'd used it on one boy in my fifth-grade class who kept taunting me after school. I broke my metal lunch box over his head then got him into the headlock, banging his face against the street until he was crying and pleading for me to stop. Soon after, the boy's father came to my parents' house, demanding to see who had injured his son. I came shyly to the door – me, a girl. The father was flabbergasted: his son had failed to mention that a *girl* had beaten him up, and the matter was quickly dropped. My own father, of course, had never been prouder. I could take care of myself, by God.

Thankfully, though, Phillip and the others are starting to leave me alone. They seem to be getting bored with my silence. Our boat shoots through the Kiwai Island straits, which forms the delta of the Fly River, and the jungle is getting close. There is something arresting about this jungle, something which speaks to that primordial human fear in me of the unknown. Phillip and the others might be miles away from me now; they barely register in my thoughts. Staring at the jungle, I have never seen this before: a world so complete that it wants no one. A place that reduces human beings to a kind of vermin scrambling up and down the waterways, struggling on the shores. All of us in the boat have become dwarfed by the giant rise of enormous trees that stand in a frenzied buzz of insect sound and bird chatter.

We officially enter the mouth of the Fly River, and though the river is nearly a mile wide here and I can only see the jungle on the shore to my left, already a feeling of claustrophobia starts. I'm wary and scared of Phillip and the others, being alone and the only woman among them, but I'm even more wary of this impressive expanse of jungle. I can't identify a single tree or animal. None of it is familiar. Not yet. I think I can imagine how the first

127

explorers must have felt. Their excitement and un-
easiness. As we go further up the delta, a few families
pass us in large dugout canoes propelled by outboards.
They wave as we go by, gaping and pointing when they
catch sight of me. My presence is so unexpected that the
children inside keep looking at me until we can't see each
other anymore.

The mouth of the Fly is becoming more narrow now,
and I can see the opposite bank. A few islands rise out of
the middle of the river. Our boat clings to the left-hand
shore, puttering below the reach of enormous trees, their
vines hanging down, as wide around as a person's head.
More villagers drift past us in small dugout canoes. They
freeze when they see me, eyes staring, paddles held docile
in their hands.

Finally, the jungle breaks and we pull up at a village
called Severiambu, composed of small, thatch stilt huts.
When we motor the boat up to the shore, an alarm
spreads throughout the entire village. Dogs bark and
children scream in such excited delight that the sound is
almost deafening. Suddenly everyone in the village who
can walk, limp, or hop has lined up on the shore above us
– a long line of dark bodies. They smile and point and
wave. Naked children peek out at us from behind their
mothers' legs. Dogs bark ferociously until they're kicked
into silence. And the younger women, strangely shy and
more cautious, stay in back of the crowd and watch with
their heads bowed.

I follow Phillip's lead and step out of the canoe onto
the muddy shore. My hiking boots are no good for this,
and I quickly take them off. This is a land, I see, which
prefers bare feet, and which requires one to get used to
mud.

We've only just climbed up the shore to the village
above when a man comes up to us and shakes my hand.

'I am head of the village,' he says in good English,
looking at me with a hint of suspicion. 'Why have you
come?'

I tell him that this trip is for my thesis for graduate

school. I don't want to assign a purpose to what I'm doing – and couldn't assign a logical purpose even if I tried.

'I'm sorry to ask these questions,' he says, 'but people sometimes come here. We sometimes have trouble with the Ok Tedi people.'

In these parts, if you're white, it usually means you're working for Ok Tedi, the giant gold and copper mine many hundreds of miles north, right in the middle of New Guinea. But though the mine is so far away, the politics reverberate across the whole country. Ok Tedi doesn't like to brag about the fact that it has already managed to seriously pollute the Fly River and its other tributaries. Instead, it makes much ado of its monthly payment plan to the tribes, which is used to build everything from community centers and schools to solar-powered lights. Apparently in this village of Severiambu, the local people regard the Ok Tedi agreement as being less than ideal.

As the village chief shows me around, a crowd of children follow, laughing and running in circles around us, taking turns trying to touch me. As far as villages go, this is one of the larger ones with a population of about 500 people and surely twice as many dogs. The people tend to cook outside, in Melanesian-style fire pits, and their diet is a basic one of sago tubers, bananas, yams, coconut, with the occasional fish thrown in. The men of the village often leave on hunting parties into the swampy jungle in search of wild pig, wallaby, and the large cassowary: an emu-like bird that yields enormous drumsticks. In the old days, these were the only sources of protein to be found, but the Dutch colonists, lamenting the lack of meat (and also good game hunting, as New Guinea hasn't many large land animals to pursue) imported the squat rusa deer. An invasive species, it multiplied quickly throughout the south of New Guinea, flourishing in the enormous wetlands and providing local tribes with the once exotic taste of venison.

We won't stay long in Severiambu. It's getting late and Phillip wants to reach the village of Daumori, further upriver, so we can spend the night there. To the west, the sun has lost its edge, retreating close to the top of the jungle. In a land without electricity, our days are dependent on available light, and our travels must stop by dusk.

We get into the boat again, and the entire village lines up once more to see us off. I take out my camera. Every time the flash goes off, the children squeal and dash away, quickly returning to wait excitedly for that split-second moment of the flash.

Daumori. It faces the Fly River island of Adulu, an island overgrown with jungle, where, I'm told, the Magic Fire Spirits live. The spirits can be seen at night, riding the Fly River in their dugout canoes, fire trailing behind them. These spirits also live in the sky, up by the stars, and visit their brothers on earth by riding down on a path of fire. Their job is to seek out bad people. Few are safe; the spirits' justice is fierce and irreversible. When they come to you and touch you, their fire goes out and you will rot and die. The body will wither. The inner flame dies.

The children of Daumori tell me these stories, their eyes wide. They truly believe in the Magic Fire Spirits, telling me that the spirits turn invisible when they land on earth, and that as soon as they touch the unsuspecting bad people, the sinners begin to rot. A marvelous idea! I picture the world's tyrants decaying away, skin peeling, extremities falling off. At last, reduced to a skeleton of their old selves, the bad men stare in perplexed awe at the night sky . . .

I ask the children if they'd like to hear a story, and they all nod enthusiastically. In my stuttering Pidgin, I tell them a Tahitian story about the White Lady.

A man was walking along a path by the beach at night, and he saw a light following far behind him. He hid behind a bush to wait for the light to appear and discovered that it was a beautiful woman *tupapau* – ghost – with pale skin and long white hair. He watched the ghost woman, whom he called the White Lady, walk along the beach, stop and suddenly disappear. The next morning he went to where she had disappeared and discovered the grave of a woman who had drowned. That night, as he again walked upon the path by the beach, he saw the light of the White Lady following him. He didn't know that she was a kind spirit – in Tahiti, kind spirits are warm lights that follow you and keep you safe – so he was very scared. He went to her grave, unburied her body, and drove a stick through her heart. Then he buried sea urchins and sea cucumbers all over her. This worked to drive her spirit away, for tupapau don't like anything from the sea, and he never saw her following him again. But from that day forward he was never able to keep his own fires lit, and he could never feel warm.

The kids clap in delight and tuck their knees inside their T-shirts, shivering from the cold. Cold! I can't believe it, since the days and nights in New Guinea are always so sultry. I sit with them on the bank of the wide river, my legs dangling over the edge of the shore, the Fly River lapping below. The moonlight covers me, and I think of the story about the White Lady, how the man killed her kindness without even realizing it. The Fly's pale water drifts past, the breeze creating tiny waves. I wonder how much kindness from others I have also killed, all out of a fear of getting close to anyone.

The children want to hear more stories, so I tell them about more Tahitian ghosts; they can appreciate the tales of animal spirits following lone travelers into the night. The night seems to grow thicker around us as I talk. Only the flames of the huts' cooking fires intrude on the darkness.

I start to run out of stories and ask the kids for another one of their own. They tell me about the evil spirits – *masalai* – that inhabit the swamps behind Daumori. All dreams, the children explain, are actually spirit wanderings, the soul leaving the body. So what the masalai like to do is to come to Daumori while a person sleeps and his or her spirit is out wandering. They will wake the person up suddenly, thus preventing the individual's spirit from returning to the body. In this way the masalai are able to steal people's hearts. The next morning, people walk around the village without a heart and never even know it! Soon, though, they grow weaker and realize the sorcery of the masalai. So they must try to get their heart back, which is no easy thing to do. First, they must find their spirit, which has been wandering around lost for so long that sometimes it can't be found at all. But if they do find their spirit, they must wrestle it to the ground and force it to enter their body again. Only once this happens will the masalai return during a person's sleep and give them their heart back . . .

I ask the children if they've ever met anyone without a heart, and they all nod. They all know someone, and sound off names. I start to fear that some clever masalai visited me at some point in my life, and so I have been forced to travel the world in search of my lost spirit, so that I might get my heart back again.

In the distance, some village men beat on enormous, hollowed-out logs – *garamut* drums – singing and practicing dancing. The children explain that a woman in the village has died, and so the men are preparing for a large funeral feast in a week. All the Kiwai people from as far away as Daru and Port Moresby will congregate in Daumori Village to attend this event marking the death of one of their wantoks; whether such visitors are actual family members or not is irrelevant – the Kiwai people remain faithful to the entire tribe and are strict about practicing mortuary customs. By not having such a large feast and its attending activities, everyone would risk offending the spirit of the deceased woman. The result could be catastrophic: sickness overruning Kiwai villages, hunters having difficulty acquiring food, people dying young.

The men's songs are droning, mesmerizing tunes, that drown out even the sounds of the crickets. As I sit in the moonlit darkness, the immensity of the water and jungle

surrounding Daumori makes me feel as small and incon-
sequential as the most distant of the stars. The children
pretend not to hear the calls of their parents and keep
me company. Some of them ignore the reprimands of
the older kids, touching my hair every chance they get.
Above us, the stars reign. Whenever I look at the stars,
everything else ceases to matter. I've always known this,
yet I so seldom looked at them back home. City life
prevented it. And so did all the daily responsibilities that
consumed my life – getting a master's degree, teaching at
an elementary school. Here in New Guinea, the brightness of the night sky overpowers us all in the village; it is
an imperious presence we pay homage to. Our own lights
could never hope to drown it out.

'I wish some moments would never end,' I whisper.
'Why do they have to end?'

A couple of children start to braid my hair. All around,
the jungle sits in weighted silence.

Finally the stories run out, and the children grow tired.
I say the Kiwai word they have taught me – 'eso,' 'thank
you' – and head back to the hut where I'm staying. On the
way there, I'm struck by the sight of a bush that seems
bewitched. Thousands of white lights swirl around it,
diving and flashing and rising up into the starry sky. I
imagine that it is here, in this very place, that the gods of
the universe create the stars and send them up into the
heavens. I cautiously step toward the bush, discovering
the cause: fireflies. A bush alight with them. Thousands
and thousands. On the branches, they scramble upon
each other and compete for space. When I hold out my
arm, hundreds of lights descend upon it, blinking and
colliding. I wave my arm, and the lights take to the air
like fairy dust. Hundreds more swarm about me while a
few intrepid ones fly off into the night.

This evening the Old Ones want to tell me about when
the missionaries came to Daumori.

Their voices sound like low murmurs. The dim kerosene lamp reflects off of their blind eyes – glimmering

blue cataract eyes that don't move yet possess an un-settling omniscience. The woman is ninety-five years old, the man ninety-three. They sit quietly in the corner of the hut with the kerosene lamp's light playing on their white hair and the dustiness of their skin. I sit near them, and a man from the village, Salle (pronounced 'Sal-LAY') acts as tranlator.

They were children when the mission men had come. The mission men wore black clothes, carried strange objects with many leaves inside. (Salle laughs. 'A book!' he says to me.) The Old Ones had heard of such things, and had seen such strange creatures before, so they weren't scared. But maybe the mission men were, because they never stayed long in Daumori. However, one man finally stayed behind. He showed pictures of a *waitman* with long hair, which is called Jeesis.

The men of the village did not like this mission man, so one night they hit him over the head and killed him. Then they made a big fire to cook him. They ate his book with the leaves, and his clothes and his body. They ate everything except the tough skin he wore on his feet. ('His shoes,' Salle explains.) That part tasted terrible, and couldn't be easily cut, so they had to throw it to the pigs. After that, they didn't see a mission man for a long time. They didn't see his Jeesis for a long time, either.

'They know I'm not a missionary, right?' I joke to Salle.

He laughs. 'Yes, don't worry.'

'One thing I'd like to know.'

'Yes? Please.'

My curiosity is too much for me. 'Did the missionary taste good?'

Salle translates for me. The Old Ones mumble back in their tribal language, nodding their heads.

'They say,' Salle says, listening, 'he tasted like an old pig.'

Never believe anyone in this country when they say that something is nearby. Salle had claimed that an hour-long hike through the jungle would get us to this village of Isua, which is in the land of the Gogodala people, a tribe that is supposed to include a number of talented artisans. If local tribal art interested me at all, I should go.

It sounded easy enough at first. Just an hour-long hike. The Daumori people had told us that there was a well-traveled path, and though Salle hadn't had reason to be on it since he was a boy, he did recall that the journey to Isua was pretty straightforward. In the meantime, Phillip would be staying behind in Daumori, getting drunk with his friends on some beer I had bought him. Everyone was happy.

It was my first jungle hike, and I started off naively thinking I might only have to get my feet wet. The ground was saturated and muddy, and I followed Salle's lead, going barefoot. We entered the jungle, hiking for a short time down a well-trod trail that meandered through smaller trees and patches of sago palms, their droopy fronds carrying rows of inch-long needles, which lay like booby traps designed soley for the bottom of my feet. The local people harvest the pith from these sadistic palms, pressing the tasteless white starch into balls and baking them in the cinders of their cooking fires. I'd tried the stuff, and longed for some greasy fast food.

Now, though, after an hour of scrambling through mud, we're not anywhere near Isua but are in a clearing, the jungle cut back to make room for Daumori's taro crops. Tiny grasshoppers let off such a high-pitched droning that I can barely hear Salle.

'A swaama!' he says as he machetes away some brush. 'Bii kaapu!'

'What?'

'A swaaamaa!'

My feet suddenly plunge down several feet and I'm submerged in black muck.

Salle walks back to see if I'm okay. 'I told you it's a swamp. You don't listen to me.' He helps to pull me out. We're both laughing hysterically. I'm so covered in the pungent black swamp mud that Salle nearly topples over from his cackling laughter.

'Come here, come here, come here,' he says, eyes tearing.

'What?' I clamber through the mud and stand next to him.

He holds his arm next to mine, wheezing. 'You are like me!' He pinches my skin, covered with black swamp mud, and cackles. 'And you are now a *bus meri!*'

But I'm not a *bus meri* – a 'bush Mary,' a woman adept at getting through the jungle. At least not yet. That seems an Indiana Jones-type title you have to earn, and it's still a slippery, muddy world to which I'm completely unaccustomed.

We start moving again. The sun has an enervating effect, feels like liquid seeping into my skin and body, sucking my energy and weighing my every step. I try to follow Salle across a narrow tree trunk that traverses a part of the swamp, but I inevitably slip and fall in, sending large white birds fleeing from the reeds.

Salle is laughing so hard he has to hold his hands between his legs. 'You make me piss!'

Our trip is slow-going, and I can't see an end to the swamp before us. I stop and suggest we abort the mission and return to Daumori.

Salle shakes his head. 'We are going slow because of you,' he says.

I cross my arms. 'You never said anything about going through a swamp.'

'Schoolboys cross this way every day going to the mission school in Isua.'

'That,' I say, 'is pretty unlikely.'

He continues to blame our poor speed on me, but he falls into the swamp a number of times himself and starts cursing his friends in Daumori.

'My friends said this path is dry.'

'Dry?' I say. 'Salle, this isn't a dry path.'

'They are not good friends. They tell me lies. They play a joke.'

Salle busies himself with thinking of some kind of appropriate retribution while we take turns freeing each other's legs from deep patches of muck. A thick metallic smell rises from the mud, and when it gives way to swamp water, I'm relieved: though the water is up to our necks, the smell is less offensive and we can move more quickly. I wade behind Salle. When we reach more shallow areas, I observe cute black inchworms trying to climb up my body. As Salle starts slapping and smearing them off of himself, I realize that my friends the inchworms are, in fact, waterborne leeches.

I stop, letting out a chorus of Oh-my-Gods.

'Don't stop!' Salle screeches.

'I've got leeches all over me!'

'If you stop, they jump on you easy. Always move. Fast, fast.' He dances in the water. 'Fast, fast, fast.'

I sprint past him through the water. He catches up with me, chopping away some reeds with his machete.

'They go everywhere. You must search your whole body,' he says.

'Everywhere?'

His hand is on the back of my neck, and I feel something being ripped from the skin. He shows me the leech, his hand bloody.

'Look everywhere.'

As soon as we hit a patch of dry land, I look. Everywhere. I put a nervous hand up my shirt, under my bra, and feel a rather large, slippery thing resting there. That the creature has somehow wriggled itself in and attached itself *there*, reaching a shocking size, is a bit too much for me.

'Oh, Jesus,' I say.

In a frenzy, I pull out my small bottle of rubbing alcohol and pull up my shirt. Pouring it down my bra, I send the bloated creature writhing to the ground. Salle has been watching it all and laughing, the bastard.

We find Isua at last. In terms of kilometers on a map, it isn't far from Daumori, yet its people, the Gogodala, speak an entirely different language so that Salle can only communicate in Pidgin. Considering Daumori and Isua are separated by that swamp we've just gotten across, I'm not surprised that two distinct languages evolved – apparently I'm not the only one who thinks it's crazy trying to cross a swamp. Language differences aside, though, the Gogodala people look and act no different than the Daumori people, wearing T-shirts and living in the same style of raised thatch hut I first saw in Severiambu. The cultures, Salle tells me, are very similar.

I sneak off into the jungle to remove leeches from several other ingenious locations on my body. When I come back, Salle tells me that Isua hasn't any art to speak of, that the village of Balimo is the cultural mecca, and that Balimo is rather a long way off. Still, the missionaries had made their way to Isua through the jungle, and built a road to link it with their mission in Balimo. It is one of those bizarre roads in PNG that connects only two neighbouring villages, going nowhere else, and otherwise being completely surrounded by virgin jungle. A couple of trucks had been delivered to riverside Balimo to take Isua's villagers to and from Jesus Christ and His teachings. The trucks, both out of commision now and rusting on the outskirts of Isua, herald a return to animistic ways unless they can be fixed. At the very least, they herald an end to my quest for a glimpse of some of the celebrated local tribal art.

Salle hadn't been planning on spending the night with the Gogodala, so we have a quick lunch of tasteless sago biscuits and decide to head back to Daumori. Before we leave, I discover yet another leech – it's a big, fat one curled complacently around the underside of my big toe. Nonchalantly now (maybe I'm becoming a *bus meri* after all?), I borrow our host's lighter and burn it off. I'm hoping it's the last one on me, but Salle reminds me we'll have to go back the way we came. Back through that swamp. I contemplate more leeches, more mud and sweat and unrelenting heat.

'I'll be going faster this time,' I assure him.

'Yes.' He nods. 'Good.'

*   *   *

It's the next morning and I leave Daumori. Phillip, hung-over, reluctantly pilots us away, his friends staying behind. As I had suspected, his buddies had only come along for the free ride, and Phillip is now solely in charge of the boat. That he has an obligation to me, and isn't able to stick behind with them to get drunk off of the remaining cases of beer, leaves him in a surly mood all day. He barely says a word as he sits in back, controlling the outboard. I don't mind. I like the silence, and now we're entering a stretch of the river that is completely uninhabited, making our human voices seem, at the very least, obtrusive.

It's mile after mile of jungle on either side of the ever-narrowing river. Mile after mile of gigantic trees rising from the very edge of the water, their branches quaking with the movement of creatures I can't see or identify. But the most daunting fact is this: a glance before or behind, a glance in any direction, yields nothing but the sight of a long, empty river and a seemingly unmolested jungle pressing in from the shores. It has looked like this for millenniums. I pretend I'm going back in time.

In 1876, Italian naturalist Luigi Maria D'Albertis must have seen a river that looked almost exactly the same. A man with as much of a penchant for collecting tribal artifacts as natural specimens, he put the crew of his steam launch through a forty-five-day odyssey up the Fly River. They covered some 800 miles, and – long before Ivan Champion traveled up these same waters in 1926 – he became the first Western explorer to view the interior of New Guinea via the Fly. En route, he fired rockets at any villages he encountered. When the terrified villagers, who had never seen a white man or his fireworks, ran off into the jungle to hide, D'Albertis and his men came ashore to ransack the huts and steal any artifacts they wanted. That included sacred objects from the *haus tambaran* – spirit houses – and the skeletons from burial scaffolds. D'Albertis was completely unrepentant and wrote: 'Exclaim if you will, against my barbarity. I am too delighted with my prize to heed reproof!' Little wonder, then, that the Fly River tribes soon found white men so palatable.

Our dinghy careens over the waves of the Fly, past islands thick with jungle. Smaller rivers have started to flow into the Fly so that it's hard to tell whether we're still following the main route. The sun burns into my skin, turning it red beneath all of the sunblock I lather on. I hide under a wide-brimmed Australian bush hat I bought in Cairns. Phillip has a towel tied around his head so that he looks like an old lady in a babushka. We make an odd pair, traveling on this empty expanse of river. An entire day has gone by and we haven't encountered a single person. Just jungle. This interminable jungle.

With the sun setting, we pull up on one of the islands. Using some empty 'Meat Spaghetti' cans, I help bail out the foot of water that's leaked into the bottom of the boat, while Phillip uses his machete to make us a clearing for a cooking fire.

'Maybe ghosts will come,' Phillip says suddenly, as he pours kerosene on a pile of wood.

'Ghosts?'

'This is their island.'

'Are you scared of ghosts?' I get out of the boat and wipe my feet on the grassy shore.

He spits, and sets some logs ablaze with a match. 'When I was a boy, I was scared.'

'Who are your people?' I ask him. 'You're not Kiwai?'

He laughs. 'No, I'm not Kiwai. I have two tribes. My mother is Yongom. My father Gowarabari.'

'Where are these tribes?'

'The Yongom are north. The Gowarabari are east by Kikori. Far from here. Like your American people are far.'

'In America there are many different kinds of people, too.'

'What tribe are you?'

I smile. I've never thought of my ancestry as being a kind of tribe. 'I'm Czech,' I say.

'I never hear of this tribe. Do they speak English?'

'No. They speak Czech.'

'Do you speak this language?'

'Just a little,' I say.

Phillip lights a cigarette and blows a thick stream of smoke through the gap in his front teeth. His eyes settle on the jungle, silhouetted by the last orange traces of the sun. 'Why don't you speak more of your language?' he asks, like a reprimand.

'I don't know.'

'How can you talk to your ancestors?'

I push some brush into the fire. 'I can't,' I say.

Phillip humphs. We eat our dinner of canned mackerel and bananas in silence, and the sky soon blazes with stars so numerous that I can't make out a single constellation. I wonder if, by staring at them for a while, I can catch some Magic Fire Spirits speeding down to earth. I see nothing, though. Perhaps it's a good sign? Our tiny fire, like some caveman's flame in the midst of an ancient plain, is the only respite from the night. Here in the solitude of the jungle, I see that ancestors connect one with the land and give life meaning. They define who you are, and tell you that you're never alone. Back home in the States, though, ancestors hardly seem to matter at all beyond the drunken cheers of a St Patrick's Day parade.

I realize why I envy the indigenous peoples of the world. They know where they belong. They have a place they can connect with, landmarks that speak to them from far back in the past. I have to content myself with being a rootless entity called American, an immigrant's offspring.

It's nearing the end of the next day, and Phillip reveals that we aren't on the Fly River anymore. We're heading westward, he says, inland, toward a village called Suki. I'm assuming we're going there because it's a place to spend the night.

The Fly had narrowed even further today, had been broken up by islands and always seemed to be going in several different directions. My map is of little use, as the rainy seasons change the appearance of the Fly each year, sometimes completely altering its course. Only someone like Phillip, I realize, can easily pilot the Fly and get in and out of a place like Suki. If it wasn't for Phillip, I would be utterly lost in this land.

Utterly lost. The thought unsettles me. Phillip has been less than congenial today, and we've seen no sign of anyone. No canoes filled with waving villagers. No boats plying the Fly. Just an entire day of gray water and jungle: a world that still doesn't want us, that shows not a single sign of human habitation.

I pull down my bush hat over my face as the sun glares down from between some clouds. Suddenly Phillip cuts the motor. We drift backward and bump against a patch of *pitpit* – wild sugarcane – and he promptly lights up a cigarette.

'I will need more money,' he says all at once.

'More money for what?'

He picks something out of the back of his teeth and flicks it into the water. 'Petrol,' he says.

I look at him from beneath the brim of my hat. Does he think there's a gas station just around the corner?

'I already gave you five hundred kina for petrol,' I say. 'That's a lot of money. That's more than enough money.'

'I need more money. It's not enough.'

I look at all the filled petrol jugs. 'Forget it,' I say.

His tongue runs over his lips. He won't look at me now. He sighs and looks everywhere else but me. 'I think you're a crazy *wait meri*,' he says.

'You're probably right.'

'Look what I'm doing for you.'

'I'm paying you,' I remind him. 'A lot of money. You agreed to it back in Daru.'

'Yes, yes. But you are a crazy *wait meri*, and I am crazy too, for taking you up this river.'

'Then you shouldn't have come to me, telling me you'd

take me.' I reach in my backpack and pull out some canned spaghetti.

'I think you are crazy.'

'You want some spaghetti? I'm going to have lunch now.'

'I want more money for petrol.'

If he's trying to scare me into forking out more money, it's not going to work. I'm not scared of him. He's just one man. Not a very large man. He'd have to be holding a gun or knife or something for me to be scared of him – and his machete, I note, is by me. The only thing that *does* worry me is what I'd do, where I'd go, if I somehow got separated from Phillip. He must know this, know my disadvantage, and is planning on using it for all it's worth.

I look at him again, catch his eyes. I can feel the anger and frustration in me burning.

I take out my Swiss Army knife and pull out the can opener. Holding the can over the side of the boat, I slowly open it.

'I will need more money,' Phillip is saying.

I slam the blade into the top of the can, wrenching it open. 'Reverend Anna said I shouldn't give you more money, remember? She said you got plenty. And you did.'

'Reverend Anna . . .' Phillip starts to mumble in a tribal language. The wild sugarcane rubs against the side of the boat, leaning in toward us. I wonder how long we're going to sit here discussing this. I'm not going to give in.

I eat the spaghetti with the largest blade of my knife. It's a disgusting meal – I wouldn't be surprised if the spaghetti was canned around 1945 – but I don't care. I have to eat something, haven't eaten all day.

'You want some?' I ask Phillip, offering the can.

'No.'

He looks out at the swampy land surrounding us. Just lots of wild sugarcane, the surface of the water blazing white from the sunlight on it.

'Then can we go?' I ask.

'Go?' He sighs. 'I think you are crazy.'

But he rips at the outboard's cord. The engine revs, and the boat leaps forward. He tells me we're going to a place called Suki. I don't ask him why. I'm starting not to care. Just as long as we're moving.

The Suki people are a distinct tribe with their own language and customs, and they live in the seldom visited swampland to the west of the Fly River. This area is considered one of the world's largest wetlands and extends all the way across the south of the island of New Guinea. Suki itself is hidden in a maze of waterways and our route is soon so overgrown with wild sugarcane that Phillip pulls up the outboard motor and I help him pole our boat along. The narrow river we've been following has become a stream. The jungle I've grown so used to seeing, blocking out the horizon and creating a vague feeling of claustrophobia, has vanished. In its place are spreads of black water and grasslands, with only the occasional patch of forest. Suddenly I can see 360 degrees, cumulus clouds sitting low over verdant fields of *pitpit*. The sun reflects off of the water in a dazzle of brilliant light. There is no dust here to distort distance and color, and the land and sky glow in sharp clarity as if I look at them through a special lens. It's a sopping, humid land, but it's also remarkably radiant.

The *pitpit* lets up. We enter a small lagoon. A number of small, raised huts sit in a clearing on the edge of the water. Dogs are the first to see us approach and let up a howl that brings the village to life. Naked children gather on the shore, their bellies bloated. This doesn't seem to be a prosperous village, but the kids appear content, smiling broadly at us and yelling for their families to come watch.

Phillip brings the dinghy up by the huts and skids it onto the muddy shore with a quick jerk of the outboard. The children are literally dancing in joy now, their parents cautiously approaching. Age ten seems to be the age when one starts to wear clothes, and everyone older than that has on holey shorts or a *laplap* – a wraparound cloth skirt, like a sarong. Many of the women are bare-chested, nursing babies.

I step out of the canoe and slosh through the mud to shore, holding up the fringes of my tattered skirt. The children excitedly repeat my Pidgin title of *wait meri*, white woman. I open up my backpack and hand each of them a piece of butterscotch candy. Sticking it to their palms, the kids run their tongues over the candy then show it to their parents who take it, lick it a couple of times and stick it back on the kids' hands. Women with babies tied to their backs come to see what the commotion is all about, and the kids put their candy up to the faces of babies. The babies smile and suck at it.

The men, unimpressed by my candy, stop frowning as soon as I pass out some packs of Marlboro cigarettes that I hoped to trade for supplies. Now everyone is happy. Phillip notices a couple of acquaintances of his and leaves me behind. I sit down on the steps of a wooden ladder going up to one of the huts. A woman sits down near me, and a six-year-old boy promptly climbs into her lap and starts breast-feeding.

I smile at her as if I'm used to seeing first graders being breast-fed. She smiles back. We sit and watch each other for a while. I don't speak Suki; she doesn't speak English. Suddenly she frowns, gets up, and quickly heads toward some of the other huts: a stooped, glum-looking man has just walked up to me.

'I'm Lawrence,' he says apologetically.

His English surprises me. 'Kira,' I say.

We shake hands. He looks at me shyly and rubs his chin.

'I was feeding my crocodiles. Would you like to see them?'

'Sure.'

He leads me over to a circle of high, thick logs. Standing on the stump of a tree, I peer into the enclosure and realize that nearly every square foot of the muddy water is moving. Crocodiles of all sizes nudge each other or languish about.

'One of my big ones got out,' Lawrence says. 'I looked for him all this week.'

'It's probably long gone,' I say.

'No, I don't think so. I think it is very close.'

I quickly glance around.

Apparently the crocodile business is a booming one. Lawrence explains that a full-grown crocodile skin can fetch $150 in the world markets. Half of his profits, though, are spent getting the skins to Moresby where they can be shipped out. It isn't easy to feed scores of crocodiles, either. That can take even more money if game is scarce.

'It seems a hard way to make money,' I say.

'Oh, yes.'

He rubs his chin and guides me back to the hut. There's something very somber about poor Lawrence, and I hand him a pack of my duty-free Marlboros, hoping to cheer him up.

'Good brand,' he says gloomily, thanking me.

Phillip returns with a couple of young men. They follow behind him, laughing when he laughs, waiting eagerly for his every word. I smirk: Phillip the celebrity.

Phillip points at a hut across the lagoon, saying it's the guest hut and I'm supposed to carry my pack over there. There's to be a party or something tonight, with his friends.

'You're also sleeping in the guest hut?' I ask him.

'Yes.'

'And they're sleeping there, too?' I point at his buddies.

'Yes, yes.' He spits a red projectile onto the back of a dog standing too close to him.

Phillip can't have any idea that I'm thinking back to Africa, to Mozambique, and am getting a bad feeling.

'Forget it,' I say. 'I'll sleep somewhere else.'

Lawrence steps in. 'You can share the bed with my children,' he says to me. 'This is my hut. But . . . my wife . . . we are having marital problems . . . she isn't here.'

A bare-chested, gruff-looking woman stands at a hut

146

opposite Lawrence's, her arms crossed before her. 'That is my wife.' Lawrence points weakly at her.

When I wave, she loses her frown and smiles at me. Lawrence's eyes brighten until she looks at him and her face turns grave again.

'So I'm a very bad cook,' he continues, 'but if you need a place to sleep, please stay in my children's room.'

I thank him and tell him I'd be glad to.

Lawrence made two mistakes. The first, he says, was marrying a Lowlands woman; he is a Highlander, and his own tribe's women are never much trouble. His second mistake was to move to his wife's village of Suki, because when his wife decides to hate him, the entire village hates him, too.

'No one likes me now,' Lawrence says, shaking his head. 'I have no friends here.'

Using a teaspoon, he laboriously spoons out some cassowary broth and pieces of yam into a tea cup and hands it to me. The cassowary's huge drumstick sits half submerged in an aluminium pot, and in my un-professional opinion it looks about ready to shrivel up from overcooking. Lawrence's two kids, little girls of six and eight, watch in fascination as their dad tries to serve up dinner.

'My wife took all of the forks and spoons,' Lawrence explains. He scoops out pieces of yam into plastic spray can caps, blowing wildly on his fingers after each attempt.

'Did she take the plates, too?' I ask.

Lawrence rubs his chin and nods, embarrassed.

'Where did she take them?'

'They're in that other hut. She lives there with her parents.'

That 'other hut' is a mere thirty feet away. I consider the cassowary drumstick for a moment. 'Couldn't you send one of your daughters over to borrow something?'

He licks his lips and stirs feebly at the contents in the pot. 'Oh . . . no. No . . . It is forbidden. We are having marital problems.'

A woman's voice calls from outside and one of the little girls jumps up and runs off. A moment later, she returns, bringing in a plate of freshly baked biscuits. I notice that there are only three biscuits on the plate. The girls take one each.

Lawrence smiles apologetically. 'That last one is yours,' he says. '*She* made them for you and the girls.'

'No, you take it,' I say. Poor guy.

'I can't touch it. It is forbidden.'

Reluctantly, I pick it up. As soon as I do so, the little girl – apparently with orders – runs back outside to return the plate to her mother.

Lawrence rubs his eyes and sighs. 'I'm very sorry. I'm a terrible cook, and they hate me here so I have no plates.'

I assure Lawrence that plates are unnecessary and thank him for his hospitality.

'They hate me here,' he says, stirring the fire.

I'm thinking maybe it'll help if Lawrence gets the chance to talk about his problems, so I ask him what happened. He's reluctant to get into details, though. Apparently he and his wife's family had a disagreement, and the argument can't be resolved because it involves a standoff between the traditions of his Highlands tribe and the Suki village. Their separation itself involves a very rigid set of codes that allows the wife to take nearly anything she wants from Lawrence's hut and to move it all to her own. He, in turn, is prohibited from using anything she took.

'Sort of sounds like divorce in the States,' I say.

'Does the wife take everything in America?' Lawrence asks glumly.

'Sometimes.' I smile.

He pulls out the cassowary drumstick and, because his wife took all the knives, tries to peel off the meat with his fingers. I offer him my Swiss Army knife. Using the sharpest of the blades, Lawrence still can't get the boot-leather meat to come off: he cooked the hell out of it. At last, resting the drumstick in his lap, he gazes into the cooking fire.

'I'm a terrible cook,' he says.

I pull some canned mackerel from my pack and set it down before him.

It's the next morning, and Phillip and the boat are gone. He took everything, of course – all the petrol money I'd given him, and the cans of food. I have some provisions in my backpack, but not much.

What I'm really worried about, though, is where I am and how the hell I can get out. My map isn't much help. Suki is on it, but it looks far from the Fly River. There's one of those dashed lines indicating a hiking trail from Suki, but the nearest – the only – village of any kind is a sixty-mile hike south through the swamps, to a place called Morehead. And then from Morehead more hiking trails go off in every direction. For all I know, I'd have to hike more than a hundred miles just to make it back to the coast, and my experience with swamp hiking tells me that this would be, at the very least, unpleasant. I've learned that one has to take those dashed 'hiking' lines at face value. Just because someone decides to put them there doesn't necessarily mean that an actual trail exists. For one thing, you can't really have a trail when most of it is underwater and you have to make up your route as you go along. And then sixty miles in New Guinea, through one of the largest swamps in the world, isn't a leisurely sixty-mile hike. Who knows how long it could take?

I sit below one of the huts and try to remain calm, thinking of my options. If I have to, I can hire a guide, hike through the swamp. I wouldn't *enjoy* it but I could do it. There'd be leeches, heat – God knows what. (And I still have those little leech marks on my chest.) But if I hike to the coast it'd be like backtracking. It'd be like giving up, and I've only just started this journey.

Lawrence sympathizes with me. He says he'd wondered what I was doing with Phillip. Apparently Phillip has a bad reputation even in Suki, most of the older people thinking he's a 'humbug man.'

'I didn't really have a choice,' I say. 'No one else wanted to take me.'

One of Lawrence's little girls runs over from his wife's hut and starts speaking quickly to us in the Suki language.

'Oh . . .' Lawrence glances at his daughter, then at his wife who stands beneath the hut, her arms crossed before her. 'Yes, maybe . . .'

The little girl starts speaking again. Lawrence rubs his chin and glances at me. 'There is Mr Glen,' he says.

'Who's Mr Glen?'

'A white man. He lives on a boat. My wife . . . she thinks maybe Mr Glen can help you.' Lawrence rubs his chin again.

I think about this Mr Glen for a moment. Something seems very strange. 'What's this Mr Glen doing out here?' I ask.

Lawrence feebly shakes his head.

'How long has he been here?'

Lawrence puts his hand on his daughter's head and shrugs.

'A long time. The children will take you there.'

I go in search of the elusive Mr Glen. Lawrence's older girl and her cousin, a boy of about twelve, help steady a narrow dugout canoe as I step carefully inside. The canoe is so narrow across that I can't get my hips in and have to sit on the edge. The little girl sits in front on her knees, holding a paddle; the boy stands in back to help steer. As we pull out, I keep thinking about Lawrence's crocodile being on the loose, waiting for some canoe novice like me to fall into the lagoon.

The kids, though, know what they're doing. Kids in these parts are practically born in canoes, getting their own little canoe to practice in when they become toddlers. Earlier this afternoon, I watched four-year-old kids zooming across the lagoon with paddles the size of tennis rackets, racing each other. I try to imagine some American kid trying to get in one of these canoes – good luck.

Mr Glen isn't far. We take one of the swampy byways, which leads to another, smaller lagoon bordered by dry land. At the very end of the lagoon sits a small fishing boat.

I don't see anyone inside, so the kids paddle our canoe over to the spit of land and I clamber onto the shore. Blocking the sunlight with my hand, I gaze into the boat and see a middle-aged, darkly tanned man in shorts, passed out on his stomach on a foam mattress. He has on sunglasses, his mouth hangs open. Several other little kids are already on the island with us, looking down at him and laughing and pointing.

'Mr Glen,' my guides tell me.

CHAPTER SIX

Damsel in Distress

I know nothing about this Mr Glen. As Lawrence's daughter ferries me out to his boat in her dugout canoe, I try to imagine why or how a man could decide to spend his life in the swamps of New Guinea. Unquestionably, this is a land of such brilliant colors and contrasts that even Gauguin might have found a home here. The rich blue sky bends toward green fields of wild sugarcane. Sunlight radiates over the land, clarifying the distances, making the dark swamp water appear iridescent. Yet, despite such pure, primordial beauty, no one lives here but the Suki people. Perhaps it's for this reason that Mr Glen stays within reach of Suki Village? I wonder if even the most jaded or misanthropic of people can completely leave the embrace of humanity.

Mr Glen's boat is anchored in the middle of the lagoon, and as we approach I consider yelling out my presence to let him know I'm coming. It couldn't be every day that he's greeted by an American woman stranded in the swamps.

But this very fact makes me want to delay the meeting. My incongruity leaves me strangely embarrassed. How do I explain my presence to someone when I have yet to explain it to myself? And how do I tell him that I am, in a sense, desperate, the man I'd hired to pilot me up the Fly River taking off in the night? I always try to rely on myself, find it amazingly hard to ask someone for help, but today my ignorance and helplessness feel overwhelming.

Our canoe knocks against the side of the boat. I throw my backpack on a shoulder, grab hold of the boat's ladder, and start to climb up to the deck.

A great Australian-accented voice booms out: 'I'm going to cut off the balls of whoever's climbing up this boat!'

I get back in the canoe. I'm slightly consoled by the fact that I don't have any balls, but Lawrence's daughter is wide-eyed, and she looks on the verge of paddling away.

Our canoe hits the side of the boat again, and again the great voice sounds out: 'You've got ten seconds!'

Lawrence's daughter, terrified, starts paddling. I grab hold of the ladder to pull her canoe back against the boat, and yell out, 'Mr Glen? Can I talk to you?'

'Who's that?' But the voice has softened. 'You a Yank?'

'Yeah. I'm kind of stranded out here, and I'm wondering if I can talk to you. Just for a minute.'

There's a pause. Then: 'Oh, yeah. Yeah, that's all right. Come on up. Watch your step.'

I look to Lawrence's daughter as if she could advise me – she's still terrified. When I step out of the canoe onto the ladder, she promptly paddles away.

'You won't cut my balls off, will you?' I ask as I climb.

'No, no. No worries.'

'You're sure?'

'Yeah. What's your name?'

I tell him.

'Yeah,' says the voice. 'I just talk that way to the kiddies. They're always trying to get on the boat. No worries.'

I'm thinking, *A hell of a way to talk to the kiddies*. I make it up to the deck and hoist myself over the side of the boat. Mr Glen is still lying exactly in the same place he was when I first saw him: on his stomach, on the foam mattress, bare, oily back exposed to the sun. He greets me with a finger, says 'G'day,' and pushes his sunglasses further up. He tells me his name, asks for mine again.

I look at the cluttered deck. It's full of metal piping,

153

long steel tubes, fishing nets and tackle, tools, tarps, boxes of canned food, bottled water. And beer. Lots of beer: SP – the Papua New Guinean brand.

Glen says, 'I can count on one hand the number of white women I've seen in the last couple of years – not counting missionary women. They aren't quite the same thing, if you know what I mean.'

I think I know what he means. 'I've kind of had some problems,' I tell him. 'I hired this man, Phillip, to take me up the Fly River in his dinghy, and he took off last night, stranding me in Suki Village.'

'He left you for good?'

'Yeah,' I say. 'It looks that way.'

'So you paid this Phillip to take you up the Fly,' Glen says, scratching his chest, 'and then he nicks off on you, and you don't know how to get out of here.'

I nod.

Glen starts to laugh uproariously. 'This Phillip proves my point about PNG,' he says. 'Time is the only thing that ever changes here. Have a seat if you can find one.'

I shove some boxes out of the way and sit down in the shade of a canvas canopy. Glen sluggishly rolls over to face me. The act of turning over seems counter to his nature, though, and he has the painfully slow and laborious movements of a turtle trying to pull itself across the sand.

Slowly, he reaches for a pack of cigarettes lying on the mattress. He tediously shakes one out and offers it to me.

'No, thanks.'

'All righty. Just being the gentleman.' He guffaws.

'Thanks.'

He lights it for himself. 'So this Phillip leaves you,' Glen continues, 'and you're stranded. You should know that my boat's buggered. I haven't gotten around to fixing it yet.'

'Well, I'm just wondering what my options are – what you'd do if you were in my situation. How you'd get out.'

Glen takes off his sunglasses and rubs his nose, revealing a startling pair of blue eyes that glance at me curiously from his tan face. He has a thin, wiry body, and the striking indifference of someone rarely fazed by anything. This nonchalance strikes me the most – I've seen it before when I've traveled, but only in the most seasoned of adventurers. He is, in a word, tough. He's been around the block more than just a few times.

But he's apparently lazy, too, these days. I wonder how old Glen is. He looks somewhere in his forties, but the tropical sun has taken its toll, makes his skin look porous and burnished well beyond his age. All I can tell for sure is that, from his accent, he's an Aussie. Or had been an Aussie – it's unclear now who or what he is, his isolation from the world seems so complete.

He puts his palms to his temples and slicks back his greasy blond hair. After a long moment, he approaches my question. 'How do you get out of here?' He considers this, his cigarette held daintily between thumb and forefinger. 'That is a good question.'

'I'd rather not hike through the swamps,' I explain.

'Yes!' he says. 'My God, you don't want to hike.' He chuckles. 'If you *could* hike, that is.'

'I was told that Suki Village has a place where a helicopter can land. Planes can't land, but a helicopter, maybe. Lawrence, back in the village, told me that every once in a while a helicopter comes by.'

'Your information is correct.'

'Lawrence told me you'd know all about that.'

Glen sucks slowly on his cigarette, the smoke streaming out of his nostrils. He puts his sunglasses back on and, hand behind his head, says, 'They do land here. Ok Tedi choppers come by every once in a while.' He waves over his shoulder at the spit of land bordering the lagoon. 'They land right up there. You thinking of getting on one?'

'I was thinking of it.'

'Not a bad idea if someone'll do you a favor. Take you along for the ride. They're not supposed to, of course.'

'Yeah. But I wouldn't have to go too far. Just up to

Obo, maybe, where I can try to catch a ride on a rubber ship.'

Glen is staring at me.

'Obo? You want to get on a rubber boat?' he says.

'Yeah.'

'And do what?!'

'Just go wherever it's going.'

He's interested all of a sudden and pulls himself up. 'Are you a scientist? One of those anthropologists?'

I smile. 'No. I'm just traveling through.'

'Uh-huh.'

'I want to eventually go over the Highlands and hike down to the Sepik River in the north. I want to go from south to north and see some of the tribes, learn about their cultures . . . and I want to see the jungle, too. I haven't really seen it yet. Not *the* jungle. The big one.'

' "The big one." ' Glen's still staring at me. 'And you're going just for the hell of it?'

'Yeah. Do you know when the choppers come?'

'They come when I ask them to come. I could always radio someone later on. I don't think my radio's buggered yet.'

Glen can do that because, as it turns out, he's actually an employee of the Ok Tedi mining company. He is, as he puts it, a 'public relations' person. His job is to cruise to the various villages in the mine's districts (the villages along, or near, the Fly River, which are affected by its pollution), and deliver the various payments provided by the Ok Tedi trust. This works out to about $10,000 per village per year, which has to be used for approved 'projects.' That's Glen's job – delivering and overseeing the projects. Maybe Glen helps to build latrines, install water pumps or solar lamps, create a rainwater collection facility. Whatever. He carries the supplies on his boat and the village elders choose the project. The $10,000 allows him to deliver or build one thing a year in each village, though he keeps a very loose schedule.

'My job is about ten-percent work and ninety-percent fishing,' he explains. He's been doing it ever since the mid-1980s, when an Ok Tedi tailings dam burst, flooding the Fly River with hundreds of thousands of tons of mining by-products. Ok Tedi, on the verge of getting sued by an Australian law firm acting on behalf of the local tribes, agreed to an out-of-court settlement to provide for the local people in financial and developmental ways.

'That settlement was the best thing that ever happened to me,' Glen says. 'I got paid to fish.'

He stands up and scratches his chest, then suddenly runs toward the end of the boat. '*Waaga-waaga-waaga!*' he screams, waving wildly at the kids watching us on shore. When they run away in terror, he unzips his shorts and takes a leak into the water.

'Goldfish Bowl Syndrome,' he says as he pisses, his cigarette dangling from the corner of his mouth. 'Never could get used to it. Drives me crazy.'

I want to be polite, look at him as he speaks, but now he's shaking himself off in front of me.

'Can't stand it,' he says. 'Drives me crazy.' He turns, zipping up. 'Doing the other is worse. They can't take their eyes off my arse.'

'Goldfish Bowl Syndrome?' I ask.

'I'm like a fish trapped in a bowl here. Always being watched. Can't escape it. See, look, there they are.'

I look. He's right. I recognize Lawrence's daughter in the returning crowd. There are a couple of men, now, too. Just standing there, watching us.

'Can't stand it,' he says. He flicks his cigarette over the side of the boat and lies back down on the foam mattress. 'Can you drink warm beer?'

'Yeah.'

'Well, then. How 'bout getting up off your bum and getting us some of that Dutch courage. Over there. In that box.' He raises a lazy hand and points somewhere in the direction of the cabin.

As I go to get the beer, I ask him if this isn't a lonely life, being out in the middle of nowhere for months on end, having to drink warm beer and being watched by village people whenever he takes a piss. Doesn't it get a bit much?

'What you mean is, do I get sick of a life of wanking?' Glen smirks as he takes the bottles of beer from me and opens them.

'Uh, yeah. Sort of.'

He hands me one of the beers and sits back against the side of the boat.

'I would be lonely, I suppose – *was* lonely until I got the Missus.'

'The "Missus"?'

'The Wife.'

Life on the boat, out in the swamps around Suki, would have been perfect, he insists – except for the fact that he kept getting horny. Horniness drove him from the idyllic life, up into the Highlands, where he found himself a woman from a local tribe to be his wife. Ok Tedi would then occasionally fly him out to see her, which was often at first until she got to be a 'pain-in-the-arse.' He always had to bring fish and other goodies for her, and apparently she had a habit of demanding his paychecks and insisting on holiday trips down to Australia to go shopping for, among other things, 'women's undies.' Glen says she had a particular penchant for fancy underwear. For a long time he obliged her, even setting up a small store in her hometown, which she could run every time he went away – 'Keep her busy.' The only thing Glen hadn't counted on was PNG culture and the belief that everything in a village should be shared. His store had no chance of success. He'd stock it every time he came back, and as soon as he left, his wife's relatives would come by for their share.

'There are two ways here,' Glen says to me, finishing his beer. 'The white way and the black way. The white way isn't to give away all your stuff all the time. The black way is to just hand everything over. PNG villages are like little Communist societies.'

He seems pleased with the analogy and scratches his chest.

'You should follow the way that works for you, though,' he adds. 'If you like to give away all your stuff, go ahead.'

But because of the store debacle, he doesn't visit his wife much anymore. He's stopped going anywhere unless absolutely necessary. An Ok Tedi chopper now delivers supplies when he needs them, and he otherwise leads a hermit's life.

'You must like it,' I say. I stare out at the expanse of swamp, the sun already dipping well to the west. Not a village anywhere to be seen. Just the black water, bright green of the swamp grass and tufts of cumulus clouds sitting sluggishly in the blue sky.

'It has its perks.' He rolls his empty beer bottle down the deck. 'This is probably one of the best fishing spots along the Fly.'

'Why don't you have your wife with you? Keep you company on the boat?'

He laughs. 'You don't know the Missus. Not exactly my idea of company.'

Lawrence's daughter paddles her canoe over to tell me that it's getting late. Am I going back to the village with her?

'You can stay here if you like,' Glen says quickly. 'I'll clear away some of the garbage. I don't get much English conversation these days.'

Deciding I could use the company and conversation too, I agree.

He sends the girl off. 'They'll be back to gape at us tomorrow, don't worry.'

I watch her leave with the others toward Suki, hearing the soft *plit plit plit* of her paddle in the water. I like the sudden isolation they leave behind, my world becoming the deck of Glen's fishing boat with the sky above and the swamp all around. This world is changing to a hazy orange land, the black swamp water looking fiery, other-worldly in the quickly changing light. Insects dive about the reeds, disturbing the repose of still water, and I can already smell the coming night rising sharply from the land. A cool smell, heavy with life.

'Tonight's menu is going to be fish and Maggi,' Glen says, disrupting my thoughts. 'Unless you're one of those vegetarian types that are such a pain in the arse.'

'Sounds good,' I say. I'd better not tell him that I don't eat red meat. 'Thanks.'

He takes off his sunglasses and throws on a T-shirt. Opening another beer, he casts out one of his fishing lines. 'So what are you doing here, Miss Kira? You're not a scientist, so what are you?'

'I'm not anything official. I just wanted to see the place. New Guinea's like one of the last frontiers.' I look out at the view around us. 'I've never seen anything like it.'

'Yeah, it's different. Isn't what you'd call a tourist attraction, though.' He casts another line into the water. 'Why're you alone? Where's the husband to boss you around?'

'I like to travel alone.'

He shrugs. 'I never could figure out why, but there's two kinds of people in this world. The kind that only go as far as the front door to fetch the paper, and then the crazy bastards looking for Shangri-La.'

'Which category are you in?'

'I forgot. I don't bother thinking about that as long as the buggers are biting.'

'And how are they biting?'

He yanks on the line. 'Like royalty.'

I could listen to Glen for hours. For days. He's full of stories. Through our great feast of fish, Maggi-brand ramen noodles and warm SP beer, mosquito coils fending off the *natnats*, Glen gets increasingly drunk and talkative. I settle down to the role I prefer most – that of listener – and encourage him to tell me what life is like in this strange place, this Shangri-La he's found for himself.

It's not always a Shangri-La. He wants me to know that his job can be unpleasant, even dangerous. He tells me about the time when he went to an especially remote village for the first time in order to install a solar-powered light. Just finding the village was an odyssey in itself, and when he got there he had to explain to the village elders that they would be receiving a gift from the Ok Tedi people, and that they could choose which gift they liked the most. He described some of the gifts as best he could to them: a water pump, a rainwater-collection facility, a new building, a light.

A light? they wondered.

That's right – a solar-powered light. He tried to explain how it'd work. They wouldn't have to do anything, just let it sit in the sun. Then, at night, all they had to do was turn it on and it'd light up the village. Like magic.

The village elders were impressed and decided they wanted one, so Glen went and unloaded the materials from his boat. He erected the solar-powered street lamp while the whole village watched. At night, to everyone's amazement, the light shone brilliantly from its place in the middle of the village.

Later that evening, a pig, snuffling around the new metal object, observed something that looked like a kind of snake: the light's electrical cable. Apparently, the pig took a bite and electrocuted itself, sending the village into a panic. Suddenly this light wasn't so fantastic, and Glen wasn't welcome. Pigs in PNG are usually considered equal in value to a young child, often being worth more to a family than a daughter, and so Glen was viewed as a kind of murderer. Young men went for their bows and arrows. According to the village's deeply ingrained system of payback, Glen was expected to provide a huge compensation for the loss of the pig. Having no intention of offering any payback, he did the most logical thing he could think of: he ran. He got on his boat, started the engine, and literally fled before a volley of arrows like some character out of *Heart of Darkness*.

'I never did offer them any payback,' he says, chuckling. Nor did he return to offer the village their yearly Ok Tedi payment. He just pretends the village doesn't exist: 'I'm leaving 'em to the missionaries.'

Glen admits that that was one of the most dangerous

situations he'd ever had to deal with. Usually, he explains, it's not so bad. Usually it's a matter of strange customs making his work difficult. Take, for example, the time he tried to install water pumps under some village huts. What the people there had failed to tell him was where they buried their dead. So as he went about his job of drilling beneath the huts, he unwittingly 'went through little Johnny and Suzie' on his way to an aquifer. It was an uncomfortable situation, made worse by language difficulties – he could speak Pidgin and Motu, the two national languages of PNG – but no tribal tongues. It took some time before he could discover exactly where the other bodies were, and it became so frustrating that he nearly quit.

'You think that's bad,' he tells me, 'wait until it *floods* in those villages. Then you've got bodies coming up and floating around, having themselves a reunion.'

Glen says that children, in particular, die early and quickly in those villages. Malaria, usually. Or dengue fever and the internal bleeding that comes with the bad cases. He would return year after year, ask how little Mikey and Sally were doing until someone in the village pointed to a new mound under one of the huts. Child mortality got so bad that some parents didn't even bother naming their kids until they reached seven or eight.

'This is a hard place to live,' he says, drinking the last of his beer. 'It's not all what it seems to be.'

He stretches himself out on the mattress, picking absently at the noodles still left on his plate. Overhead, the stars brightly eavesdrop on us.

Glen opens another beer for me though I've not yet finished my last. He doesn't just smoke his cigarette now but keeps it close to his mouth, savoring its proximity. I look out at the swamp. All around us, the sounds of insects keep up a fierce cadence. Glen, I discover, is studying me.

'You're quiet,' he says.

'You're not the first person to point that out. Did you

ever think,' I ask him quickly, 'when you were young, that you'd end up in a place like this?'

'You never know anything when you're young.' He takes a puff from his cigarette and blows out perfect smoke circles. 'The whole point of childhood is not knowing a bloody thing.'

'Did you ever see yourself having one of those nine-to-five jobs?'

'Not for a minute – and goddamn lucky thing for everyone that I hadn't. Would have had one too many one morning and walked into the office with my dad's hunting rifle to shoot away the lot of them.' He takes mock aim at the stars. 'Sayonara you bastards!'

He gulps down some beer, taps his cigarette.

We listen to the silence.

Through the hazy film of mosquito netting, the stars shine dully. I listen to the boat making creaking, hollow noises.

Mr Glen's breathing keeps up a steady rhythm at the other end of the foam mattress. He sleeps with his back to me, hands clasped in against his chest like a child's. I know the dawn's coming, though it'll be a while yet. But the night has lost its completeness somehow, the coming gray arriving more as a feeling than an actual event.

I wonder what it'd be like to live in this place as Glen does. It's something of a lost paradise here. Radiant days. Pleasant nights. And everything probably looking exactly as it's looked before humankind ever arrived in the first place. It seems safe here. Lonely, but safe. I wonder what it'd be like to stay. I glance at Glen's sleeping form, as if it held some kind of answer.

But what would I miss? It's the same question a person must ask, standing with toes over the edge of a building, about to jump off. How is it that the questions are the same? Yet they are the same. Exactly the same. Always, when you choose a certain life for yourself, you deny yourself some other kind of life at the same time. Living is nothing but an attempt to champion the choice you've made.

What would I miss?

It is the mantra of the psychologists who had wanted to save me from myself. And did. *What would I miss?*

Mr Glen rolls over, sighs in his sleep. The mosquito net quivers and falls still. In the east, there is no doubt about it now: the dawn.

When Mr Glen finally wakes up, it's nearly nine. Already, the kids from Suki village are making their way over in their dugout canoes. Poor Glen never stops being a novelty for them.

'If you've got to go to the loo,' he advises, pointing to the side of the boat, 'you'd better go now, before you become a celebrity.'

I take his advice and climb down to the water while he gets some fish cooking for breakfast. When I come back up, he's lighting a cigarette and reclining on a chair by the kerosene stove.

I ask him if he could use his radio and find out if a chopper's coming to Suki.

'You ready to leave this place?'

'Yeah.'

'So soon?' But he smiles. Turning down the flame beneath the pan of fish, he goes to the radio. 'So you want to be dropped off at Obo?'

I think about this. Obo is only a small way station at the junction of the Fly and Strickland Rivers, but supposedly rubber boats frequently stop there on their way up and down the Fly. Aside from Obo, the whole area is sparsely inhabited by tiny villages, so I figure Obo is my best bet if I want to catch a boat heading further north into the interior.

I tell Glen my decision. With an expert's precision, he turns on the equipment and speaks flawlessly into the microphone. There's a crackling sound and a voice responds. A clear, friendly voice that seems to have an American accent. The two men chitchat for a while, then Glen looks at me.

'So I've got a young lady here. The bloke she hired to

take her up the Fly left her behind in Suki. I'm wondering if you're coming this way any time soon. Over.'

The voice comes back immediately. 'I can swing over there. No problem. I'm always ready to help a damsel in distress.'

They chitchat some more. Turns out the pilot of the chopper, a Jim Mead, can come by this afternoon, at around two o'clock.

I nod. Glen tells him that two o'clock is fine.

'Just remember you don't know anything about this,' Jim says over the crackling distance. 'You don't know anything about her getting on, and I don't know anything. You copy?'

'Copy you.'

They catch up on news and say their good-byes.

Glen at last switches the radio off and turns to me, giving me the thumbs-up. 'You ever been in a chopper before?' he asks.

'Never,' I say.

He smiles and nods at me.

The chopper arrives a little after two. At first I can only hear the *wop-wop* of its blades getting louder as it approaches from the sky. The landing area near Glen's boat is filling with people who, having also heard its approach, race over in their canoes for what is obviously a rare and special event.

I can understand their excitement. The chopper makes an incredible noise as it descends, everything bowing before the crush of wind from the rotors. It's an awesome sight, this amazing technology arriving from the heavens with such clamor. My hair tangles about my face and I hold it back as the great machine daintily touches the ground and steadies itself.

The rotors lose momentum. The noise subsides. As the blades turn sluggishly, I see the pilot put his headset down. The doors open upward and he jumps nimbly to the ground.

'That's Jim Mead,' Glen tells me.

Jim is in his late 40's but has the bounce and spunk of a teenager. I get the impression that he's refused to acknowledge his age. Simply refused. And though his body has given him gray hair, wrinkles, he's unimpressed by the change.

Jim waves to the people from Suki then comes over to us. He pats Glen on the back and shakes my hand.

'So here she is?' he says, motioning to me.

Glen introduces us.

'Where are you from?' His voice is confident, sure of itself.

'Chicago.'

'Chicago. I've been there a few times.'

I'm curious about the accent. 'Are you American?'

He shakes his head. 'Canadian, Kenyan, Aussie – take your pick. Lived all over. And what are you doing out here?'

'Just traveling through. No particular reason.'

He laughs. 'The way it should be.'

Glen tells him I want to be dropped off at Obo, that I'll try to get a ride on a rubber boat heading further up the Fly.

'No problem,' Jim says. 'I have to stop at Obo, anyway. But what's this about a rubber boat?'

'I'd like to try to hitch a ride on one.'

Glen starts laughing. Jim just looks at me with his pleasant blue eyes, suspending a smile.

'Well,' he says at last, 'if you've gotten this far, all the power to you.'

I'm starting to really like this man.

Glen and Jim head to the chopper to remove some supplies. I see a box full of beer – obviously for Glen. There's also a lot of food and some building supplies. Jim takes a moment to chat with some of the Suki men before handing them boxes.

He walks over to me again.

'So have you ever taken a chopper ride?' he asks.

'Never.'

'You're in for a treat.' He picks up my backpack and

swings it to a shoulder. 'Come on. I'll explain some things.'

I stop to thank Glen for his help.

'No worries,' he says. He motions to Jim. 'You're in good hands. He's an excellent pilot.'

I wave good-bye to the people of Suki and head to the chopper. Jim helps me into the front seat beside the pilot's chair and pulls straps over my shoulders, locking me in firmly.

He hands me a headset. 'This is how we talk to each other once we're up in the air.' He shows me the button to press when I want to speak. 'When you're through talking, you say "over".'

Jim walks around the chopper and jumps into the pilot's seat. He straps himself in and we pull our doors shut.

'How long have you been a pilot?' I ask him as he picks up his headset.

'Long time. I used to fly a lot in the war.'

He flicks some switches. The rotors start.

'Vietnam?'

'Yeah. That war.'

He puts my headset on me, adjusting the small microphone before my mouth. He puts his own headset on and we practice the strange new way of communication. His voice comes straight to my ears, sharp and personal.

'Ready to end your helicopter virginity?' he asks.

I nod. I can already feel the chopper rearing.

'Okay. Let's go.'

The chopper ascends slowly at first, and then *whooshes* into the air. The spit of land below, the lagoon, Suki Village appear in miniature. All around them sits that incredible expanse of swamp. This is nothing like an airplane ride in which one is hermetically sealed, the world reduced to a single view through foggy oval windows. A chopper presents the world unobstructed and gaping, only a pane of curved glass keeping me apart from it.

Jim sees my delight.

'Shall we play?' he asks me. 'I like to play.'

The chopper takes a sharp turn and edges down over the enormous spread of wetlands. The green land rushes by below. Herds of rusa deer flee before our approach, diving and leaping through the water, reeds streaming from their antlers.

Jim points at the deer, at the verdant landscape, smiling broadly. 'Have you ever seen anything like it?' he asks.

I shake my head. I wish there were some way to keep this moment in the present, fresh and unadulterated by the imperfections of memory: all the sharp, brilliant colors of the land. Blue skies, green grasses, the afternoon sun turning the dark swamp water into a gleaming gold. And no people in sight. No roads. No human beings anywhere. Jim and I like noisy gods in the sky. I feel, for the first time in my life, absolutely superhuman. I feel what it means to live.

Jim looks over at me. I fear he can see the tears in my eyes.

'And to think they pay me for this,' he says gently. Then, all of a sudden, 'Why don't we go west? You're not in a hurry to get to Obo, are you?'

I shake my head.

'Good. Let's play.'

We sail up, just below the cumulus clouds, and head due west. As we travel, Jim asks me about myself. How old I am. Where I've traveled. If I always travel alone. I answer all his questions, tell him I've got the travel bug and can't find a cure for it.

'I usually can't stay in a place for more than two years,' I laugh.

'I know about that,' he says. 'I've always been a restless sort.'

He asks me about school. I tell him about leaving graduate school, about needing to see Papua New Guinea, needing to go way into the place.

He looks at me. 'It takes a lot of guts to be a woman traveling here.'

'Or maybe just stupidity.'

'What were you studying in graduate school?'

'Writing.'

'Will you be writing about an old pilot you met in Suki?'

He catches my eyes, smiling. I nod. *Most definitely*.

Sitting beside him, I'm getting a strange feeling. It's as if we've met before – or should have. My usual reserve is gone. I feel like some giddy little girl. And there is something about this man, something so kind, so wholesome and engaging, that I can barely contain my admiration for him. Out of all of the myriad courses presented to people during their lives, Jim has taken himself here, to Papua New Guinea. His choice of the maverick life must have required him to have more guts and faith than most people ever know.

He brings the chopper down over an area of wetlands that he says is the place where Papua New Guinea borders Indonesian Irian Jaya. But there is no sign of a border down below. There are no lines of demarcation. Nothing. The land is untouched.

Jim says he's flown to nearly every corner of Papua New Guinea. He doesn't really fly over the western, Indonesian half of the island, though. For one thing, he's not supposed to – not that regulations necessarily stop him, but the Indonesians have been doing a fine job of ripping up the jungles, wiping out villages, killing people and just making a mess of the place. Jim wants to avoid messes. He saw all the messes he cared to see back in Vietnam – 'that war,' as he always calls it.

Jim doesn't like to talk too much about Vietnam, except to say that he fought with the Aussies. This actually tells me a lot, though, because when most people think of Vietnam, they think of exclusive American involvement. But I know that right at the start of the war the Aussies sent in a few of their best, their most elite. A 'crack unit,' it was called, of only one battalion. Jim must have been one of those men – a pilot for this elite unit. And he would have seen some pretty rough fighting.

Jim does tell me that he learned his piloting skills in the

war, skills that come in handy in Papua New Guinea, which, he says, has some of the toughest terrain there is when it comes to flying. PNG's mountains have a way of breaking sharply into the clouds, the weather always changing so quickly that one has to be very careful when maneuvering around the country. Reaching mountain villages, in particular, can be quite a feat.

'It's always a challenge flying in this country,' Jim says. 'But I love it here. Love it.'

'So is this your home?' I ask him.

He smiles. 'For now it is.'

He pulls the chopper northeast, toward Obo. As we fly, he asks where I've been before PNG. I know he's lived in Kenya for a while, so I tell him about my trip to Africa – seeing the wildebeest migration in the Serengeti, viewing Kenya's strange clarity of distance, clouds drifting off in one unending procession till the eyes strain on the horizon. Like PNG, that was another unimaginably beautiful land. But not the same as here, not as green, the colors not quite as pure.

'Lots of beauty in this world,' Jim says in that confident voice of his, nodding.

And then, because he asks, and because we stream over the world as if immune to it all, I tell him briefly about Mozambique and going down the Bone Yard Stretch.

When I finish, I feel strangely embarrassed, as if I've said too much – I usually don't tell people about that. I guess I figure they wouldn't understand. I left behind most of my innocence and faith in that country. It was as if I grew twenty years older once I'd left; the place still holds a part of me I'll never be able to get back. Now, when I do bring up Mozambique in conversation, it's just to say that I've been there, that I've got a passport with its bleeding pink entry stamp. But I sense that Jim would understand.

'My experience in Mozambique was nothing, though. I mean, you were in Viet*nam*.' I look at Jim. 'I can't imagine what that must have been like.'

He's silent for a moment. Then: 'You ever wonder if the only reason why we're here is luck? Plain ole luck? I wonder that all the time.'

We swoop gracefully over the green fields, then pull up sharply. Down, up, we glide in the air like a dragonfly caught on the wind. I'm laughing in delight. It's such a privilege to share this moment with someone else; I realize that, for most of my life, I've experienced my sublime moments alone – have even come to associate beauty with loneliness, as if the two are forever inseparable. Jim is teaching me that they don't have to be. He's like a messenger, and the world is beginning to tell me things. Important things.

Quite unexpectedly, I'm beginning to see this trip to New Guinea in a different way. Not as an endurance test, but as a test in a new sort of faith, a trusting that I will be shown a kind world if I can only learn to slow down. I couldn't have predicted this ride with Jim; rather, it needed to find me. Like serendipity.

'Look at this place!' Jim says. When he looks at me, his eyes are bright, alive. 'Wonderful! It's all so wonderful.'

We're approaching Obo. Jim flies the chopper low over the swampy grasslands. Some children, fishing in a lagoon, wave wildly at us as we fly overhead.

'Over too soon,' I say as the chopper nears Obo's landing area beside a few flimsy wooden buildings.

'It's been a lot of fun, hasn't it?' Jim says.

He lowers the chopper to the ground. We take off our headsets, and he turns to me. 'I'm stationed up in Tabubil. Will you ever be heading that way?'

Tabubil is the town established by the Ok Tedi company, built to accommodate its mining personnel. It's near the end of the Fly River, north of the town of Kiunga. I wasn't planning on going there – until now.

'Yeah, I'll probably make it up there,' I say. 'After Kiunga.'

Jim reaches in his pocket and hands me a business card. It reads: 'Capt. Jim Mead.'

'I live by the airstrip,' he says. 'Look me up if I can be of any assistance, okay? There's my number.'

I nod.

We stare at each other for a moment.

He unbuckles me and asks me to wait. Getting out of the chopper, he comes around to open my door and help me down, and I'm thinking that it's nice to be a damsel in distress every once in a while, if I can manage it. I'm exhausted by the idea of always taking care of myself.

I stare at Obo. It consists of a couple of crude buildings. The Fly River meanders slowly by, much more narrow and docile than it was further south by Daumori Village. Other than what I'm looking at, there's not much more to the place, and I'm starting to get an inkling of what the American frontier must have been like with its isolated and make-shift trading posts on the rivers. There are no trees or jungle here. Just grassland, nothing blocking the horizon. It's a flat, vast place.

Jim starts to refuel the chopper from a nearby metal drum. He asks a friend of his, a Papua Guinean man named Jimmy, when the next rubber boat is due to arrive at Obo.

'Four, five days,' the man replies.

Our attention is diverted to the other end of the village where a bearded man wearing only a breech-cloth, carrying bow and arrows, starts screaming wildly as he comes toward us. I see an arrow held at ready in his bow.

Jimmy explains that this man has been on the rampage for several days because his daughter's virginity had been taken by some man – an apparent boyfriend who lives in Obo. As the act went against tribal custom, the bearded man has been trying to find the perpetrator and kill him.

'Jimmy,' Jim says, 'take her into one of the buildings, please. Keep an eye on her after I go.'

His friend nods and picks up my backpack, escorting me to a nearby shed. I go inside and lock the door. I can still hear the bearded man howling outside. What kind of crazy place have I come to? It's hot here and I can't really see anything. What if the man makes it inside, comes after me? Anything's possible.

What am I doing here? I wonder. Four or five days until the next rubber boat. And what happens if, when the boat arrives, the captain refuses to take me along?

I want to get back in that chopper. Be with Jim again. Maybe he can take me to Kiunga? Then I'll go north to Tabubil, give him a call, try to see him again.

I hoist my backpack onto a shoulder and unlock the shed's door, seeing that Jim is just pulling himself into the chopper. He stops when he sees me run over.

'Can you . . . can I go with you? Are you stopping in Kiunga?' I ask.

'So you're not sick of me yet?' He smiles. He looks relieved. 'No problem. I can drop you off there.'

And it is this easy. All these weeks in PNG I've been swept up in a strange momentum that has been hurling me from one place to the next, almost as if I were running a race that seemed out of my control. Now, though, I'm consciously slowing down, am getting somewhere without the usual challenge.

Jim hurries me into the chopper. Taking my pack, he quickly puts it in back and climbs into the pilot seat. I buckle myself in and put on the headset. Jim has already set the rotors whirling. Vietnam taught him well: in a quick moment, we're up in the air, leaving Obo behind. Down below, the bearded man becomes a tiny figure sliding along a side of the shed I'd been in, bow and arrow held out before him. His quarry, whoever that unfortunate man is, is nowhere to be seen.

Kiunga is a few hundred miles due north, but we head northeast instead. Jim wants to take me somewhere special, show me Lake Murray and what he claims is some of the most spectacular and rarely glimpsed scenery in all of PNG. This is the strangest sort of 'date' I've ever been on – if I can call it that. I'm being taken by helicopter for an aerial view of one of the most seldom seen regions in the world. According to my map, the area just to the east of Lake Murray and the Strickland River is a huge, uninhabited blank extending for hundreds of miles in all directions. No villages. Nothing but swampy grasslands and jungle.

We reach Lake Murray and skim down above the water. Scores of great white birds scurry into the air, spreading wide wings. Jim shows me patches of water that appear bright red from a strange kind of plankton. White cockatoos burst forth from patches of trees.

'I do this a lot,' he says. 'I like to come out here.'

'Is this paradise for you?'

'It's got to be close.'

Jim says there are a few villages on Lake Murray, but they're far from each other and seldom visited by anyone except the people on the rubber boats. There are a couple of spots by villages, though, where a clearing has been made so a chopper can land. He's hardly ever landed, himself, preferring to see the country from the air.

'And do you like jungles?' he asks.

I nod my head adamantly.

'Good,' he says. 'Let's play.'

We head northwest and follow the Fly River for a while. The wetlands bordering it at last give way to a thick jungle. We see a red road cutting deeply into the rain forest from the Fly River village of Aiambak.

'The government's hired the Malays to come in and cut a road from Aiambak to Kiunga,' Jim explains. 'According to the deal, they get to harvest 500 meters of timber on either side of the road as they build it.'

We follow the road now. From the air, the trail looks like a bloody cut across an otherwise unbroken expanse of jungle. In his disgust, Jim hovers ominously above some Malaysian workers busy cutting up trees they've felled. They stop their work and look up.

'That's not five hundred meters down there,' Jim says. 'More like a thousand meters on each side.'

I observe the route of the road. Logic suggests that the easiest way to build a road along a relatively flat terrain is to make a simple straight line from one point to the other. The Malays' road, however, defies logic. It meanders east, heads west, edges south and creeps up north again. It's obvious what they're doing. The more switchbacks they cut through the forest, the more timber they can harvest. Their final road will end up being several times longer than it actually needs to be.

Jim shakes his head. 'What they do is,' he explains, 'they send scouts out in search of valuable trees. And when they find some, they cut their road out to the different spots so they can "legally" take the trees. And see, the problem with all this is that in the rainy season the roads turn into rivers, and then all the topsoil gets washed away into the Fly River. What they're doing is terrible. Just terrible.'

We fly over the farthest point the incomplete road has reached. There are several trucks parked down below, and men busy cutting giant trees down.

'The Malaysians ruin their own country,' Jim says, 'a third of their rain forests in Borneo cut down, and then they decide to come out here to ruin this place.'

He has completely lost his cheer. We circle around the end of the road, and the workers stop their cutting to look up nervously.

'That's a hell of a lot more than five hundred meters,' Jim says. 'I'll report them to the ministry when I get back to Tabubil.'

He flies us past the end of the red road, and there's only jungle now. A jungle so thick and vast, I'm dazed by it. We speed north. It is 360 degrees of uninterrupted green. One can scan the world in all directions and see nothing but jungle touching the very edge of the horizon. There can be nothing like it in the world.

'This is what I wanted to show you,' Jim says, delighted again.

Trees of all different sizes compete for space and light in the canopy. There are giant hardwoods that the native peoples use to make canoes: black and red *klinkii*, rosewood. Tall, stiff yellow tauns reign above all but the spindly aruka – betel nut – palms, which jut higher than the rest to bask, unobstructed, in the sunlight. In high points in the undulating canopy, great flocks of green and red parrots take to the air as we approach.

Though I'm aware of the power of greed, I still can't understand why someone would want to cut all of this down. I look at the rain forest, at those big trees and the life teeming within, and I try to figure out what would have to be in the heart of someone like the men we just saw, who can unconscionably exploit this land. Where does one's sense of reverence go? Perhaps they had none to begin with.

I wonder if Jim gets a pinch of conscience that he works for a mining company that has done its own job of polluting the natural environment. He must have made peace with the idea, somehow. Perhaps, he'd argue, it's a necessary evil, much of the huge profits supposedly going back to the Papua New Guinea government and, ultimately, the people – not, as is the case with mines in neighboring Irian Jaya, into the pockets of Indonesian president Suharto and his special friends and family.

I want to get my mind off the subject, so I ask Jim what he does when he's not flying choppers for Ok Tedi. Does he go to Australia? Does he take any holidays?

He shakes his head. He hasn't a wife or anything. 'Usually,' he says, 'I go diving. Papua New Guinea – Milne Bay, in particular – has the best diving in the world in my opinion. I'd love to start a diving business there. Have you ever dived?'

'No,' I say. 'I didn't grow up by an ocean. I never learned.'

'You have to learn someday,' he says. 'There's nothing like it. Whenever I need to get away, I go diving.'

As his eyes scan the spread of jungle below, he starts to tell me about his life here. Some days, when the loneliness gets to him, he says he'll fly off in his chopper to a deserted beach. There are many such beaches in PNG, and he says it is like landing on the very edge of the world. He spends his days scuba diving. At night, hearing only the sound of the sea, he builds a fire, pretending he's the last person alive.

I imagine taking a chopper and landing on some deserted beach, the jungle waiting sentinel-like behind me once the sand finally ends. Something about Jim's story speaks to my own traveling in search of a similar forgotten shore. There is so much I'd like to ask him about what his trips mean. I'd like to ask him about the days before he ever came here, and if he knew this would be the place where he'd end up. Because if he *did* know, then I want to find out how. Did he wake up one morning knowing where he belonged? Or was it a slow process? Did he do what I'm doing – always moving from one place to the next, hoping to get it right finally?

But too late. Kiunga is already approaching, and Jim is radioing a friend there, arranging for an Ok Tedi truck to come to the airstrip and take me wherever I need to go. I decide I'll ask Jim all of these questions when, hopefully, I'll see him again in Tabubil.

Down below, Kiunga isn't much of a sight. It's a town of corrugated iron-roofed buildings sitting near the Fly River. Nearby, I glimpse the Alice River, gray from Ok Tedi mining runoff.

The chopper descends onto the asphalt at Kiunga's tiny airfield. Jim keeps the chopper going as he unbuckles me and gets out to unload my pack. 'Watch your head,' he says, opening the door for me. The blades are loud and swift overhead. He points to a waiting truck. 'They'll take you wherever you're staying.'

The swishing of the blades makes it hard to hear, and as he leans down to say good-bye our faces brush, our eyes meet. He has his hand on my shoulder.

'I wish you the best,' he says into my ear.

And I never do such things myself, but I take hold of his shoulder, gripping it, and thank him.

'You have my card,' he says. 'Call . . . if I can be of assistance. All right?'

I nod.

After a pause, he moves away. 'Good-bye,' he yells over the noise of the chopper.

I pick up my backpack and wave to him, then walk

toward the waiting Ok Tedi truck. As I get in and sit in the front seat, I watch the chopper rise from the asphalt and sail away. Already, I'm thinking of an excuse to look him up in Tabubil. I'll come up with something. Something good. I must see him again. *I must*.

And now, suddenly, Kiunga appears.

CHAPTER SEVEN

The Silent War

How quickly life changes, sobers.

I'm staying with Pastor Michael Simak in the guest quarters of the Kiunga Lutheran settlement. It's night, and we sit outside on the platform where he gives his sermons. In a quiet voice, he tells me about the refugees in a place called Blackwater. It holds approximately 10,000 people from Western New Guinea – Indonesian Irian Jaya – who were forced to flee from the rape, torture and slaughter of the Indonesian military, the same notorious military that has been occupying and terrorizing East Timor for decades. This situation in Irian Jaya is such a common topic in PNG that I've been hearing a lot about it during my travels; I recall that several women in the YWCA in Port Moresby had fled from Irian Jaya. It seems incredible that Indonesia has gotten away with seizing half of New Guinea with most Westerners knowing almost nothing about the situation. Why? Why is it such a mystery? I want to find out. Get into the camp.

Since when did my trip begin to take on more concrete purpose? I think of Jim Mead and the chopper ride, and the idea of the world revealing important things if I can only pause for a moment to listen. Here is yet another opportunity that has nothing to do with any plan I may have concocted for myself: getting into the camp and talking to the people. I'm not a journalist, of course, but if I can *meet* with them, maybe I can write about them. Help them. I think people should know what's going on.

'I want to visit the refugees,' I tell Pastor Michael.

He studies me for a moment. A very dark-skinned, rotund man from the Solomon Islands with a prodigious appetite, he's in sharp contrast to the local people of Kiunga, who appear gaunt, if not undernourished. Smoking and chewing betel nuts, he regards me with his usual half-sardonic, half-sincere expression, as if waiting for me to change my mind.

'I'm serious,' I say. 'I want to go. I'd like to write about it.'

'Do you work for a newspaper?'

'No.'

'But are you a reporter?'

Maybe I am. Or maybe I need to be to get in. I nod. Okay, yes, I'm a reporter. I'm wondering if Pastor Michael knows anyone in the camp, and if they can help me get in.

'I have a better idea,' he whispers. 'You can meet Pastor Carl Waromi.'

Why is he whispering? 'Can he help me?' I ask.

Pastor Michael laughs heartily. When he at last composes himself, he says, 'Do you know who Pastor Carl is?'

I'm confused and shrug.

'You have never heard of Pastor Carl?'

'No.'

'Pastor Carl Waromi,' he says slowly, 'is the leader of the OPM.'

And now I'm starting to understand. I can be taken to visit soldiers in the OPM (*Organisasi Papua Merdeka*, the Free Papua Movement), which is the guerrilla band fighting the Indonesian takeover of Western New Guinea.

Pastor Michael massages his belly and watches me. I ask him about this Carl Waromi. How is it that a pastor, a man of God, can be the leader of a guerrilla resistance movement?

'You ask him,' he says, smiling.

Pastor Michael suggests I first make it to the refugee camp, then Carl will find me. However, the route to the camp has been declared off-limits by the PNG Ministry of Foreign Affairs. No one is allowed entry without official (and very reluctantly granted) permission, not that entry is as easy as it sounds. The camp isn't close to Kiunga, and it sits deep in a stretch of jungle reached by river and then the crudest of roads.

Yet, if it's out there somewhere, I'm convinced I can get there – illegally, of course. I'll go with all my resolve. No matter what anyone says, I'll get in.

But Pastor Michael wants me to know that it's a dangerous business.

If the refugee camp does indeed double as head-quarters and training camp for the OPM, a Westerner suddenly appearing there would surely be held suspect. Which makes me wonder whether I might be considered a spy – someone dangerous. I could be anyone! Which makes the real truth about me all the more outrageous. I'm an American graduate student who was in a creative writing program. That's it. About as harmless as you can get. I even write poetry. I pay attention to such silly, petty matters as beauty and meter.

So I'll need a good motive for going. A damn good motive.

Yet what do I know about hunting down guerrilla leaders and interviewing them? Can I just *visit* a man like Pastor Carl? I tell myself I can. For some reason, the idea seems entirely feasible – maybe because I'm a woman. And a young woman, too. I'd have to be the last person anyone would suspect in some jungle in the middle of New Guinea. And if I get into any trouble, I can always use my femaleness to my advantage, pretend I'm some clueless, ditsy blonde.

'Is it safe for me to go at all?' I ask Pastor Michael. 'What do you think?' Because I don't want to go on a suicide mission. Among other things, I'm looking forward to seeing Jim Mead again.

Pastor Michael shrugs. 'It will be in God's hands.'

I don't like his answer. 'Can you arrange to get me there?' I ask.

He nods. 'Some OPM soldiers are in town, and they're returning to the camp tomorrow. You can go with them.'

'Just like that?'

'Yes, like that. If they'll take you, you can go with them. But remember,' he smiled one of his mysterious smiles, 'you must do the rest.'

It's noon. Time to meet the soldiers by this river.

And what does a typical guerrilla soldier look like? I've never met one in person. I've seen photos of men from Honduras, Afghanistan. I might have glanced at them in a *Time* magazine as I waited to get a haircut or stood in a grocery line. Hollywood movies teach me that they wear camouflage and carry AK-47s, and have an overall dingy, emaciated look, which suggests the rigors of secret wars, of hiding and planning and sneak attacks.

But what about Pastor Carl Waromi?

I have no photos of him, so I must create him from my imagination. Of course he's in camouflage, a rifle hanging from a shoulder. And he must have a slight paunch because he's a leader and well-fed. He needs huge, strong arms, so I give them to him. My creation evolves, becomes more formidable. Carl's exposed black skin should glisten from sweat, and so he'll need a bandanna now to hang handy from a pants pocket. No, better: the bandanna sits damp around his thick, bearded neck. Carl must have the beard, some element of distinction. And also deep-set, terrifying eyes – eyes that can evoke a fear of God, because Carl Waromi is a pastor in addition to being a guerrilla leader.

My image starts to satisfy. It gives me courage.

No one approaches me yet. My watch tells me it's 12:15.

I wonder about the man I'm going to try to find. When had Carl turned from peaceful church duties to the bloody business of planning and executing attacks against the Indonesians? Could one really be a man of God and at the same time hate enough to issue orders to kill? I can't fathom the paradox of that and want to know how, why. Something inside me has to know, depends upon the reply. I question all I know about hating, remembering the millions of people oppressed in the world who do hate, can talk about it and justify it. And I wonder this: am I naive for the simple reason that I haven't hated? And why, suddenly, such guilt?

Because I had always considered the word 'hate' as something both unreasonable and derogatory. We must not hate. We must love. We must forgive, empathize, understand. If all else fails, we must see our aggressor or tormentor as a baby, thus always keeping in sight their hidden, helpless humanity.

It's 12:30. Several large dugout canoes have landed and are being loaded with supplies from Kiunga. How will I recognize my guides? Perhaps they've already arrived, and I don't know it. Maybe they inspect me now, trying to determine if they can trust me. No one wears camouflage. There isn't any of that Hollywood illusion at all. Beyond this loading spot, the tail end of the long Fly River flows gray from mining runoff. A jungle sits opposite. And of course there's the sun, and the heat. And a humidity that envelops and debilitates, trying to eat into my pores, burrow under my skin. I must simply wait. In Papua New Guinea, you must always wait. I tell myself I'll eventually get to Pastor Carl.

I've always considered it a fault that I think too much about everything. A simple gesture from someone can have any kind of hidden meaning; I often debate facts for days. Last night, I pondered my chances of ever reaching Waromi. Yet now, on the river bank, I don't think at all about what I'm about to do because already the fear is almost too great. My mind stays empty, numb.

The mystery soldiers appear. There are several of them and they surprise me by coming from the dirt slope behind me. They're ready to return to camp in the two large dugout canoes docked in the river. The men wear scraggly T-shirts, have very sharp cheekbones and wide noses. A few of these dreadlocked men carry little bags that – I'm told – have guns inside. From a distance, I wouldn't have noticed who they are. They wear old T-shirts and cutoff shorts made from secondhand pants, and this obvious poverty makes them blend with those around them. To notice them one almost needs to be up close as I am – close enough to see their eyes. I've never had the experience of looking at eyes so serious and imbued with rage. I'm looking at hate, a hate so deep it's palpable. I can actually see it, study it.

One man asks me to take a seat in the back of a dugout canoe. I follow his instructions, and he hands me my heavy backpack with one hand, muscular arm extended. I watch as the soldiers load on the provisions they've purchased in Kiunga town. They treat my presence as a matter of course, politely stepping by me in muddy bare feet as they rearrange and pack; no one seems to suspect I have any fears for the journey, that I am in fact questioning my sanity at this very moment.

Greetings are quick: few of the men speak any English. As they finish loading up the canoe, they arrange objects so that I might be comfortably seated in back and can stretch my legs. Though they're kind, the weight of their eyes warns me that I'm getting myself into something way over my head. But too late. The outboard is gunned up. They nod at me. We're off.

One man is to be my bodyguard; he doesn't tell me his name so I will call him John. John is a tiny man, from the Highlands of Irian Jaya. He calls me 'Sista' – Sister, in Pidgin – so I know that I've been secretly inspected and, apparently, approved. He has long dreadlocks, a wide nose typical of Highlands people, and he smiles frequently at me. His favorite phrase is 'No worries,' perhaps because he alone catches the nervousness in my eyes. He carries a dirty gray, nylon bag with a pistol inside, his smiles dissolving into seriousness whenever he inspects the far shore of the river.

Another soldier, a sinewy man whose face sinks into sharp cheekbones and a heavy brow, motions to John.

'He stay with you,' this man says. 'Good man. You safe with him.' I'm left to ponder the implicit meaning of his word 'safe.'

Rain forest speeds by on either side of us, the gray river meandering peacefully as we slice through it at an almost panicked speed. A storm is approaching but the clouds haven't reached us yet. The sun's rays creep under my large canvas hat, burning my skin. Not the place for a person with very light skin, surely. Nor, it would seem, for anyone. Along with the heat and humidity, the jungle is a dank place, full of malaria and dengue fever. Full of any number of dangers to add to the new possibility of getting shot by a sniper. I sink low in the canoe while John keeps his guard up, like all of the men. I notice that no one talks.

I try to come up with an exact plan, because the future looks too uncertain and hazardous without one. I want to know exactly what I'm doing and why. I want to have all excuses, even lies, prepared in case I need them.

I'll ask John to take me directly to Pastor Carl. Whatever it takes, I'm certain that if I can meet the OPM commander, be approved and put under his protection, I'll be safe. And then, with Carl's cooperation, I can learn about him and his people's struggles, and write about it all. Little has been written on these people and the genocide being waged against them by the Indonesians, and I start to realize the inherent power of words.

What do I know already? I'll want to check all my facts. The Indonesians seized Irian Jaya when the Dutch left in 1963. The United States, filled with Cold War paranoia, sanctioned the takeover in the hope that the Indonesians would, in return, not flirt with the Soviet Union and Communism. And so West Papua as it was known, filled with hundreds of indigenous Melanesian tribes with absolutely no ethnic relation to the Indonesians, was quickly subjugated by one of the largest militaries in the world.

Hard to believe, considering the island of New Guinea was hardly explored even up to the middle of the twentieth century. Missionaries had claimed footholds on the edges of the great jungles, had taken canoes into the swampy interior only to clash with tribes and be expelled or destroyed for their audacity. Then, in the early 1930s, the New Guinea Highlands was first explored. Imagine it: a great plateau in the center of the island, 14,000 feet high, home to hundreds of distinct tribes believed to be the first agricultural people in the history of humankind. And such a discovery when the rest of the world was colonized, mapped, known.

More amazing is that the discovery was documented on film. Australian explorer/gold hunter Mick Leahy brought a movie camera on his expedition, and so one of the most extraordinary movies of all time was made. Black and white shots show the first glimpse of the Highlands: a vast plain of planted fields to the very edge of the horizon. Here lived a people, we discovered with Leahy in that moment, who had been planting and harvesting while much of Western civilization still wandered about, struggling to survive.

Yet, the glories revealed by the camera also acted as harbinger to the end of those glories. Highlands tribes, who had never seen a white man or a camera, ran off in terror. Leahy would brag during an interview that they 'shit their pants' from fright, and watching the village people's reactions on film, he hadn't been exaggerating. In an act of bravado, Leahy takes his rifle and shoots one of their pigs in the head. As the gun *booms* and the pig falls dead in an instant, the entire village, crying, hysterical, runs off to hide.

It is like the fall of Eden in that moment, recorded for posterity on grainy black and white. When I first saw it, I was riveted. It is actually possible to sit down and watch on a television screen an abbreviated version of foreign encroachment and destruction, a chilling glimpse of what has happened to nearly every native group 'discovered' in the world. It is almost as if I were watching the arrival of Judgement Day. Thirty years later in the western half of New Guinea, the Indonesians would already have their foothold and begin the massive deforestation and genocide of the tribes. Thirty years from beginning to the arrival of the end.

And so the hate in the eyes of the men around me becomes more comprehensible as I sit in the canoe. They've seen their families massacred, their villages nearly exterminated. I begin to see that hate isn't something that rashly becomes a part of one's existence; one must cultivate it, nurture it. And the OPM men have had plenty of time.

The OPM began as a ragtag group who took on the Indonesian soldiers with bows and arrows, fighting against outrageous odds, obtaining guns from the men they'd managed to kill, striking quickly and fading into the landscape. Elusive, brave, but with hardly a chance.

Did So-and-So from a particular Dani tribe attack some Indonesian soldiers? Then go to the Dani tribe itself and wipe it out. One young man caught in the OPM could jeopardize his entire village, and so hundreds of villages have been attacked, entire tribes nearly exterminated. Men, women, children have dug their own graves: a favorite activity of an Indonesian military elite supported and trained by America's own Special Forces. So much for my childhood dreams of becoming a Green Beret.

The one thing I know about these people, the one fact that keeps resurfacing in my mind, is that to be a member of the OPM is to be an outcast. Their own villages, their own *kind*, had to turn them away. Before they fled to Papua New Guinea, the guerrillas lived in remote outposts in the jungles, fighting what they called their 'silent war.' If they chanced a visit to their family, their very presence could lead to their family's death. And so the exile, the pain of losing one's roots and identity. These men came together from all over Irian Jaya – imagine, let's say, Navajos and Iroquois fighting together – and can never return to their people. And so the heaviness I feel in their presence, that weight in a single gaze.

*   *   *

We finally dock our canoes at a place called Ramsite. It has begun to pour. There is nothing gentle about rain in the tropics. It comes down in torrents, as if to ravish the land, and we all hurry to unload the supplies from the canoe and wrap them in plastic. My legs are already covered in a dark red mud, my clothes completely soaked. I get the feeling it's going to be a very long day.

Ramsite is nothing but a small clearing cut from the thick jungle bordering the river. A few rusted petrol drums sit in foot-high overgrowth, but there's no village, nothing encouraging. I have no idea where I am, Ramsite not appearing on any of my maps. I don't even know if we stayed on the Fly. I would ask the soldiers, but due to their lack of English, they can hardly communicate with me. I'm left to guess at everything, including what the next leg of the trip will be.

The soldiers do make it clear that they want me out of sight from the river, and so I follow John up a mud hill to a crude thatch hut. It is a typical PNG hut, raised some five feet off the ground, and I need to climb a bamboo ladder to get inside. From out one of the back windows, I notice a dirt road. The rain has transformed it into a river of red mud that streams out of the jungle. If people aren't meant for this place, then roads certainly aren't.

Once again, I'm told to wait, but wait for what? Transportation? The arrival of someone else? Will Carl Waromi meet me here? I don't know. I steel myself and sit calmly, remaining hyperaware of everything around me.

An hour or so later, after sitting in silence with a group of the guerrilla soldiers constantly assessing me, the hut shakes as someone new walks inside. He identifies himself as Mr Richard, and sits down near me. My bodyguard, John, starts mumbling in a tribal language, but I know without the warning that this 'Mr Richard' is going to be a problem.

I note his neat white shirt, his closely cropped hair. His skin is lighter-colored, his facial features small. This is a man with money and some kind of position, who is clearly an outsider. I compare him to the OPM men who wear only dirty shorts and T-shirts, their hair in dreadlocks. While Mr Richard's role is unclear, he obviously isn't a refugee or member of the OPM.

He tells me he came up in the second of the two canoes that were delayed in Kiunga, and had not been informed about me. What do I think I'm doing? Where do I think I'm going?

I note his excellent English: he's been educated in a city somewhere.

'I want to go to the refugee camp,' I say bluntly. I keep my face expressionless.

'Yes. But you cannot do this, you know.'

He immediately asks for my passport. I calmly deliver it, and he studies it for several minutes in silence. He flips through all the visas and entry stamps, studying each one assiduously. I wonder, trying to hide my smile, what possible meaning a Zimbabwe or Madagascar stamp might have.

Finally: 'Who are you? Why do you want to visit Blackwater Camp?'

I have my pat answer all ready. 'I'm a tourist. I'm interested in the art and culture of the tribes of Irian Jaya.'

'There is none of that in the camp. They are refugees, you know.'

'I was told that there is.'

'Who will you stay with? Do you know anyone?'

I tell him I was given the name of a Pastor Carl Waromi, that I could stay with him. I wait to see how he'll react. His reaction will tell me a great deal.

Richard laughs sharply and looks all around, as if the whole world could share in his amusement. 'This is impossible,' Richard says at last.

'Why?' I smile now. I must change tactics, warm up to him. I pretend I have no idea whatsoever who Pastor Carl is and shrug apologetically.

Richard won't tell me anything, just glances through

my passport again. I watch him squinting at the visa for Tanzania.

'What is your job?' he asks, his eyes suddenly meeting mine.

I have the concentration I might have during a job interview; I can't afford to miss any signals. I tell Richard the truth. Whenever possible, I decide, I must give the truth because lies can more easily incriminate me.

I explain that I'm a student, in English – creative writing. I've never been able to explain creative writing to anyone outside the US (nor in it, come to think of it), but I give Richard what details I can. No, I don't write for newspapers. I make stuff up. *Stories.* Pretend.

He doesn't understand.

'I make up stories. Like dreams. All pretend.'

'Do you write for newspapers?' he asks again, annoyed.

I'm forced to say one of the stupidest things I've ever had to say: 'I write love stories.'

Richard looks at me with interest. Amazed that my lie has caught his attention, I decide to play the role of ditsy tourist. Just being a twenty-four-year-old 'girl' will help do the job for me, I know. I've often relied on my age and gender to get me into places that are technically off-limits, counting on my ability to fit the stereotypes held by officials. Who suspects a young woman of anything? Usually, though, I put on makeup, wear my contacts, fix up my hair, but I've had no time to prepare for Mr Richard. The most I can do with him is giggle and smile a lot.

Richard is a hard one, though – he isn't smiling back. I realize I must find and project the persona that will best suit him, will gain his trust or – even better – his dismissal of me.

He says he works for PNG's Ministry of Foreign Affairs, the very people who don't want me going to the camp. He just happens to be visiting the camp and has been fortunate enough to catch me trying to get in. He is deciding, now, what to do with me.

I find myself looking for comfort in the stares of the

guerrilla soldiers. I note with interest that they refuse to leave me alone in the hut with Richard. This fact, in particular, makes me feel a strong apprehension for the first time.

Richard, meanwhile, wants to feel me out with his questions.

'Do you know what Blackwater is?'

I decide to seem even more naive, more ridiculous. I will have to flirt with him.

'A refugee camp,' I say, 'with lots of great art.' I fluff out my hair and hold his eyes.

He gets angry. His dark eyes hold mine in an obvious attempt to intimidate. 'I have told you,' he snaps, 'there is no art in Blackwater.' He still fingers my passport.

His questions become more pointed, his demeanor more aggressive. So I'm planning on staying with Pastor Carl Waromi? I must know who the man is.

I shake my head. The pastor in Kiunga gave me the name, said I might stay with the man. That's all. I smile and shrug.

It's getting harder to smile. There is something profoundly cruel about Richard. I feel desperate to get away from his presence, as if he were contagious with something so awful, so base, that I'm scared of catching it. Of course I don't know what I'm sensing, but fear is rising in me, and it isn't a comfort to see that John and the others obviously loathe this man.

Still, I play dumb and ditsy. It occurs to me that I've probably smiled more in the past half hour than I have in the last month. Typically reticent, I become garrulous now. I chitchat in a manner that would astound the people who know me.

I talk about absolutely anything. The idea is not to shut up. Yes, I like the art of Papua New Guinea. I've just bought some Sepik River masks – now that is a cultural mecca! The Sepik River, wow! Has he ever been? The mosquitoes though – my God. They're all *over* the place . . . Does he know if the people from Irian Jaya have a similar artistic tradition as the Sepik People?

191

Richard doesn't know. He isn't sure. But if I'm going to Blackwater for art and culture, I'm going to be quite disappointed.

I keep going. Now the Asmat people are the carvers, aren't they? Amazing paddles, amazing bowls and plates. I've seen an American TV special, *National Geographic*, I think, that showed these people in Irian Jaya who actually lived in tree houses, too. Who wouldn't love to see such a thing . . . ?

I can see that Richard is dismissing me – slowly. His hard gaze softens. He even starts returning my smiles. But he still won't allow me to go to Blackwater, which is seventy kilometers up the mud road outside. It's forbidden, he reminds me. No one is allowed to go there unless they have special permission from PNG's Ministry of Foreign Affairs.

'I wish someone had told me!' I fake indignation. 'I was told you could just visit the place!'

'No. Who told you this?'

'Everyone! Now how am I supposed to get back to Kiunga? Great!' I pout. I look at the OPM soldiers and back to Richard in mock frustration. 'Is anyone heading back to Kiunga?'

He's staring pointedly at a page of my passport now, at the Indonesian visa I have there. He notices it isn't stamped yet. 'Are you going to Indonesia?'

I pause. 'Yeah, after I leave this country I may swing by there. I have a friend who's doing research there. On coral.'

'Coral?'

I nod.

'What will you do there?'

'I'm going scuba diving.'

'Diving.' He smiles slightly, as if at the novelty of such an idea. Stupid American tourist.

'*Deep sea* diving,' I say. 'There's great reefs.'

He slaps the passport closed and hands it to me. And then, smirking, he suddenly tells me I can go to Blackwater. His strange permission is obviously a kind of joke now. I want to go to Blackwater? He'll send me, the stupid tourist, and I'll wish I never wanted to go.

I thank him repeatedly, driving him in annoyance to his feet. A Mr Henry, an aid worker, is coming up in a third canoe, he tells me. A Land Rover is waiting to take Mr Henry to camp and I can go with him. But Richard wants me to understand that he's breaking the rules, and that if the PNG Ministry of Foreign Affairs knows he's allowing me to go illegally, he could lose his job. Then, with a regal wave of his hand to dismiss my new onslaught of thank yous, he exits the hut. My smile instantly vanishes, I make a 'fuck you' gesture at Richard as he leaves. John laughs while I wonder, bleakly, what I've just won and whether I want the prize.

John, to the protests of his friends, comes forward and whispers something in my ear.

'Mr Henry, Mr Richard – they are not friends of OPM.' The OPM men mutter that he should be quiet, not say anything more, but John leans closer. 'They are not friends, you understand?'

I look him in the eyes, nodding.

It strikes me as strange that I don't fear being with these guerrilla soldiers, in a hut in the middle of nowhere. Instead, I fear the men who will be in the Land Rover with me. Richard I already know to be untrustworthy, but now there is another like him, a Mr Henry.

Mr Henry, the 'aid worker,' turns out to be an Australian Baptist minister. At least, that's what Richard tells me. When this Mr Henry first sees me, he laughs so loudly that everyone at Ramsite glances his way. His first words to me are, 'So you think you're coming with? On holiday, are we? Forget it.'

A tall, thin man with brown hair, beard and hard blue eyes, he immediately dismisses my presence with a flicker of his hand.

'Richard said I could get a ride with you,' I say as politely as I can. 'I'm supposed to stay with Pastor Carl.'

Henry snorts. 'You *think* you're going to stay with

Pastor Carl. You're not doing anything we don't tell you to do.'

And what to say to that? I stand silently, dumbfounded. Traveling in a place with very few foreigners tends to exaggerate the significance of the chance meeting with one. I assumed, when I first saw him approach me, that he would be happy for this coincidental meeting. But not at all. Henry seems to have resented me instantly.

I look to Richard and project my best look of innocent helplessness.

'I told her she could go,' he tells Mr Henry.

Henry glares at him. Not prepared to argue with his friend, however, he relents and growls that I can hitch a ride in the back seat of the vehicle.

Our Land Rover skids and roars across the muddy red road, the sun almost set, the rain constant and severe. Jungle stands on either side, a dark green barrier. The road itself is swelled with water as if it were another river. A long red river.

Henry and Richard carry on nonstop chitchat, two friends catching up on news after a long separation, while Henry drives the lurching vehicle across the mud road as if engaged in battle. He shoves the gearshift knob forward, yanks it back, the engine whining and pleading as Henry forces it through the pools of water and mounds of red clay.

'I think this is the way we went this morning? Huh, Richard?' Henry's voice maintains a steady timbre, a voice that hasn't once given itself away to emotion of any kind. I sit in the backseat, wary of him, wary of absolutely everything.

Richard says a prompt yes because Henry's voice is the kind one fears. All hell would break loose if, for a fraction of a second, that steady voice raised its pitch.

It'll be hours until we reach this place called Blackwater. Hours of being slammed around the backseat, staring at the silhouettes of two men who can literally do whatever they want with me. I'm convinced that Henry isn't a Baptist minister, though why he pretends to be one

I'm not sure. Already, the complicated politics of the situation becomes obvious to me. So much suspicion, so many lies, and an odd hodgepodge of countries – Switzerland, Australia, Japan, even America (though America's name is whispered, is more confidential) – rumored to have mysterious interests in a part of the world that most Westerners have never even heard of. And here I am, already a player in it all. I start to wonder whether Richard and Henry are actually taking me to the camp. John, the soldier who calls me Sista, is the only person I trust. And John was left behind at Ramsite.

Richard makes the sudden announcement that I won't be staying with Pastor Carl. He and Henry chuckle about this as the adrenaline runs through me. I can feel my heart beating yet I can't calm down. If Blackwater isn't on any maps, then this road doesn't exist. I'm going somewhere that no one is supposed to know about, and that no one ever sees. But more importantly, I'm going there illegally and who can ever track me down? If something happens to me, no one will ever know. I'll just disappear. No trace.

In my mind, I tell those two silhouettes in the front seats that if they try to do anything to me, I won't make it easy for them. Rest assured.

Richard turns around and informs me that I'll be staying with Mr Henry. Again the whispered conversation, the chuckles from the men.

I contemplate the specter of Henry, not knowing what staying with him means. Will a man who so obviously resents me let me stay with him in his house? I doubt it and I decide to try to get some clues.

'I'm sorry about all this,' I say to him. 'I was supposed to stay with Pastor Carl. I really don't mean to impose on you.'

'Well, you are imposing,' he snaps with a certain brutality to his voice.

I take a deep breath. It's important that he doesn't hear my voice shake. 'Look,' I say. 'I need to know where we're going. I need to know where you're taking me.'

Henry snorts. 'Where I'm taking you! I don't think you have much choice in any of this, do you?'

Henry jams the Land Rover into first gear, the engine howling as the car charges through some mud. I see it's no use trying to get any information from this so-called Baptist minister, and give up.

I decide to continue my ditsy charade: if they believe it, there's a chance it can keep me safe. No matter what, I must pretend to be innocent and gregarious, though they don't know with what determination I'll fight them if they try anything.

'I'd never be able to get through this! Never!' I say to them. 'I would have been stuck way back. I can't even drive a stick shift.' Forget that my car back home is a stick shift. Forget Back Home altogether.

I ask basic, stupid questions, the expected kind. When Henry answers, always curtly, I respond eagerly to even the most cursory response.

'Australia, huh?' I say. 'It must have taken a lot of courage to come out here and leave all that behind! Was that hard for you and your wife?'

Because it comes out that he has a wife, stranded in the midst of this jungle along with him. Somehow I'm not comforted knowing this. It doesn't soften the edge to Henry's voice, doesn't make me overlook the fact that the questions he asks me are clearly not friendly queries. Like Richard, Henry interrogates, though subtly. He uses my name a lot when he asks me things, personalizing, numbing the motives behind the inquiries. But I'm not fooled. I give him plenty of conversation fodder, tell him about my paleontologist brother, about the animals I saw on my trip to East Africa. I tell him things that I think might spark a friendly human response from him: can you tell me how you got there? What was that like, Kira? But Henry has his own agenda, his own questions.

He forces the groaning car over the muddy ruts, the rain forest now a spread of blackness. The entire world is encapsulated in the beams of the headlights. The windshield wipers squeal, sweeping away the pouring rain. I watch them, my arm aching as I grasp the handle above the door, each knuckle bony white as I hold on to keep my whole body from slamming against the roof. I watch the wipers and wait for Henry's next question, struggling always to determine the motive behind his queries.

'What is it you study in school, Kira?'

'English,' I say. 'Creative writing.' I tell him in my brightest, most amiable voice that I like writing stories about stuff. Just stories about weird people I've met, strange things – stuff like that.

'Love stories,' Richard throws in, sneering.

I wait.

'You write for newspapers, Kira? Magazines?' Henry's head is half turned to hear my answer. He says my name with a certain interrogator's disdain, and I note that his question is the same one Richard has already asked me twice.

'No,' I lie, 'just stuff that isn't true. Just fiction. I make up stories. It's a lot of fun to sit there and think of characters and the stuff that happens to them. I've been doing it ever since I was a kid.' I want him to think that what I'm studying is completely asinine. 'I think my parents wished I'd become a lawyer or something.'

'Uh-huh,' Henry says. 'Ever published anything?'

'Some poems,' I say. 'I write a lot of poetry.'

Henry stays silent. I study the road caught in the headlight beams. I'm wishing I never said I'm a writer of any kind. Bad judgement there. I sigh and notice that my breath wavers.

'Yeah, I like to travel,' I add, forcing myself to be stupid, stupid. 'I like to find out about weird new places and write about how weird it all is. It really gets the imagination going, being in a place like this. People live so different and there's all these new customs.'

'Like what? What "customs" would you write about from your experiences here so far?' Henry asks. Richard looks back at me.

'Well, I stayed at this village called Daumori and they

believed in these Magic Fire Spirits. That'd be great to use in a story. And the villages were so simple and beautiful, too. I've never met people as nice as the villagers I stayed with in places like Daumori . . .' And on and on. I blab now as if possessed. It isn't me speaking but some charlatan. I listen to this person from some distance away, amazed.

Henry and Richard start chatting again. I lean back, silent. I'm too weary from the talking and worrying, and am glad for a break even if it means sitting and hearing the cries of the engine and Henry's furious comments about the road.

At last, having spent six hours to go roughly seventy kilometers, we arrive at Blackwater. There isn't any electricity, and the camp now appears as darkness dotted with the occasional cooking fire peeping through the slats of palm bark huts.

Henry looks back at me, gesturing outside and smirking. 'Here's your refugee camp, Kira.'

For the first time, I don't offer him a placating smile. I come hazardously close to telling him to fuck off.

The Land Rover at last pulls up under a house that is raised some fifteen feet from the ground. By PNG standards, the house is luxurious with its aluminum siding and glass windows. No cooking fires inside this home – it has generator-produced electricity.

I feel overwhelmed with relief. I haven't arrived at some seedy building in the middle of nowhere; this is, indeed, Henry's house.

'I really didn't mean to impose on you like this,' I say sincerely as Henry turns off the engine. Staying with him is the very last thing I want to do. 'I was supposed to stay with Pastor Carl.'

'Fine, but you are imposing.'

Like an angry father, he opens the door of the Land Rover and orders me out. I hoist my backpack on a shoulder and look around. Darkness. Rain. I wonder if the rain ever stops.

We walk up the stairs of the house, and an Australian woman greets us at the door: his wife. She's completely surprised to see me with her husband, and puts a hand on her chest. So Henry *does* have a wife, and a fairly comfortable house with all of the amenities one might find in the West: air conditioning, hot water shower, refrigerator, stove. Never mind that he's in the middle of a refugee camp where babies are dying from malaria and poor sanitation, where people have to sell paintings on the streets of Kiunga to raise enough money to buy food or medicine. Only the best for Mr Henry and his wife. They must be comfortable – comfortable enough to completely forget where they are.

Henry introduces his wife as Sue. Somewhere in her late fifties, her hair up in a bun, she says hello to me in the airy, obliging voice of an eager-to-please housewife. With her friendly demeanor, she's like Henry's alter ego. Do they *love* each other, this husband and wife?

Henry ushers me inside as if shooing in an insect.

'I haven't seen another white woman for some two years,' Sue says. She's grinning broadly, and can't know the fear her husband tried to plant in me during the entire trip out here. Just minutes ago I was convinced I was going to some dank holding cell.

Henry spits out my name and Sue, ever congenial, tries it out on her tongue.

'Ki-ra. Kee-ra. Unusual.'

'I think it's a Russian name,' I say.

'Are you Russian?'

'Czech.' Thank God she's friendly, I'm thinking. Thank God someone is.

Richard announces that he's leaving and will 'deal with me' in the morning. He needs to alert the camp administrator that I'm here, and I can only assume there will be more questions for me in the morning. Something to look forward to.

Sue shows me the guest bedroom. She points out their bathroom, gives me a tour of the kitchen. She makes a proud fuss about some new curtains, and points out her silverware and casserole dishes. I realize that I'm supposed to compliment her – and do.

She has books, a television. They even have a VCR – how could they go without one, stuck as they are in a refugee camp? Their small library consists of home decorating books and thrillers. A stereo plays some classical violin music and Henry slumps down on the sofa in the small living room area, studying me.

I examine their small house and its furnishings, looking for clues about the 'Baptist minister' who keeps watching me. Theirs isn't an ascetic life of deprivation, certainly. No pictures of Jesus anywhere. No crosses up. No 'Footprints in the Sand'-type parables on the walls. Nothing. I can't even see a Bible. I'd heard rumors about Australia sending spies to pose as missionaries near the border with Irian Jaya, and I start to wonder if this 'Mr Henry' is one of them. Apparently Australia likes to keep tabs on the tensions between Papua New Guinea and Indonesia. Indonesia has been known to cross the border to attack OPM forces in PNG, and if any of these attacks erupt into a more wide-scale assault on PNG itself, Australia – like a big brother – will have to come to the aid of its ex-colony. That could mean, in the worst-case scenario, war with Indonesia. They don't want that. They'd rather placate Indonesia, pretending to commiserate with its plight against the OPM 'secessionists' and throwing it political crumbs.

I turn to Sue. 'How long have you been here?'

'Oh, going on four years now.'

'Long time.' I shake my head sympathetically. Sue strikes me as someone unwittingly trapped in her husband's life. If 'Mr Henry' is not who he seems to be, Sue instead appears to be a genuinely dutiful housewife.

'What do you do here?' I ask her.

Henry sits up, angry. He knows there's a motive behind my questions.

'All right then. Kira,' he says, 'time for bed. I've got work tomorrow. Sue . . .'

Sue smiles apologetically and ushers me into the guest

bedroom. 'Sleep as late as you like, all right? I'll see you in the morning.'

She shuts the door, and I can hear Henry whispering to her outside. Their voices momentarily rise in volume. Climbing into bed, I note how the sheets are clean, neatly pressed. I haven't been in such a comfortable bed for weeks. I tuck the mosquito netting under the mattress and stare through the foggy gauze, listening to the rain. More questioning tomorrow. More of Henry.

I feel almost as lonely as I did back in Mozambique after I'd run away from the soldiers and was waiting for the night to end. Here is when the idea of traveling by myself seems like insanity, like masochism at its worse; when I most need someone to hold and comfort me, there is no one. Just the furious banter of my own thoughts. And the fear.

What should I do? So many worries. I'm sick of worries. The rains make road travel hazardous, so I don't know how I might get out of the camp. I contemplate a week – two weeks – stuck in this place. But no. I won't stay here that long. I'll leave. I'll just get up and go, the hell with what 'Mr Henry' has to say. I'll be all right. I'll hike back to the river. I'll do whatever I need to do to get back to Kiunga.

Staying with Pastor Carl is apparently out of the question. They don't want me getting anywhere near him. I wonder what they fear. Will Carl tell me things that they don't want the world to know?

In the morning, dreading having to leave my room, I peek out the window. Jungle. Everywhere, jungle. The rain falls lightly now on a land soaked and steaming with wetness. This camp seems to tentatively exist in a jungle that keeps encroaching and needs to be cut and burnt back. There is the one road into the camp, and even with a four-wheel-drive vehicle and unusual patience, passage often becomes impossible. The road can turn into a river, as it had last night, stranding everyone. Stranded . . . For the first time in my life, I understand what that word means. But I can't allow myself to feel trapped here. I refuse to feel trapped. I'm determined not to spend another day here.

But no putting off the inevitable now. I will have to leave this luxurious room, a holding cell until Henry can get rid of me. I berate myself for having wanted to find Pastor Carl in the first place. Maybe I've seen too many movies. *You don't actually go out and meet a rebel leader.* This is crazy.

I take hold of the doorknob and sigh. I half expect the door to be locked, but the knob turns and the door opens. I peek into the living room and, as if diving into cold water, walk out.

'Well, hello there!' Sue calls from the kitchen. Still enormously friendly.

'Morning,' I say.

'Have a seat! I'll get you some tea and breakfast.'

'Thanks.'

Henry is at the dining table, drinking coffee, the remnants of his breakfast lying on a plate beside him. As I walk into the room, he merely levels his eyes at me and says nothing.

I take a seat opposite him. I greet his angry look with my own. I want him to know that I'm a match for him, that he's not going to intimidate me.

'Your story must have been good,' is the first thing he says. He whispers it so his wife can't hear.

'Pardon?' I keep my eyes leveled on his, waiting.

'You got Richard to believe you and let you come here. But I'm not stupid, you know. You think I'm stupid?'

He glares at me. His whole body seems to twitch in anger.

I stare back at him and don't say anything.

Sue brings me a cup of tea, smiling, and returns to the kitchen.

'You're a writer,' he says quietly. 'I know what you're up to. You may have fooled Richard and however many other blokes, but not me. I'm on to you.' He points his finger at me for emphasis, like some school disciplinarian. 'I am *on* to you.'

I just look at him, faintly amused.

But the scene around me becomes surreal. Sue enters, blithely oblivious of any tension, and sets down some plates and food. She sits beside Henry and folds her hands for prayer while her husband does nothing but scowls at me. I look out the window, tapping my teaspoon against the tablecloth.

Seventy kilometers. Maybe I can sneak out of this house and hike back to the river? I could probably do seventy kilometers in a day. Or, if the thick mud makes this impossible, I can always camp along the way. Dangerous, yes, but anything to get out of here.

Henry finishes his coffee and abruptly gets up. Sue tells me it's time for him to go to work. I wonder what his work is.

His cold blue eyes on me, he says, 'I'll see you when I come back.' An order.

And he leaves.

Sue smiles as if in apology for her husband and offers me some toast. I decline, squashing the tea bag with my spoon. Now I hear a familiar voice: Richard. When he calls to me from the front door, Sue disappears.

'Good morning,' Richard says.

He's more friendly today, I notice, so it's back to the ditsy charade. 'It sure is wet out, isn't it? Wet, wet, wet.' I run some fingers through my hair. 'So I really can't stay with Pastor Carl, huh?'

Richard laughs. He runs his eyes over my face. 'You don't understand about Carl. Do you know who he is?'

I remember Henry's words: *Your story must have been good for Richard to believe you.*

'No,' I lie. 'What's wrong with him?'

Richard sits down in the living room and tells me all about Carl, explaining that he's a leader of one of *two* factions of the OPM. He says Carl is the 'stupid' leader.

'Really?' I say.

'Carl is very uneducated, and he's too political and

reckless with his people. He's not smart like the other faction's leader. He will tell you many stupid things. Many stupid political things.'

I nod my head and try to look disappointed by this sudden revelation about Carl. 'But I never wanted any trouble. The pastor in Kiunga gave me Carl's name and said he could show me some art. I never wanted any trouble, Richard. I really didn't.'

Saying his name causes his face to light up. He actually nods and leans toward me. 'Carl is a stupid man,' he says. 'A troublemaker.'

'Yeah. I don't want to make any trouble.' I look down shyly, helplessly.

Richard sighs and, almost as an afterthought, reluctantly points outside. He tells me that some of Carl's men are waiting for me near the house. He supposes I can go with them . . . to see Carl. He supposes it'll be all right.

'But no politics,' he says to me. 'I don't want you to discuss any politics.'

I nod my head vigorously. 'Okay. I promise. I hate politics anyway.' I giggle.

I get up and look out the door. My bodyguard, John! And three other men I don't recognize, waiting for me on the front lawn. John looks up and sees me and we smile at each other. Too grandly, I fear. Richard catches our grins and frowns. But too late. I grab my backpack from the guest room and head toward the door.

Sue walks in and mumbles something about my leaving and how her husband is 'expecting' me when he gets back. I barely hear her. Henry can kiss my ass. Quickly, I leave the house and greet my three 'bratas,' brothers, sent personally by Pastor Carl Waromi. They flank me and guide me away down the muddy red road, Richard and Sue looking on from the front door of the house. I don't bother to say good-bye.

My excitement erases any fear about where I'm going and what will happen next. Henry will be mad as hell to discover me gone. I laugh and John laughs with me. All of us are full of a sense of victory.

The men with John know Pidgin and they speak to me.

'We did not think Richard would let you come with us,' one of the men says.

'*Mi save*. I didn't think so either!' I say.

We all giggle like school kids who have gotten away with a prank. And yet here I am tramping with three OPM soldiers, through a camp I'm not even supposed to be in. Already, I talk with them about the forbidden 'politics,' like a naughty child. I know I'm walking through the dangerous territory of a war and a cause now. I start to feel the press of their plight, and the urgency of gathering as much information as I can.

Whenever the soldiers address me now, I notice, they call me 'Sista.' Sister.

My feet slosh through the road's red mud, which splatters on my shins. John marches ahead, wearing my backpack, naturally adept at walking in such conditions. I nearly slip several times trying to keep up with him, but I make sure I stay at their speed. Though it's a seven-mile walk through the mud, I want to know what it's like to live in this world, to be a soldier on the march, ignoring sweat and heat. I don't want to disappoint them by falling behind.

We walk for a long time, taking various side roads and trails. Overhead, the hot sun appears. I can see they're all used to this. John's arm muscles bulging, he grips the straps of my backpack as he walks. He is a small man – they all are – yet such power in that body. My 5'7" height makes me the tallest of the group, but their individual strength amazes me. These men are, indeed, soldiers. I picture them with rifles, on the march in some dense forest across the border. What do they think about then? What are they afraid of? Do they feel fear as I know it?

I watch my companions more closely now, noting their position – they all surround me. They have a serious, all-business attitude. Their eyes scan the jungle on either side of the road as they hold the little nylon bags with guns inside. They are, I realize, protecting me. Which explains why all four were needed to come retrieve me this morning.

I'm being guarded. From what? From whom?

But this information comes too late to be processed. Suddenly the road we're on opens up. Huts now, and in the distance a group of people waiting for us in the middle of the road.

As we approach the crowd, drums start beating. It's a large crowd, filling a yard in front of a sizeable thatch hut. People back up to make a corridor for my passage. Most of them wear elaborate native dress: grass skirts, cassowary-feather headdresses and bright red tufts of bird-of-paradise plumage, white paint swirling along the contours of their bodies. Everywhere, such dazzling color, such fantastic ornamentation. Some men wear only penis gourds, their faces painted a charcoal black, pigs tusks jutting through their noses. Women, bare-chested with brightly woven *billum* bags hanging down their backs, smile at me and shush their children as I walk by. Little girls shyly duck behind their mothers, peering out at me, their faces accented by dots of white paint and wreaths of beaded flowers.

My senses can't take it all in. I have never – not once during any of my past travels – experienced such an instant and thorough disorientation. So much is utterly new. There is so much splendor and pageantry. The drums sound like a communal heartbeat, urging me on though I can barely contain my confusion and excitement. Have I come at an opportune moment, just as they're preparing to have a celebration? Or – and surely there is a mistake – are these people gathered like this for *me*?

A middle-aged man approaches me, dressed in incongruous shirt and pants. He wears glasses, is thin and delicate-looking with a slight smile and solemn eyes. He slowly extends his hand.

'Pastor Carl Waromi,' John says to me.

I'm momentarily shocked. I nod and vigorously shake his hand. Here is the man I never thought I'd see.

At last. Yet I don't expect this man. He looks like a mild-mannered preacher, someone studious, solitary . . . shy. There is nothing ferocious about him, and my image of the warrior-like guerrilla leader in camouflage fades to reality. Yet, for all of his monk-like humility, Carl has the same strikingly fervent eyes as his soldiers. And there is also the look in them of a man burdened with the very survival of a culture. Carl is a sort of living Messiah, still unable to deliver his people, and this failure – the pain of it – rests in his eyes.

Carl takes a lei of red and yellow hibiscus flowers from a woman beside him and puts it around my neck. Solemnly, he leads me away.

Flashes of light. I look to their source. A man in Western dress snaps picture after picture of me. As I make my way through the painted, excited crowd, this photographer positions himself so that he can get shots of my face from a variety of views. Profiles, up close, head-on. Not casual shots, I realize. Not for records of nostalgia. And with this realization comes a panicked feeling. These pictures of me now: for what reason? To be able to identify me later? Each time the camera goes off, I cringe. Though the people seem to welcome me warmly, a group of plainly dressed men look on from the sidelines, faces grave. They keep leaning toward each other, whispering, their eyes never leaving me: I've come to the camp without any forewarning. Who am I? What do I want?

Pastor Carl directs me toward a wooden bench beneath a shelter of palm bark planks. He sits down and pats the seat beside him: everyone is to see that I'm his guest. I realize that this entire celebration is meant for me. For *me*.

I want to tell them that there's some kind of mistake. I want to ask them to stop so I can apologize, explain that I'm only a student. Really, only some backpacker who had decided to visit their camp. On a whim, really. On some half-formed scheme that I'd be able to write about them. I'm a nobody. They *need* to know this. I'm no one important at all.

I feel like a visting queen, though – am one, perhaps, because to them I'm Hope. No one comes to their camp. The world has forgotten them. And then, one rainy night, mysteriously, a young white woman comes up the muddy red road . . .

Someone sets up a microphone, and the man who was snapping all the pictures of me now stands behind it and tests it with a tapping of his hand. Some small, cheap speakers are placed on the grass, a buzzing generator giving them life as he rattles off some Indonesian into the microphone. Indonesian? I'm in Papua New Guinea, have been using Pidgin and English all this time. And now a different world, which speaks a different language.

Pastor Carl leans close and whispers into my ear: 'Whatever you have to say to me, wait until we are alone. What is your name?'

Introductions haven't even been made; I've been too swept up by what has happened. I tell him my name and he writes it down on a little notepad. This he hands to the man behind the microphone who speaks in excited Indonesian. I hear my name announced to the entire camp. I realize I'm to make a speech.

'Remember – say nothing,' Pastor Carl says as I get up and approach the microphone.

The entire crowd of people falls silent and watches me, this complete stranger, addressing them.

'I'm glad to be here,' I say, searching for words. 'I have never been with such a special people before. I have never seen the kindness and generosity I'm seeing now . . . I want you to know that I will never forget you. You will always be in my thoughts and prayers.' I remember a dash of Indonesian to allow me an exit: '*Terima kasi banyak*. I will not forget you.'

Everyone claps. The drums start beating again and Pastor Carl beckons me to the seat beside him.

Entertainment now. Dani warriors creep across the field in front of me, imitating a war dance. They glance about, slide forward, their blackened faces searching for enemies. Their bodies move flawlessly to the drumbeats, smooth, sliding advances, spears raised. The Dani were among the first to resist the Indonesians, doing so with bows and arrows. Not surprisingly, they were among the first tribes targeted for genocide by the Indonesian military.

The Dani warriors charge each other, letting loose war whoops and cries before quickly running off. New dancers assemble. These are the Mamberamo people, from the north of Irian Jaya. Hooded women join together, singing sharp syllables of some tribal song, their woven tulip bark skirts swishing.

All these people had come a long way to get to this refugee camp in Papua New Guinea. They endured week after week of harsh travel through the lowland swamps in order to reach the border of PNG before the Indonesian soldiers caught up with them. Thousands, mostly women and children, died from malaria and other sicknesses along the way. Often, the Indonesians waited for survivors at the border, shooting them as they appeared, or rounding them up to torture and slaughter in military camps.

It is those who had managed to escape to PNG who dance for me now. They pretend to be paddling a large canoe, the type they would have used in the ocean where they come from. Women sway their hips and dance in a distinctive Melanesian way that reminds me of the Maori I saw in New Zealand. Swishing, twirling, the women pretend to be on a large fishing boat heading out to sea.

At last, everyone gets up for a large circle dance. People draw me in. We walk around and around, our feet landing to the beats of the drums. My hands rest around some women's shoulders; because I'm a foot higher, they need to reach up to hold on to me. To the casual observer, I couldn't be more incongruous-looking with my T-shirt, light skin and blonde hair, while the women beside me have cassowary quills through their noses, are naked from the waist up and covered in white paint. Yet, here we are together, holding each other's hand, enjoying the dancing and the song while hoping for the return of a stolen homeland. There is a tragic air to this dance – to all the dances – which are born of a communal suffering and sorrow. I wish I could somehow alleviate everyone's pain, but I don't know how. The world feels like such a profoundly cruel, indifferent place, that I have trouble fathoming the existence of a God. I wonder how they are able to hold on to their Christianity, their faith.

A little girl called Mastina, wearing a bird-of-paradise headdress, runs up to me and strokes my arm. She smiles grandly, the kind of smile that would surely cause even a murderer to pause, and presses in beside me. I put my arm around her and we dance to the beat.

The drum grows softer. In the distance a lone man sits before his hut and strums on a guitar. I hear the words to his song. They're in English – he is singing to me:

> *'Rosy, you will go far away*
> *Don't forget us,*
> *Don't forget us,*
> *We will set our country free . . .'*

I've talked to many people. The celebrations will go on late into the afternoon. Carl at last invites me to his hut, into the headquarters of the OPM. Like all the huts nearby, it sits on stilts above the ground and is built from palm-bark slats and thatch. Inside, however, everything has the modern taint of politics. Amnesty International posters sit framed on the walls. There is a large picture of Irian Jaya that says, 'West Papua is my home,' above a West Papuan flag of white star on red beside blue stripes. None of the refugees calls the land they've left 'Irian Jaya'; they call it West Papua, instead, which I adopt for my own vocabulary.

I wonder what important decisions are made in this room. Who dines with Pastor Carl while discussing the fate of West Papua? What thoughts, sad or hopeful, weigh on Pastor Carl's mind as he sits at this table before me?

So many eyes on me suddenly. Pair after pair of eyes as Pastor Carl's officers, the most important soldiers in the

OPM forces, crowd into his hut to greet me. Hard expressions now. None of the smiling and graciousness of the people I danced with. Here are the men who fight the wars. Here are the people who can – and do – die.

Each man is introduced separately then steps forward to shake my hand. I shake each of the smooth palms, feel the men's strong grips and see the resolve in their eyes. In a world so lacking in heroes, I'm suddenly surrounded by them. I start to feel embarrassed and guilty: I can leave this camp and its troubles. I can return to my country knowing it is still there, belonging to me.

After all the introductions, I sit at a table with Pastor Carl's lieutenants. Just the four of us now. Plates of ripe pineapple, fried banana and cassava rolls are brought out. It's a huge feast for me in the midst of such poverty. Pastor Carl says grace for us and instructs me to eat first. Only after I've had my fill do he and his lieutenants help themselves.

Now, it is all business. I tell them that I want to write about them and so they talk to me for hours. Outside, the light grows soft with the sunset as I hear story after story of Indonesian atrocities. I scribble down notes until I realize that each story blends into the next. Always the same: pregnant mothers being raped. Their own family members set aside as examples and killed in front of them. Entire villages massacred. Mass graves . . . they can get me locations and photographs.

Yet, strangely, these men don't ask what might be the most common question of victims of genocide: why doesn't the world care? Rather, they're convinced that the world *does* care and *will* help, and I'm intrigued by this. What gave them such an idea?

In answer to my question, Pastor Carl leads me outside, to the front of his hut. Bodyguards stand at a polite distance from us, vigilant with the coming night, as Carl points to five flagpoles. At the top of each is a flag: Papua New Guinea . . . West Papua . . . the United Nations . . . (the last two fascinate me) the United States . . . Japan. *America? Japan?!*

The US and Japanese ambassadors to PNG had visited Carl and given him their flags. Carl claims that they made promises to help, though he wouldn't elaborate.

Carl points to a small group of young people coming toward us, marching like soldiers. They're led by a teen-aged woman who snaps out orders in Indonesian. The group approaches in doublestep, coming to a sharp stop in front of the flagpoles. Another order sounds out. The young soldiers immediately unwind the cords in unison and slowly lower the flags. It startles me to see one of the boys staring pointedly at the Stars and Stripes as he brings it down. What American child looks with such genuine reverence at his or her flag?

The young woman barks out a second and third order – she would make an excellent Marine drill sergeant – and the flags are folded and folded again in perfectly prac-ticed form. Held out like offerings, the children carry them up into Carl's hut for safekeeping. This ritual, I'm told, is repeated every day at dawn and dusk.

'I know the US will help us,' Carl says, nodding at the empty flagpoles, 'because the US ambassador brought us your flag.'

I don't have the heart to tell Pastor Carl that surely the US government would have trouble supporting his cause. Because in West Papua there are gold and copper mines, co-owned or supported by American businesses. New Orleans-based Freeport-McMoRan owns the largest piece of the copper mines, taxes from its revenue helping to fund the very troops who are committing the genocide against West Papuans.

But Pastor Carl functions on hope – it sustains him – and so I say nothing. Besides, I don't want to be too pessimistic. In a camp filled with freedom fighters, it is almost sacrilege to lose hope. Carl will raise his flags each morning and each night to an accompaniment of well-practiced pomp. And he will pray with his people that a shock of conscience will awaken the men and women in Washington. Perhaps, miraculously, these Americans *will* suddenly forsake special interests and trade relations, realizing that people are dying in a place called New Guinea halfway around the world.

I mention to Carl that I'm interested in seeing West Papuan artifacts, so we head over to a little roofed structure that holds inside it 'a fantastic selection of artifacts from West Papua,' according to a sign. Carl invites me to inspect the objects. They are marvelous things. Bows and arrows. A painted headdress of hornbill feathers. Body armor made from woven rattan.

'If you want, you may buy. Pick what you like,' he says.

I tell him I couldn't possibly buy anything – these objects are too special.

'You choose. Please,' Carl says. He urges me.

I pick out a couple of items, including the hornbill headdress. I have no expectation of buying them, but I don't want to disappoint Carl. We take them up into his hut. The owners of the items follow us in and tell what tribe they're from, explaining their purpose.

As I take notes, Carl confers with the men in a whispered Indonesian, then smiles grandly.

'Take them,' he says to me.

I gaze at him in disbelief.

'These men want to give these things to you. Please take them.'

I immediately refuse. They're too precious.

Carl explains that the men want me to take them back to the United States, show them to people so that Americans will learn about West Papuan art and perhaps find more reason to help their cause.

That they could offer me such kindness – I'm flabbergasted. But I still refuse.

'They are yours,' Carl insists.

'At least let me pay you something,' I say to the men, though they can't understand me. When I take out some large PNG bills and hold them out, they shake their heads. I know I'm holding out as much money as they could hope to make in a year, but they refuse. No one will accept a payment.

Carl has the objects taken into the room where I'm

staying in his hut. He refuses to hear my protests: the objects are now mine.

'You are brave for coming here,' Carl says. 'It is our gift to you.' And that's the end of it.

At last, I'm about to have my interview with Pastor Carl Waromi. There's so much I want to ask him. My pen and paper out, I'm ready yet scared – scared, because behind the scholarly glasses, Pastor Carl Waromi's eyes threaten to tear over with thoughts of what he has to tell me.

But I don't want to go too quickly. I ask Carl to start with his former life in West Papua.

'When the Indonesians came, I was a theology student. I wanted to become a pastor and serve God.' He speaks slowly, pondering his words. 'Many resisted the Indonesians. They were arrested or killed. I saw many who were killed . . .'

Carl became officially ordained as a pastor in the midst of all the resistance and death. His role as pastor suddenly gave him the dirtiest work possible. Village after village requested his presence. There had been massacres by Indonesian soldiers: Pastor Carl was needed to perform the last rites.

He had never fought in his life, had only tried to serve God, and the takeover by the Indonesians tore him apart. At first he had questioned God, though secretly and only in his thoughts. Why would someone come after his people and steal their land and murder their children? No answers. Not yet.

What he must have seen . . . Carl's eyes gaze wistfully at a single place across the room. He had performed last rites over entire villages that had been destroyed. Women and children, he says, had been raped, had dug their own graves. Men had been beaten then buried alive – a favorite act of the soldiers. And then there were the bodies of those tortured to death.

Pastor Carl calls it a vision from God, what must have been his breaking point. He says that God came to him one night and told him what he must do. He must resist the Indonesians. He must be willing to give up his own life. Though a fully ordained pastor, he became one of the top men in the OPM and helped to organize a coup in 1974. No one suspected him of subversion. And who would? Looking at Carl is to look at someone bookish, docile. But it's there. In the eyes. And the Indonesian authorities must not have looked in his eyes.

The coup, which Carl had helped mastermind, failed. Most of the ringleaders were caught and tortured to death. Carl managed to flee to Papua New Guinea with thousands of others. Now he has no way to communicate with anyone left behind; it was – is – too dangerous for them should he try. And besides, there are no telephones in Blackwater. No electricity except for a rarely used generator. Carl will probably never know how anyone is, whether they're safe. I know that all the questions must be eating him alive, kindling hate. I wonder again how a pastor, a man of God, can hate with the same fervor that he loves. I realize that it has something to do with forgetting. Carl has lost his ability to forget; he has become an unwitting prisoner of memory.

I remember the story of one of the women, Anna, who spoke to me earlier. When still living in West Papua, she had received a knock on her door in the middle of the night. When she got up to answer it, Indonesian soldiers burst in and seized her husband. They took him away to a nearby military camp. He was accused of being in the OPM, but a typographical error saved his life – his name had been spelled incorrectly on an informer's list. The soldiers still tortured him nearly to death. Their favorite tool was pliers.

I met Anna's husband. When he tried to be polite and smile, I could see a gap in his lower teeth.

'How do you forgive those soldiers?' I'd asked Anna. Like everyone in Carl's camp, she is very religious. 'Is it possible to forgive them their sins, like Jesus would?'

Forgiveness – her forgiveness – seemed like hope to me. The world had felt poised to hear her answer.

Her eyes drifted away. 'I can't forgive them,' she

apologized. 'I can't. You see, I saw their faces. Those who did it. I *saw* them.'

And she will always see them, I know. Her future will never be hers, just as with Pastor Carl, because her past traps her in a single image of cruelty: a soldier's face. She had *seen* the soldiers, the humanity in them. And so the most painful question in the world – why?

In the dim light of Pastor Carl's meeting room, left to myself at last, I shake in the sultry heat of the jungle night. My pen quivers out words into my journal. I keep nervously retracing letters, trying to understand.

I write a mess of confused thoughts:

I used to walk in the clouds, reading all my books on Buddhism, stoic philosophy. Trying to live life without that quiet desperation. But what do I know from it all? What to help me now?

Taoists encourage experiencing the present to remind us that we're alive. Which reminds me that I *forget* all the time. What a thought, the idea of being alive and not knowing it – like some flesh and bone automaton. And what would the world be like if everyone simultaneously realized their aliveness? No time for wars and massacres. Only time to study the breath and to learn.

I pause. I study my breath.

They say that babies breathe naturally, from the diaphragm. And that, at some point, children stop breathing from their diaphragms, suddenly begin to breathe from the lungs. I wonder if that is when the first evil starts, at that enigmatic moment when the breath changes?

I slowly put my journal down. I'm experiencing a sort of tingling feeling.

Suddenly, without explanation, the world has frozen. I

see it as if I've seen it before. The feeble, generator-induced light, the shadows of the thatch roof, the length of the table, the slice of a post splitting light on one side with a shadowy, indiscernible dimness on the other. I've seen it all . . . a dream I had shortly before leaving on my trip. Every object on the table – leftover plate of pineapple, pile of silverware, crumbs pushed neatly to one side – I remember this exact scene.

Outside I can hear the bodyguards talking softly, their voices competing with the monotonous tapping of rain on the roof of the hut and the distant buzz of a generator. I strain to see deeper into the moment, to try to learn something. Because if this *is* déjà vu, if this moment is imbued with something inexplicably mystical, I hope to divine some answers.

The rain taps, the men's voices fade, the lamp flickers to blot out the precise scene I remember. Time starts again. Or seems to. I look at a book Pastor Carl has loaned me, which sits open on the table. I'm still at the part about the massacres and tortures. Third paragraph down, left-hand side of the page. Estimates of the numbers of innocent West Papuans slaughtered in an Indonesian retaliatory campaign against OPM resistance. Pastor Carl's wife shuffles in the back room, whispering to her daughters, who help with putting away food. Whispering because I'm that strange entity called 'important guest.' I have never felt less important in my life, wined and dined as though I were some American ambassador. Or worse: as if I were someone who could somehow produce miracles, summon the power of gods or nations.

It's the next day. More dancers have gathered to perform for me. More feasts have been prepared. I hear more stories about the injustice. In a break from the festivities, Carl guides me to a couple of huts where artisans work, his bodyguards surrounding me. I'm getting sick of being protected. It's too much now, the idea of snipers in the jungle, of someone ordered to kill me because I might tell

217

the world what I'm hearing from Pastor Carl and the others. There are certain disgruntled refugees, too, who might think I'm a spy, Carl explains. And members of the other OPM faction, too, could have reason not to trust me.

The list seems long – all these people who might want to kill me. Pastor Carl shows me the painted *kundu* drums some men are making, but I barely see them. The fear I feel has become as much a part of reality as the men in front of me. I look out at the jungle several yards away, a green wall that could be concealing anything, and feel an incredible desire to escape.

But there is an itinerary to follow. More dancing to come. I'm escorted back to Pastor Carl's hut along the muddy red road.

It's evening. For the first time, I tell Pastor Carl about Richard's interrogation. Carl wants to know everything Richard asked me, and my mind has been so used to replaying the events of that late afternoon that I easily recall each question.

When I finish, Carl tells me about Richard being an Indonesian informant. In every human rights book on Irian Jaya there is a mention of twelve OPM lieutenants extradited to Indonesia to be tortured to death, but it shocks me to learn that Richard had arranged these arrests.

Carl is furious. He says that Richard had lied to me; Richard has no authority to prevent me, or anyone, from coming to the camp. Clearly, Richard had been acting on behalf of the Indonesians and was trying to prevent me from speaking to him or any refugees. All the stories I've heard about atrocities are precisely what Richard wanted to prevent me from hearing. If no one from the outside learns what's going on in West Papua, then how can the world have the proof to care?

'You are very clever to change his mind and let you come here,' Carl says with a wry smile.

But I'm starting to feel terrified because, as I tell Carl,

I have a ticket to fly into Irian Jaya so that I can continue my trip across New Guinea. And if Richard works for the Indonesians . . . and if they know I've been a guest of OPM leader Carl Waromi . . .

'Not good,' Carl says. His face has gotten serious again. 'Did you show Richard your passport?'

I nod.

'Then he has taken your name. He will give them your name.'

'What does that mean?'

'When you arrive in Irian Jaya, the police may be waiting for you at the airport. Or they will find you in town.' He explains that men will be paid to report my departure from PNG; being a lone, female foreigner, I won't be very hard to miss.

'What will they do to me?' I ask Carl.

He purses his lips and says nothing: does he need to tell me about the rape, torture, deaths of foreign human-rights investigators caught looking into atrocities?

I picture myself being arrested by the Indonesians. Carl has given me the names and stories of Westerners who had been caught investigating the West Papuan genocide. One of the women, raped and tortured while in custody, was at last deported to the United States and now works in a human-rights group. Others, of course, hadn't been as fortunate. They are the ones with their photos on the Amnesty International posters papering Carl's walls; it is debatable whether any still live.

So I won't go to Irian Jaya, obviously. But I'm trying to understand how Richard, some man I'd never met before coming to the camp, to whom I'd never done anything, would have turned me – my life – over to the Indonesians for some cash. If I'd not told Carl about my talk with Richard, had simply followed my plans and flown to Irian Jaya, who knows what might have happened to me?

'He is a terrible man,' Carl says, commiserating.

But a powerful man. A man who can play with lives and get away with it.

When I ask him about Henry, Carl shakes his head. He

doesn't know much about the Australian except that no one in camp likes or trusts him. It occurs to me now that everyone out there falls into a 'good' or 'bad' category. There is no in-between. No gray area. Richard had categorized Carl as a 'troublemaker.' Carl's soldiers had earlier categorized Richard as 'no good.' Me and You. Bad Guy versus Good Guy. The identification seems necessary given the circumstances, but it makes human life so unimportant, a simple matter of semantics.

I ponder the category Richard had put me in. By thus separating human beings, Richard is able to sleep at night. He hadn't sent twelve men to gruesome deaths; he'd merely sent Them – those Others – away.

Carl can see the emotions rising in me, but he doesn't know what to do about it. Better to accept my declaration that I'm tired and let me retreat to my room for the night.

I hide behind the muslin mosquito net around the bed. It has the dual function of keeping both the mosquitoes and the world away. I feel sick and wretchedly alone, and only after several moments does it occur to me that I am softly, steadily, pounding the bed with my fist.

When I appear the next morning in Carl's hut, one of the OPM soldiers approaches me and asks the most extraordinary question I've ever heard: would I like to have Richard 'jumped'? I try not to consider what he means. Will a group of them make an effort to catch Richard off-guard, kick him a few times, thrash him across the face? Or will they do worse? Of course, they can do worse. Will they beat him to death and leave him to rot in the jungle?

I think I know what they mean. I also know that by asking me personally, they're offering me a kind of favor. Perhaps Pastor Carl had told them about my shock the previous night when I found out that Richard would turn me over to the Indonesians. Their offer, then, is meant to make me feel better. Revenge is, to them, straightforward and necessary. A part of life. And because I'm their guest of honor, Hope to them, I'm offered what they may consider their greatest gift yet – the power to decide a man's fate.

I excuse myself and return to my room to lie down again. I've reached a point where I can no longer consider any more questions. I want to sleep, but can't, and so lie immobile for the rest of the afternoon, trapped in my thoughts. I nearly nodded at the man who made the proposition. *Yes, do what you have to do.* Because I know what it means to have anger reach such a level that you want only to destroy the source. I know what it is to hate.

At last, I appear from my room. Pastor Carl asks if I'm okay. He hasn't seen me all day.

'I've been a little sick,' I say.

He tells me that little Mastina, the girl with the incredible smile, has been asking for me: she has a present for me.

Pastor Carl leads me out to the front of his hut. A group of children, some of them the flag raisers from the previous night, play soccer in the last light of dusk. They stop when I appear, and come to gather around me. Soon Mastina joins us. She hands me a bird-of-paradise armband, a part of her dancing costume.

I thank her. I feel like crying. For them. For myself. For all of us.

'Tell me story,' she asks, excited.

'Story from America,' one of the boys says. And suddenly a whole crowd of children nod.

All around us, the jungle turns black from the coming night. Some benches are brought out into the middle of the field and I sit down in the midst of the children with Mastina on my lap, her little legs dangling. The bodyguards stand nearby. They don't pretend to be interested in the proceedings, to be polite, because they have a job to do.

One boy announces that he learned a story about a *wait meri* called Cinderella. He points at me. That's what I am, too: *wait meri*. White woman, in Pidgin. Cinderella had long blonde hair just like mine, the little boy says. She looked very sad like me, and worked very hard in her hut.

Mastina speaks up. She tugs at her dogtooth necklace and smiles fantastically. She wants to say that Cinderella is sad because she danced with the *bigman*'s son and had to leave afterward. But they found her and she got married, and she was very happy for the rest of her life.

All of the children are delighted. A couple of the bodyguards also smile for a moment because, it turns out, they've been listening to the story. Guarding us with their guns and listening to what happened to Cinderella.

I look up at the darkening night sky but can't recognize any stars. There are too many. In this part of the world, all the stars blur together, a hazy, disorienting spread of light that – I know – would normally captivate me. But right now a man's life lingers before me with the question, 'What will you have us do?'

Luckily, the children start to tell more stories, stories they've learned in the camp's school about Snow White and a boy called Aladdin. In the distance, a lone man strums on his guitar, singing. The words are still in English rather than Bahasa Indonesian or his tribal language. He sings about freeing West Papua and going home. Finally, finally, going home. 'We will never forget you, West Papua,' he sings. This, I know, is the story the kids don't tell. Desperate to go home, they learn instead about fairy godmothers and rubs on brass lamps.

The children's hands tug at my skirt as they ask me to tell the story of Peter Pan.

Do I even remember it? In the Melanesian tradition, everyone is accustomed to 'telling stories,' and so these New Guinea refugees, Melanesian to the core, greet me in respectful silence as I begin at last to try to tell my story in Pidgin, which they understand better than English. Someone called Wendy comes to mind. Her escapes to Never-Never-Lands out the snowy window. I try to explain snow, but they've never seen it before. Here it is hot, always hot.

'Imagine being so cold, you shake. *Yupela save?*' I say.

'Like malaria,' one boy says, pretending to shake.

No one smiles because everyone knows and dreads the return of their malaria.

It's getting late and the mosquitoes assail us from all sides. Mastina uses a handkerchief to keep them from my bare legs, and I finish the story as best I can. Finally, reluctantly, the children leave to go home.

The bodyguards pat their kids as I walk over to Carl again. It's back to his hut and surely more stories. Stories about friends disappearing, about more people being shot. I will miss the fairy tales and Cinderella woes.

A soldier takes me aside – the same man from before – and reminds me of the question he'd earlier asked. He is still waiting for an answer.

I want to ask him why I have a right to answer him. I'm just some student, traveling around. Should I be able to give such an answer?

Mastina runs up and gives me a second armband decorated with the bright red bird-of-paradise feathers, so I won't forget her.

'For Cinderella,' she says, smiling.

Her appearance has startled the bodyguards. But only for a moment. Mastina's brother draws her close and she wraps her arms about his leg.

I tell the man a firm no about Richard.

He nods. 'Okay. That's okay,' he says.

But this evening, as I lie on my bed, my inability to act on my hate feels like a weakness, a character flaw. Yet I discover, surprised, that the hate in me is gone. I feel disgusted with myself, as if I were a traitor to these people. But I've learned this about hate – it requires constant vigilance. Because to not hate for an instant is, in a sense, to be left stranded: what should I do if I'm not hating? Love? And should I love everyone? How do I even begin?

Too many questions, and never any answers that can satisfy. I find solace in the thought that, unlike Pastor Carl and the rest of his men, I won't have to live and breathe their life. I can always leave this jungle. Go home.

I feel an overwhelming urge to go to sleep.

Mercifully, I do.

At five in the morning, Carl's oldest son wakes me up in a rush. A car! Returning to the river clearing at Ramsite. They must put me on before the roads become too bad with the rainy season and it is impossible to leave.

I quickly gather my things by flashlight, and these are taken out to the truck that sits in the rainy dark. It's all so unexpected that I haven't time to say good-bye to anyone except Carl, his son and a few of his lieutenants. We all stand in the deep red mud as I shake each of their hands.

'I won't forget you,' I assure them.

Pastor Carl and I hug – I'm actually hugging an OPM guerrilla leader. But not for long. The downpour wants to drown us, and the driver ushers me quickly into the cab. In the next moment, the camp is gone.

During the long, muddy drive back, I remember more than anything the warm smile of little Mastina, who gave me the armbands. She will have to live the life of the exile. Uprooted, growing up in poverty and unable to return home, what will she do with her life? What future? Her stories will always be someone else's fairy tales as she gathers up what identity she can from the ashes of her people.

Back in Kiunga, I plan to leave the next day for the mining town of Tabubil, where I'll catch a plane out of this region of PNG. Pastor Michael offers to drive me up to Tabubil himself, and so tomorrow afternoon we'll make the 100-kilometer trip north.

Tabubil is Jim Mead's town. Though we were together less than two weeks ago, I try to remember what that time had been like. While I see the chopper rides again, the beauty he showed me, it all feels like some pleasantly recalled dream, something not of this life. How *could* it be of this life? Because here is John, my bodyguard, still beside me in Pastor Michael's house in Kiunga. He and the other bodyguards will sleep here, guarding me, and will accompany me all the way to Tabubil tomorrow. So how could Jim Mead and his chopper rides exist with this reality? *This* wretched reality in which someone, not liking the idea of my being with Pastor Carl, may try to find me, do something to me?

I stay in my tiny room in Pastor Michael's house, curled up on the bed. I would give anything to be back in that chopper with Jim again, hearing his confident voice, feeling as if the world were revealing secrets to me. How did I get where I am? This new reality has nothing to do with chopper rides or beauty, or suggestions of love. It has to do with terror and escape. Desperate escape from more of the insanity and cruelty of life.

It's late in the afternoon before we get access to a vehicle and can head out. As we leave Kiunga in a Land Rover, traveling up the mining road toward Tabubil, John puts in his lap his little nylon bag with the gun inside. I'm sitting in the backseat beside him, forcing myself to look out the window as I try to stop all the crazy thoughts. Doesn't help. We climb up into the mountains of jungle, and to my left, across a deep river gorge, lies my first glimpse of West Papua. There it is, the very land from which Pastor Carl and his men fled. The paradise gone bad, and the place I can never visit now.

John sees what I'm looking at. So close, the land of his childhood – the place for which he is willing to give up his life. He can actually look at it, as it sits just out of reach.

As we finally descend from the mountains toward the sprawling new town of Tabubil, I make a decision. I'll get a room in the only hotel in town. It's expensive, I've been told, built for mining personnel, but I'll pay the money if only to get away from having to be guarded anymore. I have to be on my own again. My sanity requires that I be on my own so I can try to make sense of what I experienced in the camp.

Then tomorrow, first thing, I'll fly out of town and leave it all behind.

*   *   *

My knife lies within reach beside me. I have the second bed in the room pushed up against the door. A chair is propped up under the doorknob because I've seen this done in the movies. I feel like I'm in a movie, some horror flick or cheap thriller set smack in the center of the island of New Guinea, in the small town of Tabubil. Outside is thick jungle. Jungle everywhere, and the heat that comes with it. There's nothing else I can do but wait in this tiny trailer and hope the man will go away.

His lock-picking has been a subtle, scratching sound as if squirrels were scraping at the doorknob. But it has stopped now. He works instead at removing the bars from the far window, but with no success yet. He's reluctant to make any noise, is very slow and methodical.

For the past several hours this man has been coming to my trailer, trying to get in. He's not a drunkard. Not a thief, because his persistence is uncanny. I know only this: he must get into the trailer. He must get in because – and only because – he knows I'm inside.

I can't leave, make a run for it, because that's what he wants; he waits for me. Sometimes, when I think he's gone and I look out the window, I catch sight of him close by. A short man, dark skin, a beard. From afar he looks like a typical Papua New Guinea Highlands man – he looks like anyone. But this isn't good enough; I must see him up close. I must look at the face of this person because I feel a need to establish a humanity between us. If I can look at him, then I'm convinced he'll stop and go away.

It is now around three A.M. There is actually a TV in the room, the first television I've seen in months, and the only channel I can get is MTV out of Indonesia. Madonna flickers on the screen. Without the volume on, she flashes like senseless, garbled images, a cacophony of color. I lie on the bed and finger my Swiss Army knife, listening to the man's attempts to get in. Who is he? What does he want with me? To think these questions even for an instant makes the adrenaline rush through my body, warning me to stop. I stop. My eyes hang heavy and I drift off for a few minutes, a half hour.

I wake suddenly. The feeling I have now holds me in a bizarre sort of numbness, as though life were suspended for a moment. The curtain doesn't cover the trailer window completely: there is a single space in the bottom corner. In that space, watching me, is his eye. He blinks and the white of the eye retreats for a millisecond into the darkness outside then reappears. I lie still and stare back at him. The MTV images flicker and dance, sending shock waves of colored light across the dark room.

We look at each other for five, ten minutes. Such a long time, seeing each other; I don't think I have ever been so intimate with another in my life. His eye keeps blinking. My body is heavy, trembles as I meet him with my stare. My life is splitting into a before and after. I know this, but can't stop anything. I can't prevent the change in me.

At last, on the verge of losing the last of my sanity, my eyes somehow close. I don't care if he gets in. I don't care about anything anymore.

A dreamy consciousness takes me back to that moment when I went in search of OPM guerrilla leader Pastor Carl Waromi. Again and again, I trace the events that led to this night here in Tabubil. My watch ticks beside my bed. It is that quiet. A night silent, fitful, urgent.

I wake from something that resembled sleep, though there weren't any dreams and I was constantly on the edge of waking. My knife now rests under my hand, but I don't remember putting it there. As always, though the man is gone, I listen for the sound of him trying to get into the room.

Dawn now. A dull gray light outside and I see the uncovered corner of the window where the man had looked in at me from the darkness. I still remember staring at him in that strange communion we had, though he wanted – I'm convinced – to kill me.

I will never know what sent him away. Perhaps it was that moment when we finally saw each other, as if with a certain recognition? Seeing is everything. It creates a pause, allows for thought, a realization of the aliveness of the other and the worth of that life. In a lightning flash of comprehension it will come: we all breathe! Every one of us!

It may come as a revelation.

But if I get sick of wondering about this, and I will, I can always say he just gave up – that's the easiest way to forget, to bury the memory.

Outside a cleaning lady is sweeping. I move the bed away and unlock the door. Slowly, knife in hand, I open it and look around. I don't see anyone but her, so I venture outside. Bird song now. The heavy, mossy smell of the jungle. The woman looks up and smiles at me. She can have no idea of the night I've had.

I go back inside the room and gather my things. Numb, vaguely conscious of being a part of something too political and incomprehensible, I rip out all the journal and notebook pages I wrote in Pastor Carl's hut, gather all the used rolls of film, and put them in the bag with the artifacts to mail home. I shove the bag into my backpack and leave the room behind.

I walk, barely conscious of direction. There has to be a post office somewhere. My knife is still in my hand. I like the feel of it there, but I want a bigger one. Something better. I walk into a store and buy a machete for ten *kina*. It's big, over a foot long. I swing it in my hand as I head toward the main area of town.

I see a post office and walk inside. Buying a box and some wrapping tape, I pack up the artifacts with my notes and film, promptly taping it all shut. People look at me: I'm wrapping the package violently, running the tape around the box again and again. I keep hoping Jim Mead will suddenly walk in, see me, help me. But I won't allow myself to call him. I'm punishing myself for the terror of last night, for getting myself into something way over my head. When will I ever learn? *Forget about Jim. Forget about him. This is what you deserve. Thinking you can just go to a place like Blackwater Camp. How long are you*

going to be such a stupid little girl?! How long is your
life going to be worth nothing to you?

I write down my Chicago address and throw down
money so it can be mailed. But I can't wait for the
change. I have to leave and head for the airfield. Tabubil
speeds by me in a blur of Toyota pickups and private cars.
Mud – I'm walking through mud. A change in course
now, my hiking boots soggy, filled with ooze. I hear the
sound of an airplane arriving, and I go toward the sound,
my feet squishing.

I reach the airstrip and the shack that is the booking
office. Where do I want to go? Doesn't matter. I book a
seat on the first plane out, a four-seat mission plane
bound toward some remote village called Fiak, not on my
map. I'm told it's a tiny village to the northeast, in the
foothills of the Central Range. Good. The fog will clear
from the mountains of jungle around Tabubil allowing a
plane to take off. I will be taken up and away and
deposited somewhere. Anywhere in this world will do,
just as long as I can begin to forget. I must teach myself
how it is done.

I board the plane as the fog lifts. As we are at last
preparing to take off, I see a chopper landing in the
distance. A door opens and a man jumps down nimbly
onto the tarmac. I remove my baseball cap and press my
face to the foggy window, watching him. I watch him even
as my plane takes off down the runway and speeds me
into the air.

Part Two

CHAPTER EIGHT

Long Way Too Much

Our tiny plane drifts by the gigantic peaks of the Central Range, the unsteady drone of the engine keeping us airborne and godlike. I hide behind my sunglasses. I keep my face expressionless. No show of what I'm feeling now. The only thing I ask of the world is that it leave me alone.

I don't want to think about anything, much less about Blackwater Camp and my time there, but I can't stop the thoughts. Pastor Carl had hoped for a foreign film crew to come and document his people's plight, but I couldn't guarantee anything. I know a few budding film people, but only a few. Getting them or anyone to the camp would be virtually impossible. For one thing, there are too many Blackwaters around the world. Too many places full of a forgotten people yearning to be noticed by someone. And besides, would anyone I know jump at the idea of getting into an off-limits and dangerous camp in the midst of a New Guinea jungle, where one actually needs a bodyguard to get around?

The mountains of the Central Range reign on all sides, sharp splinters covered with jungle. Clouds cling to the peaks, winding and trailing mist down the slopes. No people anywhere down below. No place to put people, these slopes too sharp, the valleys too steep. It's a harsh beauty, but a beauty nonetheless, which tries to break into my depression for a moment long enough to be heard. I ask this world why it teases us with such beauty.

No answer.

The shifting clouds paint light and darkness across the jungle, capturing trees in flashes of sunshine only to dash them in an instant by shade. Our plane is like a crudely whittled piece of balsa wood, at the mercy of wind currents and weather, barely substantial enough to keep aloft. Yet, the pilot is at ease. This flight is, to him, routine, even as the world violently alters around us with the swift movement of the clouds.

The pilot speaks into my thoughts, his voice matter-of-fact: 'Fiak's coming.'

I nod. It occurs to me that I haven't said much since getting in the plane. I've just answered his basic questions: what's your name? Where are you from? Speaking to him through the microphone on my headgear makes my every word come out loud and crucial. When I told him I'm from Chicago, it sounded so earth-shattering that I shut up, embarrassed. But after Blackwater, followed by that night in Tabubil in the hotel room, I don't want to tell anyone anything. My paranoia is overwhelming. I can almost believe that someone is following us in another tiny plane, coming after me. And here again in my mind is an image of that man who tried to break into my hotel room last night. I see him staring in at me, his single eye blinking in the darkness.

I'm starting to wish I never went to that camp, or had any ideas of finding out about the OPM's cause. The moment you commit yourself to a cause, become a participant, a player, there are stakes. The riskier the cause, the greater the stakes. It's easy to understand the reason for apathy, then, because it takes nothing and demands nothing. It allows for peace of mind in the confidence that others will wage the wars and then magnanimously pass on the rewards. All I want is blessed peace of mind, and it occurs to me that the only time I found it was when I was with Jim Mead.

The missionary pilot asks what business I could have in a place like Fiak, but in a few minutes my explanation won't matter at all. We'll reach the place. He'll be gone and we'll never meet again. But now I have to think of some lie to tell him, because the truth would sound too crazy: that I'm ready to completely give myself over to this world, have it do what it wants with me. I don't care anymore. I just want to get lost in these jungles. If I get out, I get out.

Through the urgency of my headgear's microphone, I tell the pilot that I want to see some remote place, a Papua New Guinea not in the guidebooks. I want to try to get from Fiak to the Sepik River on foot or by canoe. How will the local people view me? Will it make any difference, my being a woman?

My explanation sounds pleasingly academic, like an experiment in women's studies.

The pilot nods politely and says only, 'Fiak is remote, that's for sure.'

He's a pilot for the New Tribes Mission, a US-based group focused on Papua New Guinea, with a goal of bringing the gospel to its most inaccessible tribes. For a fee, the New Tribes' planes will drop off unaffiliated passengers along their route, which is how I've ended up flying through these mountains in this little four-seater plane. In back is a local Tabubil man, Sammy, who heard we were going to Fiak and decided to come along at the last minute – apparently he has a sister in Fiak whom he wants to visit. And so it is the three of us, in this fragile little plane.

The pilot points down below and I see Fiak for the first time. A tiny dotting of thatch huts sitting in the crotch of some high mountains, Fiak couldn't have a population of more than a few dozen people. The airstrip is short and muddy, and the pilot carefully descends toward it. I keep imagining the worst, a sudden loss of control, our plane spiraling down toward the little village like a wrapper tossed from the sky.

The plane is in perfect control. It feels paper-light as the pilot brings it toward the ground and lands it with a delicate thud. From the village, a crowd of people rush to the airstrip to watch. Men in tattered shorts study us. The women stand some distance away; they wear T-shirts or are bare from the waist up with wraps of old material around their hips. The clothes and airstrip tell of New Tribe ministrations, yet those appear to be the only tangible evidence of any Western interference. I wonder how New Tribes conduct their work out here. Do they focus on one particularly zealous individual in each of the villages they reach, molding him or her until they can confidently move on to the next place? There must be a system, a means of ensuring that none misplace or lose their new faith.

In the village, chickens and pigs run about in a frenzy as more people rush out to the landing strip. The pilot turns off the plane's engine and climbs out. A couple of men come forward to shake his hand while Sammy and I get out. I look around. There are only steep mountains of jungle surrounding Fiak, a giant, lush barrier. A stream borders the village, flowing off into the depths of the valley.

It's not clear how one gets out of Fiak other than by air. I realize that senselessly entering this jungle could be suicidal. Yet I know that it *is* possible to make it to the Sepik River Valley. In 1938, Aussie explorers Jim Taylor and John Black made the first crossing through this region, canoeing down May River, which must be close by. I remember the details of their trip, in particular, because they were attacked while trying to cross this very range of mountains; one of their porters died with an arrow in the heart and four other men were wounded.

Wonderful. I hope such hostilities are a part of the past. I look at the mountain range they must have crossed, wondering how or where they did it. It's not too late. I can get back on the plane, be taken to some comfortable town – if any such town exists in PNG – and then fly home, abort this crazy adventure. But the momentum has begun. I must make it to the end, wherever that end is. At the very least, I will try to do what Taylor and Black did.

I turn to the pilot. 'Do you know the name of that stream?'

'It's a river,' he says. 'May River.'

I open my map. May River appears as a major artery of the Sepik River, yet I must be near its source because it's only a trickle here in Fiak. Fiak isn't on the map, so I take out my pencil and put a mark where I think it might be.

'Is this where we are?' I ask the pilot.

His finger moves us further into the Highlands, into the midst of the Thurnwald Range. A village to the north, Hotmin Mission, appears to be Fiak's nearest neighbor. Hotmin, just out of reach of the mountains, rests in the more swampy lowlands that marks the beginning of the expansive Sepik River Valley. Getting out of Fiak will mean getting out of the mountains altogether.

'Is there an easy way out of here?' I ask.

He's already heading back to the plane. 'You can fly out, if it's an emergency. Otherwise,' he smiles and points to the jungle bordering the airstrip, 'walk. At Hotmin you can probably get a ride in a canoe. They're river people down there.'

The pilot gets back in the plane and waves good-bye to me. I stand with the village people and watch it take off into the air, retreating like a fragile bird over the nearest mountain. I stand where I am for a while, having no idea what to do next. The people of Fiak stand with me, studying me, until I decide to head to the village – what little there is of it. The thatch-roof huts are raised off the ground, a smoky wood scent emanating strongly from each. Chickens peck beneath the huts. Puppies fight with each other in the dirt until a young boy shoves them apart with his foot. A couple of old women who remained behind in the huts during the commotion stand against the frames of the huts' entranceways, looking at me. Their hair is white and their breasts rest flat against their chests. I wave at them, but there's no response.

As I walk through the village, the families of each hut step back, away from me. The few huts come to an end and I retrace my steps. A couple of women return to their work of peeling heart-sized taro tubers. Squatting, they dexterously hold the slippery taro with their toes, slicing off the rough skin with a knife. In between each cut, they look at me curiously.

You need a plan, I tell myself.

Some small children playing outside see me approach and run in terror into the huts. As if it were some extreme lesson in internationalization, the mothers drag the screaming kids back out, forcing them to touch me. They kick and cry wildly, until they finally tear themselves loose and run away. Now a couple of old women appear beside me to stroke my hair with their hands. One woman yanks out several strands and holds them up to the sun. Others coo and pet my arms, as more of my hair is ripped out. They urge their relations to come touch the *wait meri*. I realize I've become a kind of carnival spectacle: everyone must touch me, everyone must take his or her souvenir strand of hair.

Fearing I won't have any hair left by the end of it, I head to the little trickle that is May River. It's only about a foot deep here and so there aren't any canoes. Obviously this river isn't useful yet as a waterway to transport people or goods. Not far downstream, the mountains rise sharply on both sides of the water.

I put down my backpack and sit on the bank, gazing at the mountains all around me, their tops obscured by clouds. That other village, Hotmin Mission, is an unknown distance to the north, but it couldn't be very far away. Only a couple days' hike through the jungle, surely, if the pilot's directions were accurate and my map is to be believed. I decide I'll try to reach it.

I turn to a man standing near me and ask him in Pidgin how far Hotmin Mission is. He takes a step back and stares at me. I wonder if he understood.

'*Hotmin klostu dispela hap?*' I ask the people in shaky Pidgin. Is Hotmin close to here?

No one answers.

'Hotmin,' I try again. '*I stap longwe o nogat?*' Is it far?

'It's far,' a man says in English. I recognize him as the other passenger in the plane, Sammy – the man with a sister in Fiak. He looks upset, tells me that his sister married a Hotmin man and doesn't live in Fiak anymore. He came to Fiak all for nothing, will have to wait for the next plane home, whenever that will be. It could be weeks.

I tell him that if it's possible to walk to Hotmin, I'm doing it. I look at the mountains, covered by jungle. It seems as if Hotmin is on the other side of them. Just a few of these mountains to get over. How bad could a few mountains be?

Sighing, Sammy says he'll come along with me, and I wonder if he knows what he's getting himself into. Coming from Tabubil, he is the equivalent of a well-fed, sedentary city-dweller in this village of emaciation. He has a paunch and wears a clean dress shirt and pants. He flashes frowns of disapproval at the overall inconvenience of his predicament here, and at the gathered villagers surrounding us. Sammy asks in his fluent Pidgin if anyone knows how to get to Hotmin. An older woman – she tells us her name is Mila – says she's willing to lead us there for twenty kina. She wears a threadbare gray T-shirt and holey skirt, her thin body covered with the telltale round lesions of flaking skin and itchy sores called *grile* in Pidgin – ringworm, common among the forest people here. The ringworm has even infested parts of her scalp, making her short hair look patchy. Sammy isn't thrilled about Mila, I suspect because she's a woman. He crosses his arms and asks if anyone else would be willing to guide us, and I have to cut in to remind him that I'm the one who's going to be paying the twenty kina. I tell him I want Mila to guide us, and she runs off to get some food for the trip from her hut.

A man offers to come along as porter for my backpack (which weighed in at an embarrassing forty-three pounds at the Tabubil airport), but I tell him no thanks. I always lug my own stuff. Having someone else to do it would make me feel like some haughty, pampered English aristocrat on an elephant safari. And, in this case, I'm also nervous about embarking through the jungle with two men I don't know, all of my possessions on me. Papua

New Guinea expatriates are full of stories of foreigners getting robbed, raped in the bush. Just Sammy is probably OK, but not anyone else besides him and Mila.

Mila comes back. With no further ceremony, we follow her down the muddy airstrip just as a heavy rain starts. The mountains are starting to disappear in cloud and fog, giving the illusion of a flat landscape and a straight-forward journey to Hotmin. I change out of my hiking boots because the mud is too thick and my boots keep getting hopelessly stuck in it. Sammy does the same. No one, I notice, ever wears footwear in the PNG jungles except clumsy foreigners.

Mila glances over her shoulder at us, smirking as a mother would at the silly antics of her children. Machete in hand, she is already far across the airstrip and entering the jungle.

One can describe the jungle of New Guinea in a book, can show it in photos, but these are a poor substitute for the real thing: the choking humidity, incessant rain and mud, sharp plants, red ants, leeches, monotonous wailing of insects. PNG's jungle is a dim, entangled labyrinth of vines and giant trees that block out what light from the sun manages to make it through the rain clouds. Only the path below my feet reassures me of direction, of an end to the endless green.

Inexplicable sounds come from the depths of the jungle – crashes, cawing, screeching. Only a person from one of the local tribes could adequately explain the sounds, the sudden rushing in the undergrowth and rustling high in the canopy. Traveling through this swampy jungle feels like being in a ceremony I don't understand. Where to put my feet? What to touch and not to touch? Can I step here? Is there something ahead of me that I can't see?

Every step I take is tentative. Traveling with con-fidence must be learned, and only Mila moves effortlessly. No wonder she laughs at us so much. Sammy and I are always splashing and slipping behind her. There is none of the leisurely feeling I've gotten from hiking back home.

Here, the jungle enfolds us in its tangled innards as if we were traveling through the belly of some gigantic beast.

The rain is torrential. In the heavy humidity, I can't tell the difference between water and sweat. I plow through the knee-deep muck of our trail, my pack weighing me down, sinking me deeper into the mud. It's important to maintain the speed and keep up with Mila, though, so I rip my legs from the mud and force them forward. My skirt is worthless for jungle travel, catching on bushes and causing me to trip. I stop to change into jean cutoffs, but Mila remains on the move. She stops for nothing.

The rule of the jungle is speed. Even Sammy knows this as he lumbers behind Mila and me, not letting himself fall too far behind. The local people don't usually measure jungle distances mathematically. It's easy enough to say that one place is X kilometers from another, but that measure of distance doesn't take into account mountains or swamps, rivers to ford or dense foliage to chop through. To say a place is 'only twenty kilometers away' marks you as a greenhorn, because traveling across a twenty-kilometer spread of 10,000-foot-high mountains could be – and has been – an expedition in itself.

Instead, distance is judged by the time it takes a healthy man, going at a reasonable speed, to get from one place to another. This distance will naturally change according to factors out of his control, such as the rainy season or a drought. Not surprisingly, concepts of distance as old as the tribes themselves have arisen to describe distance in arguably more accurate terms than the West's obsession with empirical measurements. Instead of a numerical reply to one's question 'How far is it to Hotmin Mission?', distance is defined as: close (*klostu*), fairly close (*klostu liklik*), fairly far (*longwe liklik*), far away (*longwe*) and very far away (*longwe tumas*). The terms appear vague, as if they were invented to annoy Western sensibilities, but to Papua New Guineans each statement has clear meaning, taking into account natural obstacles. If a place is *longwe tumas*, a person would probably think twice about making the journey; the destination may not look far on a map, but the journey itself will be quite grueling.

Uneasy about how difficult our travel has been thus far, I stop Mila to ask her in Pidgin, 'How far to Hotmin?'

Her answer isn't comforting: '*Longwe liklik.*' It's also becoming hard to discern our route, the jungle quaking in the heavy rain.

I look at Sammy and he shakes his head in frustration. Mila turns around and raises her machete, the chopping and mud-sloshing continuing. We're starting to lose all traces of a path now, and it's worrying me. Mila calls to us, letting us know that we're going too slow, and we both speed toward her like obedient children.

We plunge through a patch of thorny sago palms and slide down a muddy slope to a river. This is a swiftly flowing river, its bottom covered with smooth, slippery granite stones. Our going is slow now. The water comes up to my thighs, and my feet try desperately to cling to the stones as the current rushes past. My heavy backpack makes it difficult to balance, its extra forty-three pounds weighing down every step. My knees start to shake, and it's not long before my steps become extremely painful. I joke with myself, tell myself I'm on a special mission to carry a dead body across New Guinea. The dead body causes me to slip from time to time, bruising my shins, the river dragging me along until I can right myself. Sammy offers me his arm and, together, we all struggle through.

In this painful, laborious way, we slowly follow the course of the river. The hours pass and the rain begins to let up. Mountains rise sharply on either side. I reckon them to be at least 6,000 feet high, though it's hard to be sure with their tops cut off by clouds. When we reach a sandbar, I suggest we stop and rest. The sun, hot through the intermittent rain, is declining toward the west. I don't know where we are, and can only hope Mila knows. Sammy asks her in Pidgin how long we're going to be walking through the water like this, but she just smiles and says nothing.

Sammy shakes his head in frustration. 'She is crazy.'

I consider the possibility of following a crazy woman through the jungle. Or could it be that she finds Sammy and me utterly absurd as we try to understand and accept the environment she's known intimately since birth? We are like children, completely dependent on her, and I wonder if she sees us, above everything else, as a Man and a White Woman – the two things that, in colonial times, would have automatically accorded us higher status than her. Surely Mila is old enough to remember the first arrival of whites in her village (considering Fiak's remoteness, it wouldn't have been so long ago). Her knowing Pidgin tells me that she's probably had contact with them for a while. She would have been taught to use the Pidgin words of 'masta' and 'missus' whenever addressing whites, and to refer to her own children as 'pikanini' – a word that, incredibly, is still in widespread use today. But now, Mila is able to assert herself as a capable woman, to show us what she really thinks of the old hierarchy and hegemony. There is no question that she is king out here.

She smirks at us and speaks, and I can make out her Pidgin this time. She says she's going to Hotmin – which means we're going, too, because we could never get back to Fiak on our own. There is nothing for us to do but move on.

We reach our first mountain. It doesn't gradually rise but shoots skyward at nearly ninety degrees.

'Are we climbing this thing?' I ask Sammy.

'I think so.'

Mila is already guiding us toward it, and now we're not hiking anymore. We use tree roots and branches to *pull* ourselves up the mountainside. I reach blindly among the jungle plants in search of handholds, sometimes grabbing onto the spiny stems of plants, other times reaching into swarms of red ants. I don't even allow myself to think about snakes, though a couple have slithered away before my sloppy approach. I'm slithering myself, chin in the mud, body sliding up the side of the mountain. When I need to rest, I wrap my arm around a tree root or branch and shove my knees into the muddy slope. Four thousand, perhaps five thousand feet of this to get over – I don't even want to think about it.

And the rain! It pours incessantly now, with that raging, apocalyptic determination one sees only in the tropics. I take a large step and can't find a place to put my foot in the muddy slope. The weight of my backpack pulls me backwards, and I slide down with the rain and mud, crashing through patches of ferns to land several yards below. Bruised, cut up, I'll have to climb the distance all over again, and here is where I find myself wishing that I *did* have a porter. I have to carry this backpack with me up these mountains while the others have virtually nothing to carry.

I take out my water bottle, drink the last of my water. Surely there'll be another stream or river where I can refill. Just have to get over this one mountain. That's all. Hotmin Mission will be on the other side.

The jungle booms with the rhythmic patter of rain on leaves, plants bowing and lurching from the heavy drops. The slope below shows no sign of our passage.

'How are you?' Sammy yells down at me.

'Terrible!'

'We're near the top.'

'Congratulations.'

I wedge my foot in the mud of the slope and wrap my arm around a tree root to rest.

'Are you okay?' Sammy yells down.

'Okay,' I yell back. 'Resting.'

My head is throbbing. I'm thirsty and suck rainwater from my T-shirt sleeve. *What am I doing here?*

I flick a centipede off my leg. A sharp pain in my head zaps me with metronome-like regularity – a sure sign of heat exhaustion – and Sammy is once again yelling to me, encouraging me to start climbing.

'Okay,' I order my feet. 'Let's go.'

When I make it to the top at last, I throw off my backpack and collapse to the ground. Nothing can make me go a single step more. Sammy apparently feels the same way and is gathering brush that he can use to make himself a lean-to. There's no source of water in sight, and he does what I'm doing, sucking water from my clothing.

Though having endured such a grueling day, Mila looks almost relaxed. She sits with her legs crossed, watching me with amusement as I try to extract thorns from the soles of my feet. I see no slivers or cuts on her body. Aside from the ringworm patches, she looks entirely unscathed.

'How far is Hotmin Mission?' I ask Mila in Pidgin.

'*Longwe tumas*' – long way too much. I suspect my slow climbing has single-handedly increased the 'distance' for us.

I look to Sammy. 'Hotmin seems to be getting farther and farther away.'

'Yes,' he says, frowning. He throws down the brush he's collected and glares at the jungle.

It rains all night. It rains through the makeshift lean-to Sammy built over me, a continual stream of drops landing on my face. And then there are the mosquitoes. Even in the rain, they aggressively swoop in and inject their proboscises in me the moment they make contact. I burrow under layers of clothes from my backpack until the incredible heat and humidity make me wonder whether I'd actually prefer the mosquitoes. Instead, I compromise: I leave my arms uncovered and lather them with mosquito repellent. But these mosquitoes are so ingenious that if I scratch at my arm, rub an elbow against the ground – anything that removes even a square inch of repellent – they find that single chink in the armor and move in.

Mila sleeps with a large leaf over her face, knees curled in against her stomach. She never made a lean-to, and instead covered her body with brush to protect her from the mosquitoes and rain. I haven't seen her move this entire night – though I've certainly been awake often enough to notice if she did. I tried doing the same thing, but it didn't seem to keep the mosquitoes off me. I can't understand how she, or anyone, could sleep soundly under these conditions.

Sammy seems to endure the worst of it all. Before nightfall, I offered him some of my insect repellent, but he refused, calling it 'poison.' Now he rolls around every few minutes, slapping at himself and groaning loudly. I'm convinced he's trying to keep me and Mila awake, as though it were sacrilege for us to be sleeping through his suffering.

I was too sick and physically exhausted to bother trying to set up my self-contained mosquito net, but now I do. In the darkness, my body aching in pain, the rain drenching me, I take out the net and fumble with its structure. But I can't get it up – I can't see what I'm doing – and merely throw it over me. Of course the mosquitoes bite through the netting, ceaselessly. If Dante wanted a really good hell for his sinners, he should have stripped them naked and sent them to the New Guinea jungle after dusk.

The unaccountable jungle sounds seem to get worse at night, too. There must be something primordial about a human's innate fear of the dark. I was born in a world that had long been tamed and thoroughly explained, fear of the night becoming childish and irrational. Here in PNG, though, that fear is justifiable because who really knows what's lurking out there? I feel only one step removed from the darkness.

The dawn arrives as a series of slowly changing grays, the leaves and branches of the jungle gaining form instead of substance. In this eerie half-light, Mila is already up, calling to us and cutting off pieces of a powdery-gray slab of baked sago palm pith which she'd been keeping in her *billum* bag. Her sago is a hard, tasteless food she apparently made by putting balls of the pith onto the cinders of a fire. Wood ash gives it a dusty, prehistoric look, not unlike fossilized dung. Though I'm nauseous and my head still pounds, I put some in my mouth and slowly chew, pretending it's apple pie, fettuccine alfredo, deep-dish pizza. Anything but what it actually is. Funny: people in Western countries have enough money and leisure to be able to eat in order to enjoy the taste and textures of food; if a meal is burnt, people will often throw it out because the taste is ruined. But what a strange notion that is here, where the idea is simply to eat so the body will keep going, so life will be maintained.

I'm touched by the fact that Mila is willing to share her food with us – precious food, considering our predicament. It's comforting knowing that someone's in control, understanding what needs to be done for us and when. As her voice once again cuts sharply through the jungle announcing breakfast and ordering Sammy to get up, he moans miserably from his lean-to: 'Shut up, woman.'

She pushes at his shelter, and it collapses on him. He tosses off the branches, his arms and legs dotted with so many mosquito bites that it looks as if he has the measles. He wraps a large leaf around his head, pulling the edges together under his nose so that the world is condensed to a tiny peephole. Clouds of mosquitoes buzz and swarm around his head, and as he swipes madly at them, Mila laughs. Sammy swears at her in return, his loud words quickly lost in the jungle.

We make it to the bottom of the mountain. Hotmin Mission is nowhere in sight. There is still no sign of civilization, just another mountain rising sharply ahead of us. The rain has turned to a light drizzle, and we all stand and look around us. We're in a gully with high mountains on all sides. There's a small stream, and I immediately fill my water bottle and drop an iodine tablet inside to kill any parasites. Sammy has his own water bottle and fills it from the stream. When I offer him an iodine tablet, he scoffs and laughs, calling it (predictably now) 'poison.' Mila herself drinks straight from the stream, only a couple of quick handfuls. She is surely some kind of superwoman. Though strikingly thin, she refuses any offers of water from Sammy or me and doesn't appear in the least worn out from our travels. She surveys the area and I can't help wondering whether she actually knows where we are. To me, it looks the same as it does everywhere else. For all I know, we're back where we were yesterday. We could even be going in one big circle.

My legs, bloody, swollen and covered in scratches and cuts, look gruesome. I sit down on my backpack. Pulling out my Swiss Army knife, I use the tip of one of the blades to dig out some little thorns embedded in my shins. Sammy watches me, wiping sweat from his face.

'Does that hurt?' he asks.

'No.'

I work at a big thorn. It won't come out and I cut deeper.

'You are bleeding. A needle is better, I think,' he says.

I don't say anything.

'A needle is better.'

'I'll buy one when we get to the 7-Eleven.'

Sammy crouches beside me. 'I think this woman is lost,' he whispers. 'She says she forgets the way to Hotmin.'

Mila sits down and pulls up the soles of her feet. For a woman who's lost, she looks amazingly at ease. She starts to methodically remove thorns with her fingernails.

'So what are you saying?' I concentrate on getting my own thorns out.

'It means we are all lost.'

'Can't she get us back to Fiak?'

'No.' He looks behind us. 'I already asked this. She says no.'

I wonder what her answer meant. Was she saying that she *refused* to backtrack? Or, that she *couldn't* backtrack, even if she wanted to?

I glance at the mountain we've just descended. There's no sign of our passage; the jungle sprang back as soon as we passed.

Sammy examines his feet. 'We must keep going,' he says absently.

It is up and over, up and over, all day long. One mountain and now another. And *still* no sign of civilization. I drank the last of my water a while ago, hoping there'd be another stream at the base of one of these mountains. There hasn't been, and the rain has stopped altogether. The afternoon sun is piercingly hot, yet, strangely, I seem to have stopped sweating. My headache feels exactly as if two hands were trying to crush my skull, and I fear that full-blown heat stroke is on its way. The wise thing to do is to get out of the sun, drink lots of fluids, take salt tablets, try to stay cool. But of course I can do none of those things.

This jungle travel reminds me of one of the adventures I kept in my file box as a kid, where I pretended to be in the Special Forces. This particular adventure got to be such an obsession that when adults asked what I wanted to be when I grew up, I'd tell them with all seriousness: 'A Green Beret.' They'd remind me that girls – women – couldn't become Green Berets. Still, I used to check out all the Green Beret books from the library. Me, ten years old, curled up with Robin Moore's first-hand account. My favorite movie was the first Rambo movie, *First Blood*. I used to imagine myself parachuting into Laos to perform jungle reconnaissance. My missions were always classified and dangerous. I tried to imagine the heat and rigors of the jungle as described in the books I read, always asking myself whether I could take it. Whether I could survive.

But it's not a matter of survival anymore – I can no longer view the Green Berets in the same idealized way. I keep seeing the refugees in Blackwater camp, who had family members tortured or slaughtered by Indonesian soldiers trained by the US Special Forces. Did anyone in the US military stop to question what they were doing? It was as if everyone had left their consciences behind. But perhaps that is a prerequisite for joining the Special

Forces. No conscience. No remorse. Just following orders.

At any rate, I want no part of it.

I stop on the side of the mountain we're climbing. I press my face against the mud. *Jungle reconnaissance*. What the hell was I thinking? How does this kind of experience become glorious?

Sammy climbs to my side, nudging me.

'I'm resting,' I tell him. 'It's this backpack. Weighs a ton.'

'You must keep going.'

Taking my pack off, I pull things out of it – books, extra sun screen, vitamin pills – and chuck them down the mountainside. They land somewhere below, disappearing in the green. Sammy tries to take the pack from me but I yank it away. Only some irrational obstinacy keeps me from abandoning the entire thing: I will get to Hotmin with it, or I won't get to Hotmin at all. I start to pull out more things, and he stops me, seizing the pack and putting it on. Though I'm exhausted and my whole body aches, climbing is much easier without it and I make fast progress up the mountain. When I reach the top, Sammy is far behind. Mila looks down at him and laughs. I'm starting to think that her sense of humor is the secret source of her energy.

When Sammy at last gets to the top, he takes off my pack.

'I can't,' he says.

He hands it over to Mila. She accepts it without a word, but starts to fall behind as we make our descent. When we reach the bottom of the mountain, she gives it back to me, clucking her tongue at it. She must be thinking the same thing I am – that only an idiot white woman would be stupid enough to bring such a heavy, awkward thing on a journey like this. I nod. She'd be absolutely right.

Just when I think I can't go any farther, when my co-ordination seems gone and my steps are awkward and unbalanced, we leave the jungle and slide down a muddy bank to the narrow shore of a river.

Mila divides up the last of her taro. I try to eat some but immediately get nauseous. Still, she insists that I swallow some more and won't leave me until I do. My whole body feels tight, on fire. My head keeps pounding, pounding, and I can't get myself to sit up – let alone stand and put my pack back on to resume the journey. Mila keeps insisting that this mythical place called Hotmin is 'close.' All I see is jungle. Rising slopes of jungle, and not a single sign of humanity anywhere. I want to stay by this river because it's flat and shows a view of the distance. Overhead, unblocked sky offers me a retreat from the claustrophobia of the rain forest. The river is like a road, a way out of the unknown labyrinth of the wild. I can now understand why human beings have always clung to the shores.

I turn to Sammy and tell him I can't go on anymore.

It's a hell of an admission for me, but I'm simply too sick. I'm afraid I have heat stroke and could die – or am dying. Even if I wanted to be a Green Beret, I'd make a lousy one; I don't have what it takes to get through this jungle. I've failed the test. I've learned nothing from this experience except how to totally miscalculate one's environment.

'You can't stay here,' Sammy says.

'I have to. You can send a canoe back for me when you get to Hotmin.'

Sammy talks to Mila in Pidgin. She laughs at us and shakes her head. She points down the river.

'She says, "No one comes," ' Sammy says. 'No one comes up this river.'

I look down the shores of the river until it bends into the jungle. Though there are plenty of good spots for a makeshift camp, there are none of the usual signs of a human presence: crude lean-tos, fire pits, stashes of fire-wood. I know this area to be one of the least populated areas of New Guinea.

I wish I had the Pidgin to be able to explain to Mila

that I need some kind of guarantee from her; I need to know how long this race is supposed to last because I can't go on much longer. I think of what I gave up by coming to this country: all of my savings . . . James. I can see him before me. He's squatting on the sand, staring at me. There is a look of anguish on his face. His usual friendly smile is gone. He wants to know why I am doing this to myself. What's to be gained by putting myself through this kind of suffering? Am I masochistic? Do I hate myself that much?

It's not about hate, I try to tell him. *I want to know that I can accomplish something extraordinary.*

You're still trying to be noticed, he tells me. *The quiet girl, needing to be seen. This time you're really close, you know.*

To what? I try to sit up.

Death.

'Did you speak to me?' Sammy asks. He fans my face, and rests his wet palm on my forehead. 'You feel very hot!'

I watch the nameless river flowing off into the jungle. Now is the time to decide: Do I stop? Do I leave myself here?

I'm reminded of the races I used to run, and how hard it was to get around the last lap. I just wanted to collapse on the track and let someone else finish for me. But knowing there was the promise of an end to the race, a time when I could stop and rest, kept me going to the finish line. And so there must be an ending to *this* experience, too – it just hasn't made itself clear to me yet.

With difficulty, I stand up. I will keep going, and either I make it to the 'end,' to this place called Hotmin, or I will die trying.

The jungle suddenly breaks overhead – we've reached a clearing. Mila, smiling, tells us she knows where we are, that we're nearly to Hotmin. Poorly kept cassava vines snake their way up poles between crops of yams. We shove our way through some fields of sugarcane until we reach a path that edges along a river. May River? The mountains have at last ended and the sun is unobstructed here, blinding. I order my feet to keep moving. Every step must be commanded, coerced out of me. Grasshoppers assail me in single, high-pitched tones. Sammy hands me a chunk of sugarcane pith to suck on, and it has an amazing ability to rejuvenate me, to keep me going. Hotmin must be *klostu*, close. Really close.

But here, first, is the grand finale: the jungle stops before a deep, swiftly flowing river – surely an important natural barrier for Hotmin village during the days of tribal warfare. The river is over thirty feet wide, and a single thin log, barely more than a foot in diameter in its thickest spot, spans from one shore to the other. About twenty feet below, the roaring water races over rocks. This log, Mila tells us, must be crossed if we're to get to our destination before nightfall.

'You've got to be kidding,' I say. I look at Sammy.

He rubs the sweat from his eyes and crouches down, studying the river and the log going across it.

My coordination almost gone, I consider using a pole to help me balance, but the water is so swift that it would probably pull me in. No, there's no easy way of doing this. This is the final exam, and I either pass or fail miserably.

Mila goes first, of course. To add to my anxiety, she doesn't do the usual jog across the log. Instead, she puts down one careful foot in front of the other, the thin log bending and quivering. She holds her arms out on either side of her, looking like some kind of unkempt ballerina. Only near the other side does she speed up and leap to safety. Now she's all smiles and laughter. She beckons to us, and Sammy, groaning, despairing of the river, wipes the sweat from his face and begins to cross. Every move of his feet is slow, calculated. His body sways back and forth, arms flailing, bending, adjusting to the changes in balance. I try to learn from him as he finally reaches the opposite shore and jumps down with relief.

Now it's my turn.

'Go slowly,' Sammy yells. 'Hold out your arms.'

I sigh and shake my head. I try to calm my breathing. *It's over after this. Hotmin's waiting on the other side. You can stop after this.*

'Okay,' I say. 'Let's do it.'

I focus all attention on balance. I can't afford to give in to my delirious fatigue for even a moment. I test the grip of my toes around the log. I test how slippery the log has become. It's not too bad. Slowly, I step onto it. My backpack tries to pull me to one side and I lean in the other direction to compensate. Now another step forward. It's easier to walk with my feet parallel to the sides of the log, scooting one foot along and following it up with my other. I purposely don't look up to see where I am, not wanting to lose my momentum.

Slowly, slowly, I make progress. Glancing up quickly now, I see that I'm in the middle of the river. The waters surge by below. Panicking, I start to move more quickly. The closer I can get to the opposite shore, the greater the chance of being able to jump onto dry land.

As if she could read my mind, Mila steps onto the log and starts to shake it with her foot. I make a dash for the shore and leap to the muddy ground by her feet. As I glare at her, she pats me on the shoulder, laughing. Sammy shakes my hand.

'Congratulations!' he says, helping me up.

We edge around a slippery rock face, small rivulets of water cascading from a stream high above on the cliff face, and stumble down to more swampland, more cultivated fields. At the end of fields, the jungle breaks open like a great exit out of the wild. Dogs start barking. I can see huts, hear people whooping excitedly. Children gather around me, their little hands clasping, touching, urging me forward.

Hotmin.

CHAPTER NINE

Mozart and the Cockroaches

Sammy and I lie in his sister's hut in Hotmin Mission, utterly debilitated. It's our second day here and sleep, at least for me, is still nearly impossible, the bumpy palm bark floor pressing painfully against my body and its collection of scrapes and cuts. These wounds, infected and swollen, cover my legs. The slightest whiff of blood attracts flies by the droves and they frantically buzz around my legs to try to make a landing. I've never felt like such a mess and can only marvel over the stubborn resilience of the human body. To my great surprise, something or someone seems intent on keeping me alive.

In addition to all the cuts, I'm unable to eat anything because I immediately throw it up. The heat stroke took a big toll, and my head still pulses, dizziness and nausea catching me if I sit up. Now, more than ever, I wish I weren't traveling alone. I can say with certainty that there is one thing I need more than anything else right now: a pair of arms around me, holding me. I've never taken such touch for granted; the glide of fingers on my cheek, the press of a sleeping body against mine – these are comforts I've had only briefly, in the rush of relationships I was too scared to prolong.

And here I am, no longer recognizing myself. Why would I nearly kill myself in such a foolish hike through the jungle? I don't feel any different inside. If anything, I feel worse. Less sure of myself. Less confident. The hike didn't succeed in banishing thoughts of Blackwater and the refugees, or enabling me to reinvent myself. Instead, I've ended up in some remote village, sick and helpless, left to figure out how I can get out of here. There is nothing enlightening about this ordeal. It is craziness that I seem bent on perpetuating, as if I were trying to force the world to deliver some kind of truth, some reason for what any of these experiences are supposed to mean.

Sammy hasn't been getting along too well, either. He occupies another room in the hut, and sleeps most of the time. Apart from the rigors of getting here, he's in poor spirits because neither his sister nor her family are around. Weeks ago, she left Hotmin with her husband to visit people in another village, and no one knows where they might be or when they're coming back. Sammy, nearly as worn out and cut up as I am, has trouble believing that he's just made such a horrible journey for nothing. He says he'll wait in his sister's hut until she returns, which he knows could take a while. All he can do is shrug and try to accept the PNG mantra: so it goes.

Mila stops by the hut. She wears the same holey gray T-shirt she had on during our hike, her sense of humor still intact as she points at the cuts all over my legs and laughs. I try to laugh in return. Sammy, who occupies another room in the hut, comes out to see who it is. When Mila waves at him, he groans and returns to his room.

'*Bai mi go long Fiak tude*,' she says to me in Pidgin, smiling grandly.

So she's going back to Fiak already? For a moment I'm worried about her, but I remind myself that she won't have Sammy or me around to slow her down. And she can certainly take care of herself in that jungle better than anyone I've ever met. I imagine a jungle race between Mila and someone from the Special Forces. I see her arriving in Fiak long before her challengers, a sardonic grin on her face.

I already paid her many more kina than I promised her. Still, because money is pretty useless out here, I want to give her something more, something she could actually use, yet it seems as if everything I have is some frivolous Western item – travel alarm clock, Vitamin E capsules, a *Reader's Digest* – none of it of much practical use. I offer her my flashlight and some batteries, but she shakes her head and reaches toward something attached to the strap of my backpack: my hologram-eye key chain. I brought it from home, for good luck. James bought it for me in Tucson, at a flea market, shortly before I left on my trip. He held it up to the center of my forehead, saying, 'You have a third eye.' He laughed. He asked me if the middle of a person's forehead is where the 'chakra of wisdom' is located? I told him I didn't know. And I still don't. I figure Mila can make better use of a 'third eye' than I can.

I remove the key chain from my bag and give it to her. She moves it back and forth in the sunlight, making the hologram eye blink. Laughing, she waves good-bye and leaves the hut. I watch her head across the village toward the imposing immensity of the jungle, her *billum* bag hanging down her back. She is the real version of warrior – tough, resilient, strong. By comparison, I feel I am only playacting, and doing a poor job at that.

Yet, I have more or less succeeded with my original goal of making it from the south to the north of the country, from the Fly River to a tributary of the Sepik. According to my notes, my hike probably took me along the same route the Aussie explorers Taylor and Black used back in 1938 when they first entered this country. I wonder if those men had had a journey similar to mine, with a similar assortment of injuries. I do know that they would have had themselves reliable guides, and plenty of porters to carry packs brimming with palatable food and drink.

I try not to think about their possible provisions. Here in Hotmin, the food is inevitably the same: corn-on-the-cob, the kernels burnt a shiny, deep black from being cooked on cinders. The drink is grainy water tasting flat and noxious from my iodine tablets. I would much rather eat with Taylor and Black.

To pass the time as I try to recover, I'm meticulously reading everything in a *Reader's Digest* I found in the street in Tabubil. The magazine gives me a glut of easily digestible anecdotes and information, never asking much of me and never leaving me disappointed. Wanting to avoid thoughts of what I did to myself by going on such a crazy, useless hike, I read the inspirational stories of bad things happening to good people, the good people always managing to overcome. I find their stories comforting, and can actually forget the pain of my body and the flies landing on me – even the midday heat. I can forget it all.

Just as I get to the part in one of the stories where a female pilot, shot down during the Gulf War, is being discovered by Iraqi soldiers, Sammy tells me that the Hotmin people are cannibals.

'Cannibals?' I leave the Iraqi desert for a moment. 'Here?'

'They don't tell the missionaries,' he says. 'It's a secret. But they are cannibals.'

'Are you sure?'

'Yes. Some men here told me.'

He waits. I wonder if he's expecting a response of surprise.

'Who do they kill?' I ask.

'Men from other tribes – they eat them and take their spirit.'

'And those tribes kill and eat Hotmin men?'

'Of course. They take the heads from the bodies.' He demonstrates with a pretend knife.

I swat flies away and pull my flimsy skirt further over my legs.

'But it's a secret,' Sammy says. 'This is a Christian village.'

We sit in silence for a moment. The humidity is inescapable and my sweat drips onto the floor.

'Christian cannibals,' I say.

Why not? It seems the ultimate PNG paradox, a perfect example of the myriad ways Western beliefs have collided and meshed with traditional culture here. The village may have its own small airstrip, but not much else seems to have given way to Western influences. The white missionaries are gone, and although the village of Hotmin Mission still bears in its name vestiges of Christian influence, it seems to have reverted to the old ways again, like an untended plot of land gone to seed. The same must be true of other places in PNG – with over 700 tribes in the country, armies of foreign missionaries would be needed to help with the proper upkeep and instruction: an impossible task, unless members of the local people can be counted on.

My sweaty fingers stain the pages of the magazine as I return to the Iraqi desert. The world feels as if it could melt around me. Some young Hotmin children, whom Sammy says have never seen a white woman before, dare each other to scramble up the notched-log ladder to take a look at me. The question of how I got here, what I'm doing here, seems to fascinate them. I recall the anonymity of walking in a crowd through the streets of down-town Boston. No one seemed to care where anyone came from. Just the movement of bodies, the thousand separate worlds. Here, though, my presence tempts the bravest of the children to run into the hut and touch my hair.

Sammy says they think my blonde hair is magical, on fire.

I shrug. Why not?

I've started forcing myself to move around more and to get some food down, but I know the conditions in Hotmin aren't helping me recuperate. I've been told that there's an American missionary settlement a few days' journey down May River, and that they have medicine and stocks of food, but I can find no means of getting there. I must be the only person who ever wants to leave Hotmin. There are no canoes being sold or rented out; there are no people making excursions down river. No one knows when, or if, a helicopter will be stopping by the small airstrip, which swelters in the heat, unused. The only action I can take is to wait, hoping that someone or something comes up.

At least the world of Hotmin offers the comfort of few surprises and a well-ordered existence. These are what the days have become: the early morning crowing of roosters and scuffling of chickens beneath the hut, dogs barking to the comings and goings of human presence. Children play, their bare feet thumping lightly upon the pressed-earth paths of the village. Women plant and harvest, or prepare the day's meal. The men work on the huts, hunt, fish. It isn't an easy life by any means, the entire population living mostly on burnt corn at the moment, which makes them appear strikingly gaunt and undernourished. Yet, though this lifestyle is replete with its own unique difficulties, the people of Hotmin manage to avoid the frenzied, lonely, neurotic life of the West, which may explain why Westerners often glamorize these native societies. Here, indeed, are the close family ties and strong sense of community that are completely absent from many people's lives back home – mine included.

Yet, given the fact that I'm here, with nowhere to go and nothing to do but try to learn from this culture, why am I dissatisfied? Perhaps because this life is theirs, not mine. I'm still cut off from my own society; no one is yet able to unconditionally accept me to the point that I can blend in and disappear. That is how you know you're no longer a stranger – when the world around you fails to notice you walking by. Here, the people are always seeing me. Especially the children. They've started plucking hairs from my head whenever I sleep, passing them around and holding them up to the sun. I'm followed everywhere as I limp around, and can't bathe in the river with any privacy because the village people watch me from shore. I wash with my clothes on when I wash at all, looking back at the small crowd. We spend a lot of time looking at each other. It's as if we search each other's eyes for a common ground, a place where our shared humanity can meet.

But through all of this, my body doesn't heal, and so the day-to-day life of Hotmin is becoming oppressive. I think of all the backpackers I've met in the world's hostels who were quick to extol the virtues of *Roughing It*. To them, getting a terrible case of amoebic dysentery was akin to a sublime experience, an initiation rite into the sacred realm of the 'seasoned traveler.' But here, in PNG, in Hotmin Mission, I'm not sure what my cut-up body is supposed to mean. I'm not convinced that the nausea, the scanty meals of burnt-black corn and sweaty, mosquito-infested nights is necessary for something. I have little patience for the religion of *Roughing It* these days. Even the Buddha, one of humanity's most famous ascetics, knew when enough was enough.

I enlist Sammy to my cause. Does he know anyone, anyone at all, who could get me out of Hotmin and to May River Village?

There are three men going to May River, and I meet them on the riverbank. The leader's name, I'm told, is Mozart. He has a poorly healed knife scar running jagged across his face, from forehead to chin. His left eye – directly in the path of the scar – is gone, leaving a shriveled socket. His forehead seems to collapse around that missing eye, and it's so unsettling that I can barely look at him.

'You can go with these men,' Sammy tells me. 'You are lucky because they leave today.'

I don't know if 'lucky' is the word I would use. At least the other two men, somewhere in their late twenties, haven't had their faces slashed open. Still, they don't look very comforting. One man is grim-faced, silent. The other, a clown, seems to find everything perversely funny.

'They will leave soon. They wait for you,' Sammy says, as if I've already made up my mind to go with them.

When the man called Mozart speaks, I see that half his teeth are gone. He is speaking to Sammy in Pidgin, says he wants the equivalent of $400 in kina in order to take me to May River Village. It's an obscene amount of money to get to a place two days away by motorized canoe, and to which they were planning on going anyway. But being a Westerner, I'm obviously a walking bankroll to them; it's a stereotype I can understand, but can never get used to. I want to tell him that the money for this trip came from spending my summers in a factory packaging bread and croutons, six days a week. But would it make any difference? Would it matter if I told him that that factory job was so stale and spiritless that all of us employees lived for the ten-minute respites in the break room? That we scampered for the exit as soon as the clock's minute hand announced our release? No, it wouldn't matter, because the pittance I made – my $6 an hour – would still qualify me as being 'rich' here, where the GDP is barely $1,000 a year. Yet, to me, the 200 kina he's asking for is more than just money. It equals a week of my life.

I refuse to pay the amount and head back to the village. Sammy comes running after me, telling me that Mozart has changed his mind, that he'll take me for 100 kina instead.

I stop and look back at the river, its dark water curving off into the jungle. I'll need to decide – and fast.

'Will you go?' Sammy asks.

Will you go? Mozart's companion, the Joker, snickers at me like some funhouse clown. If he were doing anything other than snickering at me, I'd be surprised. Everything is as it should be. I'm already an incongruous phantom in Hotmin, and see no reason why I shouldn't go with these men, leaving one place and seeing if I will reappear at the next. Perhaps I'll end up at May River Village with my American brethren? Perhaps. But there's no certainty of that. In a way, I'm not so much frightened as curious. What will life do with me next, after what's already happened? Yet, that familiar old anxiety of mine returns: I'm a woman. I can never quite forget how close I came to being gang-raped in Mozambique.

But there *is* one source of comfort now that I've all but forgotten about: I have a machete. A machete that's over a foot long, with a sharp new iron blade stamped 'Made in Brazil.' This is the real thing, an Amazon knife, a bushwhacker's weapon. I take it out of my backpack and hold it. It's pleasantly heavy in my hand. Some may call it crazy or naive to rely on a bush knife for safety under the present circumstances, but I swear to God I would use it if I needed to. I would do some damage.

'All right,' I hear myself say. 'But for one hundred kina only.'

Sammy gets one of the village women to bring my backpack to the shore from the hut. There is quiet all around, the people of Hotmin gathering to see me, the disheveled apparition with her machete, take off. Before Mozart can put my backpack in the canoe, I look at him and his friends, one and then the other, evaluating them. Sizing them up. I don't say a word. The knife feels good in my hand.

Sammy hands me a stalk of sugarcane as a parting gift, and I thank him for everything. Sitting down in the back of the canoe, I listen to Mozart start the outboard. Our canoe putters then leaps forward into the middle of the river. I sit with my knees up, machete in my lap, my ragged, mud-splotched skirt streaming in the wind. The sun glares down at me, and I close my eyes. Sighing, I rub my temples.

I open my eyes and see only jungle now. Hotmin Mission might not have existed. Mozart takes a seat in front of me, turns around. 'You no have fear,' he says to me.

I say nothing.

'We no can hurt you. No have fear.' His eye runs over me.

Can't hurt me? Won't hurt me? Which one is it?

I pick up my stalk of sugarcane. Using my machete, I start to chop off the outer shell to get at the sweet pith inside. I chop and chop, carefully, with focus. The scraps fly off the side of the canoe and land in the water behind us. Mozart won't stop watching me.

'No can hurt you,' he says. 'Police. Come. Take me.'

I keep chopping.

'Police take me, hit me. You know?' He points to a scar on his arm, apparently evidence of that unfortunate reach of the law. In PNG, particularly outside of the cities, punishment is almost always corporal: police routinely beat the hell out of suspects.

I put a piece of sugarcane pith in my mouth, then begin my careful, calculated chopping at the stalk again, the jungle speeding by on either side of us.

Mozart points to my bush knife. 'That no good,' he says. 'I take it. Easy.'

I say nothing.

'I kill two men. With knife, like *dispela*.' He makes the motions of grabbing a knife and using it in return. His single eye looks at me steadily. 'You have fear?' he asks.

My heart is beating harshly. I don't know what his motives are for telling me this. Surely he's enjoying the warped power of it, yet is he bluffing? Is he trying to scare me for the fun of it? Or, and this is a much more disturbing thought, maybe he's actually debating whether he'll try something.

I'm determined not to show any fear.

'Police,' I remind him, putting another piece of sugarcane pith into my mouth.

'Yes, yes.' He shakes his head.

He suddenly reaches out toward me, and I hold up the knife, ready to use it. My heart is going crazy in my chest.

He pulls his hand back and laughs uproariously. 'No can hurt you!'

The others in the canoe look back and grin as I once again rest the knife across my knees. Mozart tssks and chuckles, but he turns around, which is all I care about.

I've never threatened anyone with a weapon before. Surprisingly, I like the feeling, the power of it. I clean some mud from the blade and polish it with my T-shirt. I can understand why fighting men have, through the millennia, personalized and sentimentalized their weapons. I am becoming attached to my own now, to the weight of the dirty, dingy thing in my hand.

We travel all day, making routine stops at villages where only a few families live. None of these places is on my map, and they seem temporary and isolated. At each one, we're inevitably greeted by suspicious men holding bows and bamboo arrows, reminding me of what Sammy told me about these tribes still being cannibalistic. They inspect the contents of our canoe with looks of disdain, roughly tossing around the bags of rice, aluminum cooking pots, cigarettes, bags of mustard seed pods and lime powder for betel nut chewing. They have no money, and when they want something, they run off to find produce to trade for it.

Through this entire process, it never feels as if we're welcome. The village men seem to know Mozart and the others personally, yet there is no friendliness involved during the bartering, and I don't get the impression that my traveling companions are well-liked. Me, though – they don't know what to make of me, sitting quietly in the back of the canoe with a machete across my lap. They ask Mozart questions, but he can't speak enough of their language to offer an adequate explanation. During these interchanges, I try to avoid looking at anyone, as if eye contact could somehow make the situation go bad.

The women of the villages, wearing nothing but short string skirts made from twisted bark, stay by the huts, watching us. Their arm muscles are impressively large, and they lift older children to their breasts with ease. In these parts, women are responsible for most of the farming and chores. They raise the kids, clear away the jungle for crops, plow, plant, harvest, catch fish. I often find myself glancing at them for support.

I also notice that this is the first time I've seen villages with no detectable Western influence. If missionaries came here, and I'm assuming they did, they didn't stay long. The women's bark-string skirts are proof enough of this, considering the proliferation of T-shirts and fabric in other villages. In much of PNG, traditional dress, such as string skirts, would only be worn on special occasions or for the rare appearance of tourists. But here is a place where tourists never go, and where the West hasn't gotten many glimpses. These villages probably look almost the same as they did when the explorers Taylor and Black first traveled the waters of upper May River in 1938, which gives this journey with Mozart the bizarre feel of time travel.

At dusk, we reach a village called Arai, where I'm assuming we'll spend the night. It's composed of a few huts dotting the shore of the river, each one distinguishable in the distance by the fragile orange lights of cooking fires. With the dusk, nearly everyone is inside and close to the fires to escape the onslaught of mosquitoes. There's no moon yet. The jungle near the shore seems to close in upon us, and the flickering of distant fires appears ominous in the thickening darkness.

The sound of a single garamut drum beats from one of the distant huts, a deep, resonant *boom-ba-boom*, like the beating of a giant heart. Arai unsettles me – something to do with the fires and drumbeats, the lack of people to greet us. And Mozart and the others, too, could conceivably do whatever they want to me now, if they have such thoughts. And I suspect they do.

I step out of the canoe and put my backpack on. I've had to take a piss for a while now but was scared that my companions would leave me behind the minute I left the canoe. Now, with my belongings on my back and a village nearby, I head off into the jungle. I return to see the Joker motoring off in the canoe toward one of the distant huts. The drum continues with its steady, unnerving booms.

Mosquitoes are biting my cheeks, my scalp, my toes. I do a kind of dance as I stand near the jungle, wondering what's next. Mozart lights a cigarette and crouches on the shore of the river to wait for his friend's return. The minutes pass. Finally we hear the canoe approaching. I see two dark figures inside as the canoe slows and skids against the shore. A large man wearing only a pair of tattered shorts steps out. He points at me and says something in a tribal language. There is laughter all around.

'No can hurt you,' Mozart says to me, chuckling. I look away, and he claps his hands to get my attention as if I were a dog. 'No can hurt.'

'Yeah,' I say.

The Arai man leads us to a nearby hut, which from its large size appears to be the village meeting hall. He climbs with agile steps up the notched log ladder. The Joker fumbles in a bag and pulls out a flashlight, shining it directly in my face.

'Come, come, come,' he says, clapping his hands.

I shove the light away, and climb the ladder after them. The hut is large and empty, with a high, pointed roof and a palm-bark floor, which bends and creaks beneath my every step. The men had thrown their bags down in the middle of the hut, and the Arai man is starting a fire in the cooking pit. I choose a far corner to set up my mosquito net, tying the ends to some cross beams. My net was one of my finds as I prepared for my trip: in a pinch, it can double as a one-man tent if a tarp is thrown over it. Mozart comes over to examine it, stroking the fabric.

'I want,' he says.

'Not for sale.'

'I want.' He walks around it, inspecting it.

He returns to his two frinds, telling them about it. They look over, talking in low voices. It would be easy for them to rob me, of course, and I'm starting to think that the only reason why they *haven't* is because they're too chicken shit. Maybe they're wondering if a mosquito net would be worth all the trouble, because I haven't put down my machete since first getting in their canoe.

Still, I feel fear creeping into me. My strategy in such moments is to crawl deep into myself, to pretend

I can disappear from people. I start to exist in a tiny space, my anxiety clutching me, drawing me further into myself.

I feel something crawling on my legs, and shine my flashlight down. Roaches, everywhere! Hundreds of them scramble to escape the light. They seem attracted to the moistness of my damp pack, and while they're not much more than an inch long, the hut's floor crawls with them. I can feel roaches fleeing over my feet, up my legs. I unwittingly smash and crunch on them when I walk around. My heart pounding, I look to Mozart and the others by the cooking fire. They are chitchatting among themselves and don't appear to be bothered by anything, probably because the smoke and heat of the flames keep the roaches away. I could join them, but I'm too scared: I'm afraid they might hurt me. I can't say whether this fear is rational or not, but it keeps me where I am, the roaches crawling up my legs, mosquitoes buzzing by my ears. I feel profoundly alone.

I shine the flashlight inside the mosquito net, not surprised to see droves of roaches climbing up the netting. I pull a T-shirt from my pack and shake out a handful of them. My hiking boots hold a few dozen, which I scatter onto the floor and step on. I don't even make a dent in their incredible population, though. They hide between my clothes, in the corners of my bag.

The mosquitoes are biting me mercilessly, so I climb into the mosquito net, roaches and all, and lie down, smashing several beneath me. It occurs to me that I should be hungry, but I'm not. Could be residual effects from the heat stroke – or the fact that hundreds of cockroaches are now climbing up my legs and squeezing beneath my arms as if nuzzling me. They can't get out of this mosquito net, and they try climbing up the arch of netting only to fall onto me, writhing until they right themselves and scurry off. I watch them, concentrate on them. I can feel the creatures all over me, racing across the cuts on my legs, pausing on my belly, getting tangled in my hair.

What am I doing here? I wonder. Mosquitoes bounce against the netting, trying to get in. I can hear their incessant droning.

It's common to get traveler's burnout on a long trip like this, I assure myself. The cure is to find some nice beach with other travelers around and some semblance of the familiar. Coca-Cola, Western meals, travelers bitching about some horrible bus ride through Uttar Pradesh to Nepal. Now is one of those times when I badly need a companion, someone I can crack jokes to, share anxieties with. Someone to look out for me and whom I can look out for.

Roaches climb on my face, get caught in my hair, their legs clawing at my sweaty skin. The men by the fire are speaking in Pidgin in low voices. Sometimes I can catch a word or two of what they're saying. I hear my title, *wait meri*.

I'm having difficulty breathing. I fumble at the zipper of the netting, opening it at last. I have to get out of here, out of this hut. I pull myself from the netting, shaking roaches off of me, and stumble toward the hut's entrance. The crazy, paranoid thoughts are coming. Maybe these men know I was in Blackwater Camp. Maybe they're friends of that man who had been trying to break into my hotel room? I'm certain they're planning on robbing me tonight, leaving me behind in Arai along with the cockroaches. And why shouldn't they? Why don't they do whatever they want and leave me dead in the bushes? Who would know?

It's a dark night and a slice of moon is rising. I can barely see my way out of the hut. The floor shudders with my steps, alerting the others to my departure. They call to me in falsetto voices but I barely hear them. All that matters is getting out of this hut. I practically fall down the notched ladder. Holding my flashlight between my teeth, I stride off into the jungle. Crouching, I rest my head against a tree trunk. My breaths come so quickly that I'm unable to fill my lungs. I close my eyes and concentrate on steadying my breathing, my heartbeat.

The panicked feeling won't stop. I hold my arms against myself, can still feel roaches crawling all over me. Without invitation, thoughts come of James. For the first time in a long time, I don't send these thoughts away. Yet I feel ashamed of them, for the same reason a person might feel ashamed for praying only in moments of desperation. James used to calm me at times like now. He used to bring me back to myself – even when we'd first met.

We made such an unlikely combination. James had never traveled anywhere, and I had. That was all he wanted to talk about on our first date – where I'd been in the world, what I'd done, as if I had a religion that was unfathomable to him. He would encourage me to talk, and I gorged myself on the affection in his eyes, on the grace of his touch. I started to believe that, for the first time in my life, I had found a man I could risk loving: James would not give up on me, would not let me go.

But our relationship had started with an ultimatum. I told him I'd be leaving for New Guinea at the end of the summer. I think he'd hoped that with him by my side I would no longer feel the need to go on my trip. Shortly before the departure date, he told me for the first time that he was in love with me, and suggested we go on a trip together, if a trip was what I needed. What would be accomplished by my running off somewhere alone? Particularly to some 'horrible' place like Papua New Guinea? Did I have a death wish?

I wouldn't answer him.

On my last night, we planned a special good-bye dinner at our favorite Italian restaurant – his treat – but he never showed. I didn't receive a telephone call or explanation for his absence; when I phoned his apartment, there was no answer. That night, a late-night phone call woke me. It was him. He spoke in an awkward voice, trying not to cry. He wanted to wish me good luck on my trip, and to tell me that he'd miss me.

Though it was late, I went to his place. I wore his favorite outfit, the mini-skirt he loved to run his hands up, and we ended up making love like bumbling, first-time lovers, both of us stricken with a sense of the evening's importance and finality. Neither of us knew what I planned on doing, or whether I would actually return. James knew about my foolhardiness; he was one of the few people I'd told about Mozambique.

When I left him early that morning, I knew it would be impossible to forget the feel of his hands on me. When I'd left men in the past, I always found myself missing the way they'd defined themselves through touch. James's touch was both gentle and determined – it was always trying to say, 'Let me help you.'

And I was always pushing him away.

My normal breathing returns. I go back to the hut. Once inside my mosquito netting again, I'm sure this night is never going to end. The incredible heat and scurrying cockroaches make sleep almost impossible. I keep my machete beside me, my hand resting on its cool blade, and watch the faint glow from the coals in the cooking fire. I think of James. I pretend he's here in this hut, watching me. It seems a crazy idea, though – James here, along with Mozart and the cockroaches. Still, I imagine having a conversation with him. I tell him I miss him, and that I'm sorry for just running off and leaving him. My eyes are getting heavy with the exhaustion of being on my own – always on my own – so I tell him all about my jungle trip. I try to explain how I got here, why I look like such a mess. I try to tell him that I love him, but the words feel sloppy, unfamiliar.

We're all up shortly after dawn, ready to leave. Mozart puts all of their things in the canoe, but refuses to take my backpack.

'More kina,' he says to me as he steps into his canoe and pushes aside some bags and bananas. 'One hundred kina.'

I shake my head.

'Give me *natnat* net,' he says. 'And one hundred kina.'

I tell him that I have no intention of giving him my mosquito net or any more money.

Everyone laughs. 'You have much money,' the Joker says.

I look around me. 'Where?'

'You American,' he says. 'Much money.'

I've always found it very inconvenient being an American. If people aren't trying to violently target you for one reason or another, they're refusing you visas, charging you more for visas, fingerprinting you, harassing you, arguing against some president you never voted for or some US government policy you've always been opposed to. And of course all Americans are rich – haven't I seen *Bay Watch*? *Beverly Hills 90210*?

I want to tell him that there is such a thing as a poor American, yet I know this would be futile. Even an American earning below the poverty level – as I have for all of my adult life as a graduate student – is wealthier than a majority of the people in their country. I understand this. Just being able to travel is a luxury, even if you're sleeping in some flea-infested shack out in the middle of East Africa, as I have, more times than I'd like to remember.

Funny: travel hasn't felt like a luxury for a while now. In fact, this kind of travel bears no resemblance to luxury whatsoever. The flies buzz around my legs' wounds, and I vainly swat at them. The truth of the matter is that this life presently sucks.

My stomach is tight from hunger. I have visions of the town called May River, where my friendly American brethren will offer Christian missionary hospitality. Maybe I can eat well for the first time in weeks? Maybe my body and its infected cuts and bruises will at last have a chance to heal? I'm worried about my lingering exhaustion and hunger, and about tempting fate one too many times.

At any rate, the world isn't disappointing me. It's doing exactly what I expect: Mozart and the others are getting in the canoe and telling me that I can't come with them unless I produce their 100 kina – soon. Their Arai friend smirks at me. I seem to have no choice, because staying at

Arai with the cockroaches for a second night is an option I won't consider. I open my backpack to get at my money pouch, and several roaches scamper out.

I pull out 100 kina in bills and toss them at Mozart. The money falls into the bottom of the canoe, into the muddy, petrol-streaked water.

CHAPTER TEN

Hungarian Delights

A great white house appears from the jungle. It is a glimpse of Camelot after all the swamps I've been through, all the mountains, the heat and sweat and mud. It sits on top of a hill, droning with modern convenience and affluence. Air-conditioning. Electric lights. A washing machine out back. There can be no mistaking that I have finally reached the missionary outpost of May River Village.

Mozart drops me off on shore, speeding away down the river. I watch his canoe, until it fades into the distance. Once again, I have arrived somewhere. This fact never fails to surprise me, never fails to fill me with the conviction that I must be doing something right, pleasing someone, giving the proper offerings. I sit down for a moment to rest. I am filthy, exhausted and cannot remember the last time I ate. The incongruity of the vision on the hill hurts my eyes. If ostentation is a sin, then that house is sinful. Sin designed to inspire the pursuit of a godly life. The message is obvious: follow the word of God and you, too, may someday deserve such riches. It strikes me as a wise, if underhanded, strategy in a country known for its cargo cults, those groups of people (many of them still active today) who worship the white man's technology and goods, believing them gifts from the spirit land.

I can't stop looking at the house with its adjacent church, small clinic and buildings. After miles and miles of travel down a river bordered by thick, unbroken jungle, no sight of humanity anywhere, I come upon this little kingdom. I want to meet the man in charge, a missionary named Doug Larson, who is well-known in these parts, and find out what kind of work he does here. Secretly, though, I am hoping he will take me in, as if I were a stray dog. I'm hoping for hospitality. Uncharacteristically, I'm not ashamed of this hope. Rather, I feel as if I've reached the end of my endurance. I can't go on anymore. I can't maintain the momentum. My body has begun to revolt.

I must figure out how to make myself look presentable. Infected cuts and scratches litter my body – especially my legs. Tiny thorns, left over from my jungle trek, lie still embedded in clusters in my calves. Caked mud is smeared on my feet and skirt. My hair looks greasy and tangled. I feel like some wild child, emerging from the bush. What to do? How to return to civilization?

I put my machete in my backpack. Sitting down on the edge of the river, I wash the mud off my legs, but now the cuts appear bright red on my skin. I wet down my hair and try to brush out some of the tangles, but it's a hopeless business. I know I look absolutely terrible.

Across the river, I get some stares from the people of May River. They are the unwitting recipients of the Larsons' ministrations, and I wonder if they would consider themselves lucky. Some men and women drift by in dugout canoes, holding a single baited line to catch catfish. The river literally separates their way of life from the Larsons': animism from Western theology, age-old tradition from modernization. To look from one side of the river with its thatch huts to the other with the Larsons' great white house is to actually trade realities in the blinking of an eye, and it's dizzying.

I watch an old man floating down river in his canoe. If he looks to the left, he'll see his world as the West would have it. He'll see the house, perhaps remembering when its contents were air-lifted in or sent up the Sepik River. He might hear the hum of the generator, observe the flicker of the electric lights coming on at night. Would it all mean progress to him – or loss? Because a glance to his right shows him the world that he has always known: huts sitting on stilts beside the river; children playing naked in algae-covered pools; women sitting in the sun, preparing tulip bark strips to use for *billum*-bag cord. The white house on the hill is there to convince him that the new way of life is best, and I wonder whether he believes. I wonder what it would take to make him choose the opposite shore?

A well-dressed Papua New Guinean man in shirt and pants comes over to me as I'm washing my feet off in the river. He is soft-spoken, polite, and asks if I'm here to see the Larsons.

I nod.

He beckons me to follow him up the hill. I put my backpack on and limp behind him. Stuffing my hair into a baseball cap, I wipe my face with my T-shirt and pull down my skirt as far as possible in order to hide my legs. When we reach the front of the white house, he instructs me to sit on a bench in the shade of a veranda and leaves.

I wait. And wait. I tuck my filthy, mildew-stained T-shirt into my skirt and squash a roach that has just fled from my pack. As I look for more roaches inside, I see a white man – Mr Larson? – heading up the hill toward me. I sit up, excited to finally meet a fellow American in this jungle, in this forgotten corner of New Guinea.

Mr Larson stops. He's frowning. He wipes the sweat from his forehead and stands at a distance from me on the veranda, hands on his lips. He has a pointed, angular face and narrow blue eyes that seem in a constant state of evaluation and judgement. The sunburnt skin on the back of his neck glows like peach fuzz in the sunlight. He isn't saying a word.

I introduce myself and tell him that I'm also an American. I apologize for my appearance, tell him about my hike, explain how I got this way.

'What on earth were you doing hiking from Fiak to Hotmin?' he asks, examining me with his eyes.

'That's a good question,' I say. I don't really have an answer. At least, no answer that I'd like to share with him.

He shakes his head and points his finger at me. 'You should never underestimate the jungle.'

'Yeah. You're definitely right about that.' I nod deferentially.

'You bet I am. Never underestimate it.' His eyes are looking at May River, or perhaps the village beyond it.

He excuses himself for a moment and enters the house. Air-conditioning assails me. I sit back, swatting flies away from the cuts on my ankles. A light breeze brushes past, smelling faintly of cooking fires and sun-sweetened fields.

He reappears with a robust white woman in a sundress whom he introduces as his wife, Anne. We shake hands. She hands me a glass of cold water with ice cubes inside. I poke at them, watch them bob around. I never thought ice cubes could become a novelty.

'So you're the American girl who came down from Hotmin,' she says.

She is Mr Larson's twin, frowning, assessing, disapproving. Smiles seem to pain her. I wonder if it's my appearance, my unexpected arrival? Or have I somehow given off my parents' atheist vibes? The midday heat seems to wrap itself around my head, constrict my ability to think. My head is pounding dully.

'What happened to your legs?' she asks.

'I had a bit of a jungle adventure.' I take a long drink. Only the ice cubes remain when I put down the glass. It's getting hard to keep my eyes open. The midday heat is winding, winding about me.

Mr Larson asks me what I'm doing in PNG, why I've come to his village of May River. His questions have the monotone quality of someone bored, disinterested. His eyes wander over the distant spread of jungle, flit over the river. He inspects May River Village like a general examining troops, plotting the stages of an assault. Such distraction. Such harsh contemplation.

The Larsons, it turns out, are Seventh-Day Adventists. To them, Christ will be coming *soon*. Judgement Day is nearly upon us. No wonder they're so detached and serious: there's no time to waste. Souls need saving as quickly as possible.

Already, I'm wondering if I could stay with someone in the village. But now Mrs Larson is calling over a young white woman about my age with long brown hair, who smiles excitedly as she approaches.

'This is Lisa,' Mrs Larson says. 'She teaches our boys.'

It turns out that Lisa and I have a lot in common. She's my age – twenty-four; our birthdays are eight days apart. She's a Hungarian-American, I'm Czech, and we both grew up with the same kinds of ethnic food – chicken paprika, *svickova*, dumplings and sauerkraut – our houses invaded by relatives prattling in Eastern European tongues. Now, incredibly, we find our lives intersecting in the same spot of New Guinea, both of us worlds away from anything we'd once considered familiar.

The Larsons leave us on the porch, and it's uncanny how quickly Lisa and I bond as we talk. In many ways, it's a bond of necessity, the kind that sprouts easily in a place as remote as this. I admire the resiliency that has allowed her to live in this village for a year already, with at least another year to go. It can't be easy.

'God chose me to come here,' she says, her pleasant expression turning serious. 'He wants me to pass on the good news about Jesus Christ and His teachings. I'm His servant.'

Interested in international volunteer work, she joined a youth mission group when she graduated from a Bible college in Virginia over a year ago. Holding a degree in education, Lisa tells me she had visions of being sent to some village full of children she could teach to read and write, full of people whose only education was what she would be able to give them. There seemed to be so much opportunity for her. So many rewards. She was, as she put it, 'a very willing servant.'

The missionary group ended up sending her to May River, instead, to become a freebie nanny for the Larsons' children. It must have been a disappointment.

Lisa is careful about her words; I can tell she doesn't want me to think she's dissatisfied or – worse – ungrateful for the experience she's having. Yet the frustration is there in her eyes as she describes when she'd first arrived in May River. There had been no place to put her, and the Larsons settled on an out-of-the-way hut. She went from a comfortable apartment in Virginia, having never traveled in her life, to a sweltering hut in the New Guinea jungle with virtually no amenities.

'It was really hard at first,' she whispers, smiling. 'You can feel really lonely out here. But I prayed all the time, and God gave me strength.'

The local people soon realized that she – an unmarried woman – slept alone in the hut, and a local man began knocking on her door each night. This had gone on for some time, but Lisa always politely sent him away, praying and persevering for an end to his appearances. Then one night she woke up to the feel of his hand on her thigh. Terrified, she ran from the hut. Something needed to be done, and the Larsons had no choice but to move her into a new building that had been 'reserved' for guests. Now she had a door that locked, a sink, kitchen, shower, toilet.

'Do you want to see where I live?' she asks. 'You can stay there as long as you want. I'd love the company.'

We move from the Larsons' porch to the small, two-story cement house that stands nearby. Inside, a wooden cage contains her pet cuscus, a small, spotted jungle marsupial she'd rescued from a villager's dinner table. It crawls slowly about the tiny wooden cage, its possum-like tail coiled tightly against its belly, bulbous brown eyes looking mournfully, tragically, at us. The solitude of her life shouts out from the walls papered with photos of friends, past boyfriends, family from back home; from the bookshelf filled with books, and the care package lovingly tucked under the bed, Lisa allotting herself a single Hershey's Kiss per day. She hands me two with a smile.

Concerned about my visible exhaustion, she starts a shower for me. Afterwards, she helps me clean the cuts on my legs with antiseptic scrub, then applies antibiotic ointment – I feel like a stray cat she's taken in. When I open my backpack and accidentally unleash an exodus of jungle roaches into her bedroom, she laughs and tells me not to worry. Instead, she gives me clean clothes to wear, feeds me precious corn flakes with powdered milk and water, and offers me her own bed.

It's Saturday morning, and the Larsons have invited Lisa and me to their weekly brunch. 'Strawberry pancakes,' Lisa tells me with a grin. I wear one of Lisa's sundresses and spend an hour unknotting my hair. For the first time in a long time, I look at myself in a mirror: a sunburnt, freckled apparition with wild blonde hair.

We head over, and Mrs Larson greets us at the door. This is the first time I've been inside the Larsons' house, and I'm surprised to see that it looks very much like the house of your average American family back home. Each place at the dining room table is neatly laid out with silverware, napkins, glasses. The kitchen on the other side of the room is large and fully equipped with sink and running water, range, refrigerator. I'm experiencing a kind of reverse culture shock. I keep remembering the refugees' thatch-roof huts in Blackwater Camp with no running water or electricity, unscreened windows inviting the constant threat of malaria.

I'm introduced to the Larsons' two blond boys who help their mother put out the plates.

'Do you miss home?' I ask them.

They shrug. Maybe they're scared of betraying their parents by answering my question. Or maybe they've resigned themselves to this life.

Mrs Larson offers to give me a tour of the house while the food is being put out. She shows me the bedrooms, the bathroom with a tub, flushing toilet and sink. The resemblance to a typical American house is uncanny. The Larsons have almost successfully created the illuison of being back in the States.

I remember what I've read about PNG's earliest missionaries, those hearty Dutch and English folk who set up stations on the coast and seemed to succumb to malaria and local hostilities faster than they could get anyone baptized. Such difficulties were seen as a willing sacrifice then, proof of one's true devotion to missionary work and the glory of God. Now, however, things have obviously changed. Gone is the asceticism, the martyr-dom, and in its place is the need for comfort and security before business can begin. I wonder where they would draw the line – what comforts would they do without?

'How long have you been here?' I ask Mrs Larson.

'Oh, years now. When we first came here, the people in the village were still wearing native dress.'

There is one room Mr Larson wants to show me. It's his special room, his den, which is also filled with some of the artifacts he's collected from villagers since his arrival.

He points at some stone tools, which sit on display on a tabletop like hunters' booty. 'Before I came here, these people were living sinful, Stone Age lives,' he tells me with shock. 'Look at that. They used stone. *Stone*. That's what I came to.'

I'm unable to say anything. Were I to speak, I would probably explode in indignation.

'But things have been changing here,' he says. 'I've been encouraging them to give up their stone tools. I've brought them steel.'

In less than ten years, Mr Larson has effectively wiped out a way of life. Ten years ago steel started to replace stone, and now an entire group of people has become the victim of his Master Plan. How can the actions of one man produce such devastation? Is Mr Larson qualified for such an enormous responsibility? Who approved him? Not God, surely, though that would be his answer, his justification for such arrogance. The stone tools and weapons he's talking about are considered national treasures in PNG. Once a prized bounty of Western art collectors, they've become so hard to find that the government's Cultural Ministry has launched its own effort to collect and preserve what few can still be found among the most remote tribes – unmistakable proof that PNG is on the verge of losing a huge part of its past.

'I've gotten most of the stone tools in the area,' Mr Larson confides in me. He might have just told me that he'd succeeded in inoculating an entire tribe against some insidious disease – such is his enthusiasm.

'What do you do with them?'

'I get rid of them.'

But Mr Larson wants to explain the plan he uses to get the local people to relinquish their tools. He is proud of this plan, and he flashes me a knowing, smug smile. What one must first understand, he insists, is that the tribes all work according to the laws of payback. If you give a gift to someone, he must pay you back with a gift of similar value. So Mr Larson began to hold feasts. He had special food airlifted in, and his wife used her culinary skills to produce desserts, pastries, expensive and delectable meals. None of the villagers had ever seen or tasted such fantastic foods, so Mr Larson's feasts were first-class events.

'Then I put the word out,' he says to me, crossing his arms and nodding with self-satisfaction. 'I told them that I wanted a stone tool in exchange for their attendance at the feasts.'

This strategy had worked beautifully. Mr Larson made sure he had metal axes or bush knives to pass out to everyone who came. In this way, he managed to accumulate nearly every stone tool and weapon to be found among the tribes of May River.

He stops for a moment: my lack of enthusiasm seems to miff him. But I don't even want to look at him. I'm turned toward the door, contemplating escape. I wonder what will be demanded of *me* in return for the sumptuous meal being laid out in the next room.

We head back to the lunch table, a feast laid out before

us: strawberry pancakes, syrup, toast, juice. The feast of a Caesar. Mr Larson orders everyone to bow their head while he says grace.

I'm accompanying Anne through May River Village, as I've been curious to know what a typical day is like for her. What does it mean, after all, to be a New Guinea missionary? Our presence attracts a small crowd. Little children hold out their hands, as if in expectation of gifts. She walks past them with the airs of royalty.

'Do you know everyone in the village?' I ask her.

'I used to, but it's getting harder now.' She stops to inspect a tropical ulcer on the leg of a small boy, asking the mother in Pidgin whether she's been cleaning it like she's supposed to. 'When I first came here, everyone owned only one T-shirt, so I'd tell them apart that way. I'd look and say, "Oh, there's Aia with the green T-shirt on." But now they've got more than one T-shirt.' She shakes her head in dismay. 'I can't tell them apart anymore.'

The traditional-style hut we're going to is like all the others: raised several feet above the water, sitting on the edge of May River with its back looking out at the jungle. It's made of wooden supports, palm bark floors, a thatch roof – it bears no resemblance to the great white house across the river. The inside is a simple one-room spread with a kitchen area near the cooking fire and sleeping quarters away from the smoke. A picture of the Virgin Mary, her arms outspread, hangs on the wall.

The owner of the hut is out on the deck, twisting thread for *billum*-bag cord. When she sees us, she drops everything and comes running. Anne greets the woman with a barrage of fluid Pidgin, telling her who I am and where I come from. The woman smiles broadly at me, and we say hello. She wears a T-shirt with some faint letters advertising an American university. The material is threadbare over her breasts, and her nipples stick through the lettering.

Anne reaches magnanimously into her *billum* bag. The

woman looks from Anne to me and back again, eagerly holding out her hands. Anne delays the moment for as long as she can, her hand lingering in the bag, rustling its mysterious contents. The woman smiles in anticipation, and the gift finally appears: a white plastic wall clock.

Before she hands it over, Anne sets the hands of the clock according to her own watch.

Lisa's frying pan is sizzling with the familiar sweet-dough smells of Eastern European cooking. Tonight we're to have Hungarian delights, courtesy of her mother's care packages. As she cooks, I read her extraordinary collection of May River folktales, each one neatly recorded in between her diary entries.

There are stories about the ghosts of ancestors coming to May River, stories about warriors going off on quests. At the end of each folktale, Lisa cites a Biblical story, giving its location in the New Testament.

I point out the Bible citations. 'Are you making a comparison?'

She turns to me, excited. 'The tribal stories are *exactly* like the Biblical stories.'

I'm confused. Is she a Jungian, looking for the common myths of humanity?

She motions to the journal I'm holding. 'The people in this country are already Children of God.'

' "Already"?'

'Jesus Christ visited them a long time ago. That's why their stories are the same as the ones in the Bible. They already received His teachings, but they never knew it.'

I don't say anything. I decide I'll let it pass.

I catch an entry of hers written on the page beside one of the folktales. *It doesn't feel like the Larsons appreciate me here*, she writes, and she immediately chastises herself for such a thought. Yet, she writes about teaching their boys, and how the Larsons hardly seem to notice or care. She discusses her frustration in general, until, by the end of the entry, she writes, *But I've prayed to the Lord and He's given me strength*.

I look up at Lisa preparing our Hungarian Delights. With the actions of a pro, she turns the little dumplings around, inspecting the bottoms. I can't imagine how she, so far from home yet so full of goodwill, endures the strange harshness and distraction of the Larsons in this bizarre kingdom.

Lisa takes the pan from the fire and dishes out some dumplings onto a plate for me. She puts out seasoned bread, a pitcher of Tang. For dessert, on a small plate: four Hershey's kisses. We eat until we're stuffed. Seizing the chocolate, we sit on her bed to talk like a couple of girls at a slumber party.

I'm eager to finally tell someone about my trip to Blackwater. I need to purge the experience from my thoughts, if that's possible. Lisa seems an ideal person to talk to because she still believes in innocence; I'm hoping some of her belief can rub off on me. Children's books litter her bookshelf. Like a girl with a crush, she talks excitedly about her radio communications with a young missionary in the bush.

I tell her what's happened so far: how I visited Pastor Carl and the OPM; the refugees; my night in the trailer in Tabubil and the subsequent hike through the jungle. I tell her about Mozart and his threats, and how I considered myself lucky to have gotten to May River at all. The one thing I don't tell her about – can't tell her about – is when the soldiers in Blackwater asked me if I wanted them to take care of the man who had interrogated me. For my own sanity, I must pretend that never happened.

She listens to me, her face getting more and more sober as I talk in a rushed, vague, haphazard way, wanting only to get it all out. When I finish, she looks at me, shocked.

'Everything's tainted now,' I say. 'It scares me.'

'Tainted?' She waits, concern in her eyes.

I study my hands. I never feel comfortable talking about myself.

And now I tell her what I mean. How I don't know what I'm doing here in Papua New Guinea, no longer feeling in control of my life. How a strange momentum has engulfed me, pushing me on. I don't know why I can't stop myself. I just want to find some place where I can finally slow down. Rest. Yet, I can't ever allow myself.

Lisa doesn't know what to say. Finally: 'Have you tried praying?'

'I tried when I was a kid,' I tell her.

'Maybe you could try it again. That's what got me through the hard times here. I know that God loves us. He forgives us our sins.'

Growing up the child of two staunch atheists, I would have been laughed at if my family caught me praying. But I don't want Lisa to know about my upbringing – I'm afraid it might frighten her off.

I say only, 'I always had trouble believing there was anyone out there.'

The next morning, the momentum sweeps me up again in its panicked need-to-be-gone. In a way, I'm embarrassed that I've told Lisa so much about myself when we hardly know each other. I don't want to be any kind of burden to her or anyone. My body is on its way to being healed, and it seems better to be back on my own, relying and depending on myself.

I pack my bag and say good-bye to Lisa. A missionary plane will be stopping by on its way to the Sepik River town of Ambunti, and I've decided to go along. I'm glad I'm going in this easy way. I'm not in the mood for any more tests of resolve. I'm not sure what good they did. They haven't given me any epiphanies, or changed anything about myself. The hike from Fiak to Hotmin may be written all over my body in the cuts and emerging scars, but none of it feels substantial. All I care about now is moving forward, getting to the unfamiliar.

We're both moist-eyed as I get in the plane. I know Lisa will be all right here in May River. To her, it's all God's test – the man who broke into her hut and terrified her; the Larsons and their lack of support; the scarcity of things she once took for granted. I wonder if she could have done it all without the reassurance that Someone was constantly watching and loving her, no matter how difficult things got. I envy her confidence. I've felt entirely on my own since coming to PNG, and wish I had some kind of sign, some guarantee that the world, the fates, the gods – *some*thing – was looking out for me, guiding me along. I want to know where I'm actually headed.

CHAPTER ELEVEN

Making Rain

Ambunti is the St Louis of Papua New Guinea. Sitting on the Sepik River, it is where the missionaries come to 'get a break from the bush,' while foreign backpackers find it a convenient place to head in. Tribal people pass through: women with their faces tattooed; men with the septa of their noses hollowed out, light passing through when they turn their heads. Ambunti is the gateway to all points west, the town where travelers converge to refuel and stock up before heading upriver. Here one can catch up on news, make a phone call, mail letters, even cash a traveler's check. A small police station exists to administer law and order the old-fashioned way: with fear and a big stick. The town was settled by the Australians in 1924 in an attempt to subdue the area's head-hunting populations so exploratory missions could safely venture into the interior in search of gold. There hadn't been much gold around to make it worth their efforts, but Ambunti became the most important outpost in the Sepik River region – a reputation it still holds today. It is the Last Stop. After Ambunti, the river goes on for days without offering the respite of human presence. Just jungle, I'm told. River and the endless green.

It is in Ambunti that I first hear about a famous Apowasi witch doctor living upriver. He has uncanny powers. He can heal the sick, curse the wicked. He speaks to the animals of the jungle, cajoling them until they walk into a hunter's hands. But more than anything, he's renowned for his ability to connect with the gods. He knows the proper spells, and how to lift his prayers higher than the stars until they rest at last in the right ears. The gods hear him. They answer his prayers. The lost become found; the dying, saved. He can work miracles, I'm told, and I want to find him and ask him whether the gods are watching me, helping me. I want to know what I'm doing here in New Guinea, always on the move, always traveling to one dangerous place after the next. When will I be able to stop? When will I end the searching?

Given its unique outpost status, Ambunti isn't a very big place – a pleasant town of about 1,300 people. The centrally located airstrip is its only main attraction. The village itself consists mostly of traditional and Western-style houses spread out along the Sepik River, people peacefully going about their affairs of fishing, running small stores. A missionary compound and a couple of simple guest houses face the airstrip, and I head over to see about a room. I stop off at a simple-looking shack with a corrugated iron roof – one of the town stores. Inside is the usual food of PNG, the mainstays of Australian bush cuisine: packets of Maggi instant noodles, great tins of margarine with a smiling New Guinean boy on the label holding out a piece of buttered bread, whole milk powder from France, gargantuan bottles of cooking oil, Milo bars, rice, Cadbury chocolate. I pick up a jar of the Australian black yeast spread called Vegemite, the most revolting substance ever designed for human consumption.

'It'll grow hair on your toes,' someone behind me says in an Australian accent.

I turn around to see a tall, lanky, red-headed man in olive army surplus pants and broad-rimmed straw hat, smiling at me. 'Rob Hodge,' he says, extending his hand.

Beside him is a man with curly blond hair, wearing a sun visor. Though of slight frame, he's all muscle and sinew. 'Yens,' he says with a German accent.

He spells it for me: Jens. He's from Germany, is taking his 'holiday' in Papua New Guinea. He says his girlfriend hadn't wanted to accompany him here so he has to settle for Rob. I find it odd that one would choose PNG as a vacation spot; I seem to have chosen this country for every other reason – for the raw challenge of the place, for the lack of comfort and guarantees. Jens is reminding me of the trip I might have had: going to a place merely to enjoy myself, to languish on a beach, to swim in turquoise waters. Nothing to prove to myself or the world.

I introduce myself to them. Rob inspects me, beaming like a proud father.

'Looks like you've been through hell,' he concludes.

'Do I look that bad?'

'Ya, well, your legs are not so good.' Jens points at them with a serious expression. 'All the scratches.'

I shrug. No beauty contests out here. This is what you look like after hacking yourself out of a jungle. My legs still look like war zones, covered in scratches, punctures, rips.

'How'd you get like this?' Rob asks.

I tell them about my hike from Fiak to Hotmin: the heat exhaustion, the ninety-degree-angle mountains of jungle and the never ending rain. I describe the small villages I saw after leaving Hotmin for the May River mission, and how the missionaries must be pulling out their hair and mobilizing for a new offensive because the women there were still bare-breasted and wearing bark-string skirts.

Jens shakes his head wistfully. 'I am jealous,' he says. 'I want to see that.' His disappointment is what safari goers in the Serengeti might have when told they'd missed a leopard sighting.

Rob slaps me on the back.

'You've got the blood in you,' he says. 'I'm impressed.'

I'm glad he's impressed; it's like receiving an acknowledgement that I, a woman, also belong in this place – a place that has traditionally been the playground of male travelers and adventurers. I've passed the test. I *can* do what the boys can do.

Actually, I feared the opposite response from Rob – his

being intimidated. I especially saw this when I used to run in coed races in college. If I ran as well as the men, beating many of them, they'd inevitably make excuses: 'My ankle was giving me problems,' 'I slept bad last night.' Dating men became even more complicated, and with the exception of one boyfriend who had a black belt in tae kwon do, I didn't share this integral part of my life with anyone: my physical abilities had become embarrassing. I was starting to feel less 'feminine,' as if loving physical challenge was taking away my woman-hood and turning me into some frightening, androgynous creature. I realized that so many men still wanted a woman who made a delightful fool out of herself because she couldn't throw a baseball five yards.

' "The blood"?' I ask Rob.

'You've got balls,' he says. 'I'm going to call you *bus meri*.'

I smile. A Bush Mary with balls – the male anatomy bestowed upon me to explain the phenomenon of what I've done.

Rob tells me that Jens is a German Navy SEAL officer, a 'killing machine.' (Jens blushes.) His skills are in such high demand that he's often brought over to the States to help train American Special Forces units. No wonder he is so strong, appears so physically fit. I want to know why he's chosen to commit his life to the Special Forces. What does it give him that he can't get anywhere else?

'Do you enjoy it?' I ask him.

'Of course,' he says.

'What do you enjoy about it?'

He sputters his lips. 'It's not an office job, this kind of thing.'

'Do you like the adventure of it?'

'Yes, of course.'

He sighs and looks away. I consider telling him about my childhood fantasy of becoming a female Green Beret, but I don't want to frighten him with the idea.

Rob tells me that he met Jens in a guest house in

the coastal town of Wewak, and that they flew here to Ambunti to hire a canoe and guide for their very own trip up the Sepik River. Jens doesn't have much time, but their plan is to go up some rarely traveled tributaries, seek out tribes that have had little or no contact with travelers. He asks if I'd like to join them.

It doesn't take me long to decide. We'll try to find the Apowasi witch doctor.

As we leave the store, I ask Jens what he teaches his American Special Forces students.

'It depends, you know.'

'Bombs and stuff? Explosives?'

He sighs. 'Ya, ya. I teach some of that.'

'Teaches 'em how to blow the enemy to smithereens,' Rob offers.

Jens is blushing again. 'Ya. That kind of thing.'

'Do you teach them how to conduct secret training missions?' I remember the books about the Special Forces and Navy SEALs I used to read as a kid. 'You know – scuba-diving to enemy ships and planting explosives on the hull?'

Jens looks at me curiously. 'I can't talk about it, you know.'

But we don't give up asking, Jens's reality so surreal to us.

'One thing I'm wondering,' Rob says. 'Do you know how to strangle people with wire?'

We follow the course of the airstrip, waiting for Jens to reply. We want him to tell us that yes, he's been taught to do that, has even done it once in a covert operation in some forgotten corner of the world like Papua New Guinea.

A pilot loads some screeching piglets in *billum* bags into the back of a small plane next to a coffin. Jens pulls out his camera and takes a few pictures – this is the world Jens considers bizarre. Rob reiterates his question. Wires. Strangulation.

'I'm on holiday,' Jens says simply.

Rob slaps Jens on the back again. 'We'll just get you

pissed, Mate. Loosen the tongue.' He grins devilishly at me.

We head over to the hut of a well-known guide in town. This man, Joseph Kona, says he is familiar with the Apowasi witch doctor called 'the Chief,' who is the *bigman* of his tribe. We are invited into Joseph's hut to work out the details and expenses for visiting him. It turns out that the Apowasi are far up a branch of the Wogamush River, a westen tributary of the Sepik. Their village isn't on any of our maps, the people themselves living inland from the river in a remote area. Joseph says they're visited by Westerners maybe once every few years.

We make final arrangements, and Joseph invites us to spend the night in his hut. I feel my usual burden of anxiety lifting, as I'm not traveling alone anymore and don't have to rely on myself if anything dangerous should happen. I'm with two men, one of them a German Navy SEAL. Not bad. Better than carrying a machete.

And it turns out that Rob has been everywhere. He's been attacked by hippos in the Serengeti, has made daring leaps from cliffs onto trucks in the Australia outback. He's canoed down the Klondike River, every last mile of it, and has seen the sun rise on the Alps, the Himalayas, the Andes. Rob has seen it all, and none of it was ever enough for him – until now. Now, he's content. We eat Sepik River catfish with rice before the glow of a kerosene lamp, and he sits back against the palm-bark wall of Joseph's hut, smiling a big Irish grin.

'This has got to be the one place I would most want to be in this moment,' he says. 'Here it is.'

Jens glances at him, amused. He won't be caught with Rob's moist eyes or goofy smiles. Not a word out of his mouth sails beyond the present and the practical. Jens, a warrior by profession, a specialist who teaches others how to kill, must find sentimentality a sign of weakness. A liability.

But does he hear the sound of children playing outside in the night? The soft conversations in the native *tok ples* language from Joseph's family in the back room? The banter of the frogs? There is a sense of our being told a secret now – right now. We're being let in on what should, *must*, always matter in life. The intimate sounds of life go on around us as if they have no intention of ever stopping. I wonder if Jens hears. I sit down near Rob, who is grinning mysteriously, and we smile at each other. We know. We share this night.

When we all finish eating, we head into a spare room of the hut to set up our mosquito nets. I choose a place between Jens and Rob, enjoying the safety of their proximity and relishing their company. They change out of their clothes in front of me as if I weren't here. I sit and watch them, their chests, the beautiful male bodies. Why not? I watch them until they slip into their mosquito nets – Jens in boxer shorts, Rob naked. Now I slip off my own shirt. I catch them watching me, and it's as if we belong to each other.

We three sit in wicker chairs in a large dugout canoe. 'The lazy way,' Rob calls it. Joseph sits up front, sleeping, his younger cousin, Alphonso, piloting us along. Jens is also asleep in front of me. Though fair-complexioned with blond hair and blue eyes, and wearing only a thin T-shirt and shorts, Jens is convinced that sunscreen is a useless gimmick of the West, and he refuses to wear any. His skin is red and crispy all over, his curly blond locks bleaching in the sun. Rob goes to the other extreme, wearing a long-sleeved army shirt, straw hat, pants and boots. I fall somewhere in between, in T-shirt, skirt and Australian bush hat. I keep hearing Mr Larson's words, 'Never underestimate the jungle.' Amen. I've learned my lesson.

For the first time since arriving in PNG, I'm feeling as if I might just be 'on holiday,' like Jens. I'm just enjoying the world, postponing all tests. It always amazes me how intrusive beauty becomes when the mind allows itself to rest. The body relaxes, the senses turn on. Perfection imposes itself upon the earth, and I am gorging myself on the spread of river that twists and glides to the west, to some space seemingly beyond the horizon. This feeling is the same as looking at a night sky – all the immensity, the grandeur – only here it is a feasting of color. Clouds sweep broadly across the sky, rising in pillars and arcs of gray and white. I can almost feel distant rain pounding down on some immutable shore. The river waters catch and rattle the stands of wild sugarcane bordering the river. Sunlight falls haphazardly upon the inland jungle, lighting the tops of trees in one place while another group falls into darkness. Crocodiles, the kings of the PNG waterways, slip into the water as we motor by. Joseph points at them with reverence. They're big out here, he says. As numerous as the stars themselves. He tells us that the crocodile is a special creature. In the beginning there was nothing but water, but then a giant crocodile swam down to the bottom of the sea and returned with mud on its back, creating the world.

We exit the Sepik for a small river that heads south, toward one of the largest lagoons in the country. Rob wants to see a bird-of-paradise, PNG's national bird and a species famous for its spectacular plumage, so we're taking a side trip to a village called Wagu at the far end of the lagoon.

Joseph has his reservations about taking us, though, because my female presence might emit 'poison,' which could chase the birds away. He tells me that women in PNG are believed to give off poison much more often than men, their menstrual cycles and genitals causing sickness, injury, death. Even worldly Joseph, missionary-schooled, English-speaking, a prominent man in Ambunti, firmly accepts this. He's seen it happen, he says. Couples who 'don't take the tradition seriously' will pay the price for not being wary of the female poison: the men will grow weak and die young.

Just as a town would want to separate infectious typhoid patients from the general population, women in these villages are whisked away to menstruation huts – *haus meri* – at the first sign of their monthly evil because

Joseph says they're 'full of mischief' and can spread poison. Poison is spread in the most unassuming ways. Maybe a woman sits down on her husband's chair while she's menstruating, and he sits there after her – well, he's just caught her evil and has infected himself, and chances are his health will begin to deteriorate. Food preparation and cooking must be done by another woman during this time, to avoid having menstruating women infecting the meals and causing the man's body to 'rot' from the inside out. But what the men fear most is the vindictive wife who, wanting to get back at her husband, practices 'sorcery.' Maybe she leaves some menstrual blood where he'll walk on it, or – God forbid! – is intent on spreading her poisonous sex fluids on him during intercourse. From the man's point of view, the hazards must be many, the risks great, in order to lie with a woman to perpetuate his clan.

I don't tell Joseph or anyone else that I'm currently having my period, and revel in the thought of all the poison I'm unleashing onto the world. Joseph says that one of the worst things a woman can do is to step over a man during her 'blood time.' Feeling mighty and wrathful, I make an effort to step over Joseph several times as I get in and out of the canoe during the day. The poor man suspects nothing.

After slipping across the lagoon's wide, black waters in the canoe, we reach Wagu at dusk. It's a small village of a few stilt huts spread along the water. Mosquitoes are mysteriously absent, and I walk casually along the lagoon's shore, staring up at the ever brightening stars. The night air is cool and pleasant here, and I'm surprised that the Bahinomo people of Wagu Village are the only ones to have chosen to settle beside this lagoon; it may be that fierce tribal fighting allowed them to keep this paradisiacal part of the country all for themselves.

We wake up before dawn to seek out the birds-of-paradise. Our guide, a local man, leads us up a steep slope into the neighboring jungle. We chop a path, sweating and cursing our way through the thick foliage until our guide stops us.

Two birds-of-paradise with bright red feathers taunt each other and fly into the air, their long, frilly plumage flaring about them. Rob and Jens pull their cameras out and start to take pictures, as our guide lets out a high-pitched call, hoping to attract more. The two birds fly off. We sit down and wait, flicking off the little wormlike leeches that jump onto us from the foliage and inch up our arms and legs. No birds are returning. Nothing.

Joseph is becoming increasingly furious. 'It's no good. That man – ,' he points to our guide, ' – was with his wife last night. She put smell on him. The birds smell her poison and they don't come.'

Joseph repeats this to the guide in Pidgin, and the Wagu man looks at his feet like a guilty child. Joseph is spitting and frothing in anger now, berating the silent man. Rob raises his eyebrows at me, and we try not to laugh, waiting for Joseph's tirade to end.

With the birds staying clear of us, we have no other alternative but to return to Wagu. Joseph, still piqued, tells me that if a man sleeps with a woman then goes on a big fishing trip, he won't catch anything. She leaves her evil on him, jinxes him. The animals and fish can smell her and they stay away. 'Our guide knows this,' he says to me. 'Stupid man.'

Rob nudges me, but I'm not laughing anymore. I'm starting to get really sick of women being blamed for everything. When we get back to Wagu village, I'm determined to step over both Joseph *and* the guide a few times. And maybe Rob and Jens, too.

We're traveling up the Wogamush River. The river is colored a deep, healthy black all around us from the nearby mangrove swamps. A narrow river only fifty yards across, it meanders so peacefully it seems barely to move. All is lush and vibrant in this country – I've never seen a place so rich, so bursting with light and color. Not even Tahiti had as many rainbows capriciously streaking the sky, or such large white cumulus clouds competing with the gray thunderheads that rise like anvils into the heavens. And the green! Such green, everywhere. The darker green of the wild sugarcane lining the shores, and the sultry green of the rain forest beyond. Best of all, there are no people anywhere. It is an utterly unmolested world.

We stop for the night at a fair-sized village called Biaga, on the shores of a lagoon off the Wogamush. Biaga's huts are raised seven feet off the ground, and beneath them women are cleaning and cutting vegetables. On the raised veranda in front of the *bigman*'s hut sits an enormous garamut drum made from the single trunk of a tree. It's painted with bright yellow and orange ochre, a tortoise carved on one end and a parrot on the other. A young boy plays it for us, the deep beats attracting a crowd, which welcomes us to the village. Jens, seeing some children with gaping tropical ulcers, goes into his pack and pulls out an impressive military first-aid kit filled with bandages and syringes. I take out my own supply of Band-Aids, and we spend the rest of the afternoon cleaning up cuts and wrapping them. I feel like a missionary, but with none of the proselytizing and no huge white house on a hill.

With dusk come swarms of mosquitoes, and we stop and go inside. The mosquitoes in Biaga are the worst I've yet experienced in PNG. The lagoon, while providing a steady source of drinking water even in the dry season, breeds mosquitoes by the cloudful. I sit next to the cooking fire inside the *bigman*'s hut, sweating more than I ever knew a human being could, debating whether I prefer mosquitoes to the heat. It's a hard decision, because mosquito repellent is sweated off so quickly that it's rendered useless. The only alternative is wearing long-sleeved clothes with material as thick as canvas, preventing the *natnats* from biting through. But then the thick clothing makes the heat feel unbearable all over again. Rob opts for the thick-clothing approach until the sweating sends him bare-chested to a smoke seat before the fire. Jens, the hardened warrior, endures it all in T-shirt and shorts, constantly slapping himself. We three eat canned mackerel while choking on the wood smoke and mashing mosquitoes in between bites. My clothes are completely saturated from sweat, and I find it amazing that any humans could live in these conditions for even a day, let alone their entire lives.

The *bigman*'s family laughs at our misery. The men sit cross-legged at the other end of the hut. They swat at themselves with little whisks in an almost unconscious, reflexive way. The men are all bare-chested, wearing only shorts, and I marvel at their ability to tolerate the constant assault of the *natnats*.

Rob, Jens and I finish eating and set up our mosquito nets for an early sleep. I eagerly climb inside mine. Covered in grimy sweat and the stinging traces of Army-surplus DEET mosquito repellent, I lie down and close my eyes, hoping for sleep to come quickly.

I wake up. It's the middle of the night. The front of my net has collapsed, and mosquitoes are freely feeding on my shins. I mash an entire patch of bloated insects, my legs completely covered with bumps. I could scratch my shins to the bone to get rid of the itch. This is Jens's idea of a holiday?

Inspired by his Navy SEAL fortitude, I order myself to stop scratching my legs. Using all of my willpower, I manage to lie immobile. My legs throb, and I close my eyes, listening to Jens snoring in the darkness. I can't go back to sleep, and so I wait for the morning to come.

It isn't long before Rob wakes with a yawn and rolls over to face me.

'You're awake, too?' he says. 'This has been the worst night of sleep I've ever had. I feel like I drank a whole bottle of vodka last night.'

'Yeah.'

'Let's go wash in the lagoon – how about it?'

We quietly leave the hut. The sun is just rising and no one is out yet. Rob strips off all of his clothes and, strikingly pale, dives into the water. I pass him his bar of soap, and he wraps a hand around the log pier and starts to scrub himself.

I look behind me. No one. I take off my clothes and toss them on top of Rob's on the muddy shore. Rob turns around to hand me the soap and catches sight of me. His eyes travel over me, linger on my thighs, my breasts. I don't cover myself with my hands. Since coming to PNG, I've felt the need to hide my body, my femininity, in order to keep myself safe. When traveling, drawing any attention to my gender is to invite a slew of unwanted come-ons – even threats of violence, rape. Better to put on a tough act. To carry a machete and to allow the dirt to stay on my face. Yet now, naked, all of my protective barriers fall away. I'm finally able to revel in my femininity.

I jump in beside Rob. The cool waters of the lagoon luxuriously cover me. We swim about, laughing, splashing each other. I float on my back, my breasts rising above the water into forbidden sunlight. I imagine us as Adam and Eve before the arrival of shame.

The sun dispels the early morning mist from the top of the rain-forest canopy, and now village people start to emerge from their huts. They see us, and wave and point. No one watches for long, though. To them, there's nothing unusual about a man and woman being naked in a lagoon. They go about their morning duties as if we weren't here, and only Jens, leaving the hut, looks shocked when he sees us. But just for a moment. Pretty soon his clothes are on top of ours, and he's jumping into the water.

We're on a small tributary of the Wogamush called Piyowai Creek, trying to reach the Apowasi people, and I don't even know if I could get the days and dates right now. The arching of branches and vines overhead obscures the movement of the sun so that life feels timeless here. Enormous butterflies with wings of blue and green satin flutter and cavort with each other in the patches of sunlight streaming down through the jungle.

Bright red and blue damselflies skim the water's surface, rising in abrupt swirls to settle daintily on plants lining the shore.

The bird life here would please even the most discerning ornithologist. Parrots announce our canoe's approach in a flash of green and red wings. Black-and-white cockatoos, creatures I've only see inside cages, watch us fearlessly from their perches. Joseph points out a large bird with black body, white head and an enormous yellow beak – a hornbill. As it takes off, it makes a loud, propeller-like sound, as if it were a chopper flying off in retreat. Crown pigeons with red eyes, bluish-gray bodies and large tufts of feathers on their crowns, study us from the trees. Alphonso shoots a four-pronged bamboo arrow at one, misses, and the bird flies away over the treetops with a loud whoosh-whoosh-whoosh.

The creek narrows to no more than fifteen feet across, and the water becomes shallow and cluttered with rain-forest debris. Using the outboard becomes hazardous, and we're forced to pole ourselves along. Our progress slows. Dead trees block our passage, and we're constantly getting out of the canoe to drag it over them. When we encounter large tangles of tree trunks, our only recourse is to chop them apart so we can make a corridor for our canoe. This is Jens and Rob's idea of adventure, and they eagerly shed their shirts and take up an axe. I offer my services, but Joseph and Alphonso shake their heads and grin at the idea. Men only.

Fine with me – it's full sun and 90 percent humidity.

'Move that axe a little faster,' I tell Rob from my seat in the wicker chair.

Joseph is concerned about the time it's taking us: not only is it the dry season, but there's been very little rain this year. Our canoe is now starting to drag along the bottom of the creek, making him wonder if we should forget about trying to reach the Apowasi people. He's worried there won't be any creek water left when we're making our return to Biaga. What do we want to do?

Rob is unperturbed. He doesn't mind dragging the canoe back to Biaga if he has to. Jens wants to get to these Apowasi people, see 'people who wear traditional clothing.'

'I'd still like to see the Apowasi chief,' I announce.

That settles it. We'll continue.

It's the late afternoon when Joseph says we've reached the spot where we'll be leaving the canoe behind for a hike through the jungle. The water is so low that we have to pull ourselves up a six-foot-high, muddy embankment just to reach the shore. A ramshackle hunter's hut sits in the midst of an overgrown clearing, birds streaming from the structure as we approach. The sun barely reaches us here, the jungle crouching over the hut, crowding out light so that everything appears in dim, greenish hues. Insects screech and fidget from the reeds near the creek shore. Birds high up in the canopy let out sharp calls. This place feels haunted, as if ghostly eyes of the ancestors stare at us.

We put all of our things in the hut and prepare for the hike to the Apowasi village. I trade my dingy floral-print skirt for the greater mobility of a pair of Jens's swimming trunks, and fill my little backpack with plenty of bottled water. Jens and I take our cue from Joseph and go barefoot, but Rob won't be converted – he wears his army boots, camouflage shirt, and pants.

We follow a faint, muddy path through primeval jungle, trees towering at least a hundred feet above us, vines creeping from limb to limb, hugging trunks and hanging from boughs like gigantic tentacles. Tall, skinny aruka palms compete for light with large red *klinkiis*, renowned for their strong wood, which is used by the locals for making canoes. The competing black klinkiis have wood so heavy and durable that it sinks in water and is used primarily for paddles. Every jungle plant must have its utility in the lives of the local tribes, from the food-giving sago palm to the wild sugarcane used for making mats.

Our pace is unusually fast, as if this were a bushwalking competition. Rob, Jens and Joseph are directly ahead of me, Rob slipping from time to time on muddy tree roots because he wears his boots. Jens, though, seems to be back in Navy SEAL training. He's as adept at this kind of travel as Joseph is, and easily twists and breaks off branches with a flicker of his hand. When Rob slips one too many times, Jens passes him up. Rob, unpleased about losing his place, stays right behind Jens and our pace speeds up even more. I'm reminded of Mozambique, and how all the truck drivers kept trying to pass each other. It must be a male thing.

It's been an hour of this fast-paced jungle hiking. The terrain we travel through is more swampy than hilly, and there are a number of streams we have to cross on the familiar single-log bridges I've come to hate. Jens, capable warrior, crosses after Joseph with hardly a break in speed. Robert in his boots can barely grip the wood and bungles the crossings. I try not to laugh.

The path opens up now. We see a small village on the edge of a large stream. Mountains of rain forest rise to the south, clouds languishing about them, the departing sun already warming the sky and jungle with an orange glow. Everything looks softened, as if a god were resting a gentle hand upon the earth, quieting it, preparing it for rest. The stream travels over stones, which catch the sun's light and cause it to glitter. Naked children chase each other through the water, laughing. They haven't seen us yet. No one has. The village is completely undisturbed; it is the most serene place I have ever seen.

Joseph calls out. The kids playing in the stream look at us, freeze, then run off in terror.

'They never see white people,' Joseph explains.

Jens has his camera out and is snapping pictures of the retreating children.

A man in a dingy, unbuttoned white shirt, wearing a breech-cloth and pandanus leaves around his waist, comes out to greet us. Cassowary claws erupt from the tops of each of his nostrils, and large hoop earrings made from bird quills graze his shoulders. A band of bright red and yellow beads encircles his head. A half-moon kina shell is tied around his neck – surely his prized possession as this shiny, abalone-like shell had been traded all the way from the ocean. These kina shells themselves are so highly prized that the PNG monetary unit is called by the same name.

'This is the Chief,' Joseph says.

'Does he have any other name?' I ask. I'm reminded of one of those patronizing Westerns from the '50s.

'Everyone calls him the Chief.'

The Chief's face is stern as he examines us. Rob points to a necklace he's wearing, made of tulip tree fibers woven about a round piece of wood.

'Mourning necklace,' Joseph explains.

He tells us that the Apowasi people wear a necklace whenever one of their family members dies. The necklaces contain the soul of the deceased, and only once the necklace falls off will the mourning period end and the soul pass on to the spirit world.

Joseph and the Chief chat in a tribal language, presumably about us *waitman na wait meri*, and what we're doing here. They're both laughing heartily.

The Chief says something, and Joseph translates.

'He asks if you want to take photo.'

The Chief holds out his hand. He demands one kina for every picture we want to take of him. Jens has already taken several and pays up. I look at Rob. Neither of us wants to seem like some ridiculous, camera-toting tourist, paying for a photo beside the guy in the Mickey Mouse suit. Yet we *are* tourists. Silly tourists fascinated by the man before us. And this has become a business venture for the Apowasi. It's curious that this isolated tribe knows to collect money from us, as there's nothing to spend it on and the nearest stores are in distant Ambunti. Yet, Western infatuation with money creeps into this culture just as steadily as the introduction of steel and the Gospel did on May River.

We all pay up. Rob stands beside the Chief as Jens focuses the camera. The Apowasi *bigman* looks off in a different direction, not wanting to make eye contact with the lens.

Another man, dressed like the Chief with large cassowary talons sticking out of the top of each nostril, comes forward, asks for a kina from each of us, and poses next to his friend for pictures. Rob uses his Polaroid, giving them both instant shots, and they pass these along to family members who start to emerge from the nearby huts. Jens must be disappointed: none of the Apowasi women are wearing bark-string skirts; all have converted to a cloth *laplap* around their waists and a T-shirt worn threadbare over their breasts. One old woman, however, appears in the distance wearing only a bark skirt, and Jens charges toward her with his camera. I'm embarrassed. I want to apologize to everyone for breaking into the routine of their lives, for not having anything meaningful to contribute except, perhaps, my wad of kina bills.

The Chief and his friend disappear, and about ten minutes later we hear a low-pitched, ominous whooping coming from the nearby jungle. Suddenly the two men burst forth with spears held aloft. Bright yellow paint covers their bodies. Pandanus leaves are tied about their arms and legs. They charge toward us with a sharp holler and I find myself running for my life. I retreat toward the village but am quickly cut off, the Chief's spear only inches from my face.

He smiles. I try to smile back. Thirty years ago, I may have actually been speared. Now he lowers the spear and shows it to me. He insists I run my fingers down the length of its shaft, touch the sharp bamboo point. Jens comes over and tries it out, pretending to be a javelin thrower. He calls Joseph over to translate, and thus begins a heated discussion about whether the spear is for sale and how much it costs. Rob wants a spear, too, and so the Chief's friend runs off to his hut to get some more. It's the Home Shopping Network, PNG-style, spears, bows and arrows laid out for our kina. Jens pulls off his T-shirt and exchanges it for several arrows. The T-shirt

I'm wearing could buy me two spears, but I'm not interested. I didn't come here to buy anything. I just wanted to meet the Chief and ask him to explain what I'm searching for in PNG, why I don't seem able to stop.

I wander off along the stream, watching the mountains growing increasingly pink in the declining light. If I could, I would walk off to those mountains, but with none of the rush and exertion of past travels. This time I would do it slowly, taking weeks, perhaps months, stopping to learn the names of all the plants and insects – the local names, the names that have special meaning to the people. I'd learn how one plant relies on another, how a single seed sprouts and a tree comes into being. I'd start from the beginning, learn about life all over again, if only, by the end of it, I would be able to understand why I'm here in PNG, what quakes of the soul had set me adrift.

Children hide behind the posts of the stilt huts, watching me silently. I'm the perpetual stranger. I hear Rob saying that this place is his idea of 'utopia,' but I don't know what a utopia is supposed to be, or where one could be found. I sometimes think that it is the place where fear and doubt end with the realization that around you is everything you need, and there is nothing else to find.

The old woman with the grass skirt comes toward me and hands me a few of the mourning necklaces she's made. She pats my hand, says something to me, and smiles a toothless grin. Thinking she's trying to sell them to me, I reach for some kina to pay her, but she shakes her head and speaks softly to me in her *tok ples* language. She pats my hand again and I watch her shuffle off, back bent, bare feet following the ground's well-worn path. I am beginning to understand.

'Is she selling those necklaces?' Jens calls over, his arms full of arrows.

'No,' I say.

I walk over to the Chief, and have Joseph ask him about the gods. He may find my question strange: I want to know if the gods are kind.

Joseph translates.

'They are full of mischief,' the Chief says.

'Why?'

'People want many things,' the Chief says. 'The gods hear and give them big gifts, but people don't give a payback. The gods are angry.'

'Can the gods hear us now?'

The Chief points at a bird flying across the stream. 'There. He hears.'

I have Joseph explain to the Chief that I know he has great magic, and I'd like to make a wish and have the gods hear.

The Chief tells me to wait. He suddenly points to a large crown pigeon that has alighted on a nearby tree, and nods. I look at it, make my wish. *I want to find a way to end my crazy searching.* The Chief is smiling slightly. Jens comes over wanting to see the mourning necklaces I've 'bought' and I hand them over, my eyes still on the spot where the bird was. Here in Apowasi village, life is inseparable from magic. The hunter who catches a large cassowary in the jungle has been favored by a god's magic; the little girl who grows sick and dies is the victim of evildoing. But it's not easy for me to believe. I find myself wanting evidence, proof.

It's getting late, and all of our things are back with Alphonso at the hunter's hut beside Piyowai Creek. Joseph wants us to get going, but the Apowasi chief stops us. He will do us a favor. He said he's heard from Joseph about how difficult our travel was up Piyowai Creek. He wants us to have easy travel back to the Wogamush River in our canoe, so he says he will make us rain.

Jens sputters his lips and ties his arrows together with a strip of bark. I'm looking at the sky. A few distant clouds. No sign of a storm. The jungle announces night in the dark red hues of dusk. We've got a jungle to get through, and I'm feeling nervous. I don't want to hike when it's dark out; the jungle makes me feel claustrophobic enough as it is.

The Chief goes and gets a newly cut sago palm branch, closes his eyes, and says some words in a deep voice to

307

evoke the spirit of the water. He opens his eyes and breaks the branch over the river, the pieces floating away in the current. We all watch as they knock against rocks and bob through rapids. The Chief smiles serenely: we will have our rain.

He points at me to tell me the gods have heard – I will also have my wish.

We are nearly to the hunter's hut. I've been waiting for the Chief's promise of rain, and it begins now, like a benediction. Suddenly the wind tears at the trees and lightning flashes. The dark sky wants to drown us. The path below our bare feet disappears with water and I fumble along a trail I can't see, stepping where the person ahead of me steps, feeling for footholds with my toes. The night cracks and booms as we slosh through mud, never knowing what we're about to step on.

Joseph, in the lead, lets out a squeal and knocks into the rest of us as he backs up. In the circle of light from his flashlight we see an eight-foot-long snake traveling across the mud. Poisonous, Joseph says. Even Rob hasn't a calming wisecrack now. We wait in the deluge until the snake passes and Joseph's frail flashlight beam once again bounces off the darkness of water and jungle. We're practically running now. As we wade across a small stream, the water comes up to my chest. I stop, terrified. Rob takes my hand. Cooing to me, he leads me across.

We fumble up to the hut. The rain gushes upon us, and Joseph is telling us to hurry, hurry. Alphonso stares out of the doorway at us, eyes wide. The magnitude of this storm is like nothing any of us has seen, and the night tears at the hut's thatch roof, water streaming in from myriad places. The thunder shakes the wooden foundations and pounds away across the jungle. Alphonso sits with his knees pulled in against him. Rob gives him a friendly pat on the back, but the man isn't comforted. He shakes his head, mumbles something in a language we don't understand. Joseph tells us that Alphonso knew this storm was magic – the Chief's magic. The gods are everywhere, he says to us, shaking.

We all go to bed, rain soaking us through our mosquito nets. If I should be scared, I'm not. Rather, I find myself comforted by the determination of the storm.

Dawn. The rain has ended and sunlight streams through slits in the palm-bark walls. I hear Alphonso exclaiming, and crawl out of my mosquito net to see what he's pointing at. Directly outside of the hut is Piyowai Creek. Where there was once a six-foot slope down to its waters, muddy water now surges past.

Joseph hurries us. 'This is special for us,' he says. 'Chief makes water for us. Normally, the water stay like this for two, three days, but this water is just for us. Chief said we must leave early because the water will go down.'

Our canoe, having risen with the water, floats beneath the stilt legs of the hut. We pull it over and load our things into it. Rob has his video camera out to record this creek turned river.

'Should have asked the Chief to make us some cold Fosters,' he says.

We get into the canoe and shove off. Our work is minimal; we merely let the current take us back to the Wogamush. I'm surprised to discover how swift this current is. How determined. We travel so quickly that even the outboard is unnecessary, and the giant logs that had blocked our way on the approach are now deeply submerged, only the very tips of their branches poking through the top of the water. The sun glares down on us from a cloudless sky, the heat becoming intense, yet we're speeding along as if a great wind were behind us – or a god's hand pushing us along. I'm ecstatic with the feeling of speed.

Slowly, the water returns to where it was the day before. The nearer we get to the end of the Piyowai, the more the bloated creek recedes until finally, like a gift, the current graciously releases us into the great, black spread of the Wogamush River.

'That was special for us,' Joseph reminds us.

Jens adjusts his wicker chair and leans back, eyes closed, face to the sun.

'We could use a little rainmaking back in the outback,' Rob says, beaming.

I sit in the prow, watching the tip of our canoe break the black waters. Reflections of the jungle appear on the river's surface – trees, a bird swooping across a screen of blank sky. The passage of our canoe pulls and distorts the images until they're taken by the waves. Last night's rain might have been a complete fluke. I know this. Yet, I still believe.

CHAPTER TWELVE

Rafting the Sepik

Rob and I want to build a raft and sail down the Sepik River. According to the local people, no one has ever done this before – which is one of the best reasons to do anything. In Ambunti we say good-bye to Jens, who is returning to Germany in order to help train Special Forces units. We watch him from a distance as he tries to get all of his bows, arrows and spears into a small four-seater plane. I've never seen anyone looking as satisfied as Jens, beaming with his booty.

Rob and I hitch a ride in a police speedboat to the nearby village of Kindibit, where apparently we can buy canoes, which we'll strap together to build a raft. Kindibit is small, consisting of a few thatch huts and people unused to foreign faces. The men have small tattoos on their faces, which is unusual: the only Sepik people I've seen so far with facial markings have been women. No one knows English, and for the first time Rob and I must rely on the Pidgin I've been studying. When we explain our raft idea to a group of the village people, they warn us against trying to travel in such a way. Apparently, the Sepik has a current that is often swift and can make the handling of a raft – or any small vessel – difficult, if not dangerous. The closer one gets to the sea, the worse the waves, current and eddies. If our raft capsizes, we will lose all of our things and be lucky to swim back to shore. And of course there is the problem of rascals on the river, robbing and assaulting unsuspecting travelers.

The villagers tell us that they don't take canoe trips alone, and avoid straying too far from their villages as there are long stretches of river with nothing but jungle on either side, and no place to get help if they need it. Incredibly, the rascal problem exists even out here.

Rob and I aren't deterred, though. We know the risks are real, but we're more wary of the future, and the power of regret. We don't want to be stuck with the inevitable questions: What would that trip on the Sepik have been like? What did we miss?

Building a raft is our first dilemma, and Rob applies himself wholeheartedly to this task. From his sudden commanding attitude, I know that I'm to interfere as little as possible. I sit back and let him manage the whole affair. Rob calls me over only when he needs me to use my Pidgin to barter with the villagers. Though I haggle with the men over prices, they always look to Rob for the final word. It's interesting how traveling with a man changes the dynamic of my dealings with the local people. Rob is always the one approached, bargained with, queried, the village men preferring not to speak to me about anything. Culturally, this is typical for the people of PNG: they're supposed to talk only to members of the same sex to avoid being accused of flirting. Yet, I miss being the one in charge, the person who, woman or not, must be dealt with.

Rob's raft slowly starts to take shape; I secretly question its seaworthiness. It's a ramshackle creation composed of two canoes acting as outriggers on either side of a bamboo platform. Some local men help strap the canoes to the platform with pieces of tree bark while Rob puts up a bamboo mast. He doesn't have any suitable material for a sail. Then a revelation: his rain poncho!

'Rob,' I say from my seat beneath a nearby palm tree. 'Is that going to work?'

'It'll work,' he says testily.

But before we can christen the raft – which Rob has upgraded to the category of 'pontoon boat' – and set sail, we need a quick lesson in the art of managing a dugout canoe. The ones Rob has purchased for our raft both have holes in the bottom that have been crudely plugged with clay. The village men assure us that the holes won't pose a problem, but I'm not convinced. I climb into one of the canoes and it sinks significantly. The men run off and return with two Happy Cow milk cans to use as bails, cows grinning sardonically at us from the labels.

'There are some pretty bad leaks,' I tell Rob as I bail with the Happy Cows.

'No worries.'

'Our two canoes are already half-full with water.'

He smiles and pats me on the shoulder. 'Half-empty,' he says.

I still prefer this raft to the alternative: paddling a narrow, unwieldy dugout canoe through swift currents and crocodile-filled waters. Had we grown up with dugout canoes, they might seem more viable – after all, most of the local people, including the kids, can speed around in them with ease. Yet, the vessels so easily tip and capsize on me that I want something more stable, something I can sleep on if I have to.

Our canoes, for all of their holes, are impressive works of art with large crocodile heads carved on the prows; they look exactly like the New Guinea canoes I saw on display in the Metropolitan Museum of Art. The Kindibit artisans must have spent as much time carving the canoes' intricate crocodile head with its sharp teeth, curved snout and bulbous eyes as they did on the other, more functional parts of the vessel. In the West, this might be called extravagance, a waste of time. If the purpose is to create a canoe, why bother with superfluous decoration? But in PNG, time is wasted when one makes something for purely pragmatic reasons because then nothing is honored in the process; one creates an object without meaning. As the crocodile figures in all of the local creation myths, its carved presence on paddles and prows reveals a reverence for the divine, which coexists closely with daily life.

The canoes have been bailed and are ready to go. Rob

and I buy paddles. Rob's *man pull* is made from red klinkii, a wood whose appearance resembles the rich burgundy color of teak. I buy a *meri pull* carved from a large piece of black klinkii. The Sepik tribes carve their paddles from a single piece of wood to ensure strength and durability, and every paddle is unique, a work of art. On the top of mine is a carved crocodile head, polished from handling. The finned tip is finely smoothed and sanded. It's hard to say how much use it's gone through, but the sturdy, dark wood remains undamaged and shiny in the sunlight. It almost seems a shame to use such a beautiful object for the crude purpose of paddling, yet what makes New Guinea art so special is the coming together of beauty and practicality.

As with almost every other aspect of Papua New Guinean culture, the gender roles are distinctly different from each other when it comes to canoe travel. The woman's place is in front, and she uses a special paddle called a *meri pull* – literally, 'woman's paddle.' This paddle is shorter and designed for sit-down use, and usually has a concave end meant to cut cleanly into the water. The man's paddle – *man pull* – is much longer, because the man's place is in a standing position in the back of the canoe. His paddle is sharp-tipped and functions as a rudder. The woman, then, is meant to provide most of the brute strength, while the man in back steers the canoe and helps paddle it forward. The roles are never reversed; a woman in Kindibit tells me that a man would be laughed at if he sat and paddled. Even a lone person in a canoe follows these rules, so that you can tell from far away whether a man or woman is approaching: men will always be standing up, balancing perfectly in even the most unstable canoe; women inevitably sit. All of the women in Kindibit have enormous arm and shoulder muscles as a result, as if they're long-distance swimmers.

Rob and I are ready to try out the paddling for ourselves. We load our gear onto the middle platform of our raft and say good-bye to the people in Kindibit. I take a seat in the front of one of the canoes with Rob standing in back to steer. Amazingly, the slapdash raft seems sturdy and functional. We paddle along the shore for a while, zigzagging and spinning out of control as we try to synchronize our movements and handle the raft. The entire village of Kindibit gathers by the river to watch us and laugh, children chasing after us along the shore. We finally get the hang of it as we enter a bend in the river and Kindibit leaves us. We have the world all to ourselves now.

We're starting to get used to maneuvering our bulky craft. The paddling would make an excellent workout if only it didn't have to last indefinitely. I don't want Rob to think I can't keep up with him, so rather than risk losing my 'Bush Mary' image, I put up with the constant paddling until my arm muscles scream. Rob finally suggests we 'check the canoes for leaks,' and I learn how a man might admit he's tired without losing face.

We both collapse on the bamboo platform. Our raft drifts downriver. There's nothing for it to catch on, and with no sign of rapids ahead, we're unconcerned. Whether we paddle or not, we know we'll keep heading the way we want to go, the world taking care of us. I could lie like this all the way to the ocean. I imagine us floating out toward the South Pacific islands . . . the Solomons, Fiji, Samoa . . . Tahiti. I wonder if the riots have ended in Tahiti, if the French have removed their troops. I can't imagine Tahiti as it appeared in the papers: pillaged, looted, burned. I remember only the flowers – big, bursting hibiscus blooms littering the walkways and blowing down rises in the beach.

The hours pass. We sit with our feet dangling in the water, watching a distant rise of storm clouds that we know won't ever be coming our way. Clear skies tonight, and the promise of a carnival of stars.

Normally, my lazing away an afternoon would concern me. Shouldn't I be accomplishing something? Can I afford to waste an afternoon? But nothing feels wasted now. I'm seeing more of the world than I have in years.

I'm seeing everything. All the little details. The pulse of water against my feet. Wild sugarcane nodding back and forth in the current along the shores. The sun on my face, on my cheeks. Rob beside me, his chest rising and falling with each breath.

The Sepik River rests in the soft pastels of the late afternoon, its waters reflecting the pinkish sky. No one is in sight as we drift down the middle of the river, swirling in slow circles with the eddies. Villages should be coming up if we want to find a place to rest for the night. But if no village turns up, all we have to do is pull over on the shore and camp. That easy.

As the deep orange sun touches the horizon, we paddle ourselves to the shore, to a small, stilt hut. Rob ties up our raft and calls out. No answer. The place appears abandoned. The area around the hut has been cleared away, but the surrounding jungle, encroaching toward the river, drones with the sound of insects. The hut is still in pretty good shape, and there's a pit beneath it where the previous inhabitants must have lit a fire to chase away mosquitoes. We haul our gear inside and collect firewood until it's too dark to see what we're doing. Rob gets a fire going, and we trade the annoyance of mosquitoes for the thick wood smoke.

Rob lights one of his candles. We sit as close as we can to it, hoarding its light. Marsupial rats climb the walls around us, scrounging in our food bag on the other side of the hut. Rob throws a sock at them, and we hear the panicked scraping of tiny claws fleeing across the palm bark floor.

'Not the Ritz-Carlton,' Rob says.

'The Ritz-Carlton would be too boring.'

'Pretend this is veal parmesan.' He drops some canned mackerel into my palm.

'It smells like Taiwanese mackerel caught back in 1952.'

'Might be. Hold still.' He brushes my hair back and, licking the tip of his finger, gently wipes at some dirt on my cheek. When he picks up his bandanna and rubs it across my cheek, I don't want his hand to leave.

Perhaps he knows this. It doesn't leave. It lingers. He looks at me.

'Thanks,' I say.

'I'm glad we could travel together.' He puts his bandanna away. 'I know you like to go it alone.'

'I don't know that I *like* to – it just works out that way.' And now I feel the need to tell him something. 'I remember when I was up in the Himalayas at eighteen thousand feet, the world all around me, in three hundred and sixty degrees, everywhere I looked. It took me two weeks to get up there. And just the incredible beauty of that place, and no one there to see it with me.' I look at him; he's watching me, waiting for me to go on. 'I've come to associate beauty with an incredible loneliness. The two have always gone together. I've hiked through a Borneo jungle, and all of a sudden, before me: the largest cave in the world – imagine the Grand Canyon underground, in some jungle somewhere. And no one else was there with me.'

Rob is silent, nodding gravely.

'I'm just grateful that we can be here in this hut with the rats and mosquitoes, experiencing it together,' I say.

'And you should be grateful for the mackerel,' he says. 'What would this evening be like without it?'

We laugh, choking on the wood smoke.

We reach the large village of Tambunun. Its stilt-legged huts line both sides of the Sepik, and everywhere is the lazy swaying of palm trees. During World War II, Japanese soldiers reached this idyllic village and indiscriminately slaughtered scores of villagers on the northern shore. Now, the Japanese have returned once again – Rob and I see their departing steamship, its giant waves threatening to capsize us. The sight is absolutely surreal: a luxurious ship with a Japanese tour lady on board in starched red skirt and blazer, little white gloves on her hands. The Japanese tourists, dressed in designer, faux-safari wear, find us as palatable a sight as the Tambunun villagers. They crowd to the back of the ship, pointing and recording us for posterity with their camcorders.

'It's an invasion!' Rob says. 'Where are the Australian soldiers?'

Rob tells me that cruise ships are starting to add PNG to their itinerary. They don't stop at any of the big coastal towns, of course, because half of their passengers would probably be robbed the minute they got off the boat. Instead, the fad is seeing New Guinea with the most minimal of contact. Passengers are ferried onto a steamship and, as if they were touring a game preserve, taken as far as Tambunun, where everyone is allowed to disembark to take photos of villagers and buy up souvenirs, turning Tambunun into a mecca of tourist kitsch.

The steamship noisily disappears around a bend in the river, and I want to believe that Tambunun has at last returned to the way it must have looked long before it became anyone's tourist destination – but now an old woman wearing a tulip-bark skirt and a Motley Crue T-shirt is shuffling past on shore. She stops as Rob paddles us against the muddy bank and ties up our raft.

'Hello,' I say to her, smiling.

She stares. Her Motley Crue T-shirt engulfs her tiny body as if it were a dress.

'Never did like the Crue,' Rob says to her. 'Can't stand heavy metal.'

She says something to him in her own language. With no teeth, she gums the sounds and slowly walks away.

'What do you think she said?' I ask him.

'She was telling me to mind my own bloody business.'

A new guest hut sits on the shores of the river, and Rob and I are able to have it all to ourselves. It actually has screened windows and individual rooms with mosquito nets and beds – and a toilet *inside* the hut. The luxury is almost too much for us. The cabinets in the kitchen area are well-stocked with leftovers from a group of Western documentary-makers: Rice Bubbles cereal, mashed potato powder, ketchup. A feast!

Night comes. We sit at a table digesting our Rice

Bubbles and condensed milk, Rob lighting a candle. Crickets and frogs call to each other, creating a barrier of noise outside the hut that increases the feeling of intimacy between us. Rob's face wavers in shadow as the candle's flame shifts in the breeze. He starts telling me about his business back in Australia building Mongolian-style yurts in the outback. He's considered starting up a yurt-building business in Northern California. He prefers canvas-walled yurts. They're economical. Water-resistant. They can be made-to-order.

He suddenly stops talking.

'Let's hear about you for once,' he says.

Perhaps the safety of the candlelight has something to do with his curiosity, drawing out the questions we've both been too afraid to ask. As long as the candle burns on, there is a warm space around us, a sanctuary. I wonder if I can tell him about myself. What does he want to know?

'What about your parents? You haven't said anything about them,' he says.

'Give me another question, Dr Freud.'

He smiles. 'No.'

'What *about* them?' I ask.

'Do they know you're here?'

'No.'

'Have you told them what you've been doing?'

I catch a drip of wax on my finger. 'No. But they're used to this. I've been away from home for much of my life. I went away to boarding school when I was thirteen. They don't . . . it doesn't really matter where I am. They have their own lives.'

'My father would be off his head if he knew my sister was traveling in New Guinea all by herself.'

I force myself to leave the candle alone.

'They didn't try to stop you?' Rob asks.

'They're very laissez-faire.'

'I would have tried to stop you.'

I look at Rob. His large blue eyes reflect the candle's flame. I'm not used to Rob being so candid, or concerned.

'They had their reasons,' I explain. My foot jitters but I can't stop it. I'm scared that he notices. 'I kind of . . . well, things changed. I used to be pretty good at running, and I stopped it. They called it my "ticket." I mean, I was going to be competing nationally. There had even been this crazy talk of my going to the Olympics. I think they were pretty disappointed.'

'And what, so you just quit it?'

I smile. 'I quit. I just woke up one morning and told everyone I wasn't going to run anymore.'

Rob grins. 'That took balls!'

'A lot of balls and about a year of therapy afterwards.'

'Why'd you quit?'

I sigh. So many questions. 'It wasn't who I wanted to be. I told them I wanted to be a writer. Of course they liked that one.'

Everyone has that one subject they don't like to talk about, and Rob has just brought up mine. It's a subject I don't even like to *think* about – all those years growing up with my family's complete lack of faith in me. My trying to love people who had found love too frightening and foreign. People who, as children, had been denied proper love themselves. Now, an adult, I feel like a fledgling beginning everything anew, fumbling for balance, hoping someday to take to the air in a way that feels natural.

I wish I could tell Rob about all of this, but it still feels too difficult for me. Here I am, having come to New Guinea alone, having crossed the country and gotten this far, and I'm supposed to tell him that I actually have *no* idea what I'm doing? That I'm secretly terrified of nearly everything, but most of all, my inability to change? A warning light flashes across my thoughts now: *Don't show him any weakness.*

Rob angrily shakes his head. 'Why is everybody such a bloody expert when it comes to other people's lives?'

I pick off a piece of candle wax. 'Because they're never happy with their own.'

He sighs, telling me that when he stayed in yurts in Mongolia, he realized he could make a living building them back home. Why not? So he began his own business. He doesn't make much money from it, but he's not trapped in a compromised life. He can say without self-delusion that he is doing exactly what he loves to do. That is, to him, success, and the hell with what anyone else thinks.

I smile, nodding. 'Bravo.'

Rob is suddenly delighted: 'I could never talk to my mates about these things.'

The candle keeps burning; our conversation drifts and catches on subjects with the pleasurable randomness of intimacy.

'Tell me this.' He pats my hand. 'Did you leave a boyfriend behind in America?'

'Not really.'

' "Not really"?'

'I was seeing someone but it ended right before I left on this trip.'

'So no one will come hunt me down because I'm with you now?'

I laugh, trying to imagine James – who absolutely hates the idea of traveling – coming to a place like this. 'It's unlikely.'

Rob's eyes look into mine. 'There's this really nice hotel in Wewak. The Windjammer. I'd like to treat you to a night there. I'll get us a room. We can have hot showers, a big dinner . . . spend the night together. Just a suggestion . . . Thought I'd propose it, let you think about it.'

I study the candle's flame. 'I'll think about it,' I say.

We quickly paddle our raft, hoping to reach the village of Moim by sundown. The sun is already setting, though, and there's nothing before us but river and jungle. Since this morning, after leaving Tambunun, we've seen no people or villages, and I'm starting to wonder if we've somehow left the Sepik River altogether. The Sepik doesn't always follow one clear course; over the centuries, local people have literally cut themselves short-cuts in the switchbacks of the river's natural course. And in the rainy season, the Sepik can expand into swampland and cover what was once a peninsula on a map. Lagoons appear and disappear, and a myriad different routes confront the traveler. When our maps have failed us, Rob and I have simply taken the widest course that has a current. Now, though, we're not sure where we are, and the lack of villages is really concerning me.

We paddle into the middle of the river, hoping to avoid the clouds of mosquitoes that have started to descend with the dusk. No luck. They dive at us with the speed of flies. They're nothing like mosquitoes back home, lackadaisically hovering. By the time the dark red sun disappears over the water behind us, we're covered with the insects. Paddling is impossible in the midst of our constant slapping, and we smear on super-strength bug repellent. It comes off as I sweat, though, and the *natnats* bite me with impunity. It's almost intolerable. I wonder what our German Navy SEAL friend, Jens, would have done under these circumstances. I wonder if *any*one, no matter how masochistic, could endure such an assault for an entire night. Desperate, I cover my body with the clay we've been saving to plug holes in the canoes, then put on a pair of Rob's socks doused with bug repellent. Finally, something works.

Getting to a place on shore where we can set up our mosquito nets is our first priority, yet the sun has left so quickly, clouds blocking out the sky, that it's too dark to see a suitable place to camp. We're now floating on a river we can't see, the shores retreating into a blackness so deep that the width of the Sepik looks endless. It feels as if we're drifting in the middle of a vast ocean, unable to hit shore. All light has dissolved, all form is gone. I remind myself about crocodiles, how they prefer to come out at night. I ask Rob where we are.

From somewhere behind me in the darkness, his voice says, 'I don't know.'

I stop paddling. I can't even see my hand before my face. 'What do we do?'

'Don't worry. The current will take us.'

'What if we're not even on the river? What if we're in some kind of lagoon?'

Our raft bobs up and down on this interminable black sea. I pull my legs up against me, trying to steady my breathing as mosquitoes swarm about me, landing on my scalp, my face, buzzing in my ears. The canoe is quickly filling with water.

I sigh, my breath quaking.

'Are you okay?' Rob asks, all humor gone from his voice.

'No,' I whisper.

I don't want to explain why, though – that ever since Mozambique, I've had this fear of the night. Rob doesn't even know I've been to Africa.

I hear him scrambling in his backpack. 'Here's my torch,' he says.

He comes up and hands me his flashlight, sitting down next to me in the dirty canoe water. 'We're moving with the current,' he says. 'There should be a village coming up. We just have to wait and look for lights.' His hand rests lightly on my shoulder.

'I've never seen darkness like this.' I shine the flashlight onto the water. Its feeble circle of light catches on small waves.

'That's because there's no moon.'

My eyes are open, but it's as if they're closed. 'I can't see anything,' I say. I shine the flashlight on my fingers.

Rob shouts into the blackness. No answer.

'I'm going to paddle,' he says. 'You just stay where you are.'

I listen to the smooth *plit-plit* of his paddling behind me, and shine the light out into the night. Wherever the beam strikes: blackness. I shut my eyes. My heart is pounding wildly. This isn't the place or time for me to lose control.

Suddenly, we hear a distant whoop.

'Hello!' Rob yells in return.

We see a flicker of light in the darkness, and I shine the flashlight in its direction.

'Are they friend or foe?' Rob asks in a fake British accent.

I get up now and help Rob paddle. We hear another whoop, only it's closer. Someone in a canoe seems to be heading toward us.

My flashlight beam catches sight of the carved crocodile prow of a dugout canoe. I can make out two young men inside, vigorously paddling. When they see us, they stop and smile.

'Hello!' one of them says.

'We're lost,' Rob says slowly, enunciating each word. 'Lost. Me and Mary.' He points to me.

'No problem,' they say in excellent English. 'Follow us, okay? Our village is close.'

We tie our raft to the back of their canoe and allow them to guide us off into the blackness. I can still feel my heart pounding, and I try to send away the panicked thoughts. *Everything's okay*, I tell myself repeatedly, though this hardly works. I've learned by now that I just have to wait out the feelings.

At last, like distant constellations, village lights appear. I recognize the orange hue of cooking fires. The young men tell us that we're going to a place called 'Kanduanum 2,' and the weirdness of the name doesn't help calm my nerves; I imagine us going to some obscure outpost from which no one ever returns.

Rob's thoughts are less plaintive – he's wondering out loud what happened to Kanduanum 1.

Kanduanum 2 seems a fair-sized village. A crowd of people, a couple of them holding kerosene lamps, gather on shore to greet us. Everyone is smiling and waving.

The village people help us onto shore, and a couple of women come forward to offer us some river catfish for dinner. I pass out fishhooks as gifts, and the village *bigman* escorts Rob and me to the village's official guest hut, an unfinished structure that has open walls and rests like a raised stage in the middle of the village. Strangely, Kanduanum 2 has almost no mosquitoes – it's been blessed by either a very kind god or, more likely, too much DDT.

Rob and I wash the clay and insect repellent from our bodies, and settle down to an evening with the villagers. Everyone crowds onto the platform of the guest house to look at us. As there's a missionary establishment in the village, most of the people know some English, and they tell us old stories about World War II and Japanese pontoon boats making their way past the village. Most of Kanduanum's people were terrified by the sight of such boats; some thought the Japanese were a strange new animal. A few tribesmen claim to have picked off a soldier or two with bow and arrow, and the tribe partook of an exotic new flesh.

I wake up at dawn. Something is wrong. Turning over, I see that my small backpack is resting outside of my mosquito net. I always sleep with this bag under an arm; inside are my wallet, money belt, passport. If I were truly diligent I would wear these things on me, but I've nearly destroyed most of my traveler's checks with sweat. And besides, who's going to rob us in one of these peaceful little villages on the Sepik River?

But there is always a first time. I find that only my wallet has been cleaned out; I am the first foreigner ever robbed in Kanduanum 2. Over $200 in kina was stolen – that's nearly a week of my working in the factory, packaging croutons. For some reason, the theft doesn't surprise me. I slept too well last night, felt too safe. Today, the world is reminding me not to take comfort and safety for granted.

I tell the village chief about the theft, and he looks mortified as if I just announced the death of a good friend. Drums sound out. The entire village is summoned to the meeting house, to appear before Rob and me. *Every*one gathers, which means that somewhere in the crowd is my thief. The village leaders apologize profusely to me. Their shame is genuine, their disappointment communal. Some of the people shout in Pidgin at the crowd. An old woman climbs up a ridge and starts yelling at everyone, tears in her eyes.

The village chief demands that the thief step forward and admit his guilt. No one moves. Because this is a Christianized village, I stand up to give my own speech. I tell the thief that God will punish him. He won't get away with it. He'll go to hell. Yet, if I don't believe this myself, why should he?

I wonder who did it. Is it that young man in the trench coat with the bush knife? Or maybe that sulky boy who keeps glancing away? How to know? Of course, it's impossible to know. But I'm not ready to give up yet. I ask if they have a radio in this village, because I'm going to go and radio the police in Ambunti. I'm going to radio the police *chief*, Felix Sangi, whom I declare is a good friend of mine. He will come out here in his speedboat to find the perpetrator. And when he finds him . . .

Rob calls me aside.

'Don't do that,' he whispers. 'Two hundred dollars isn't worth getting some poor bloke beat up.'

One of the village elders returns to say he used the mission's short-wave radio to contact the Sepik River town of Angoram. He says the police there told him that they don't have any petrol to come out to Kanduanum 2, but if I'm willing to go to Angoram and *buy* them petrol, then an officer will come back and start an investigation.

'I just get all of my money stolen,' I say to the man, 'and they want me to *buy* petrol for the police to come out here?'

Rob shrugs. 'Let's just go.'

It sounds like a good idea. I give up.

We load the raft with our things. As we're just about to shove off, the village leader comes up to me with 40 kina in bills.

'This is a donation for you, Miss,' he says. 'It is from our village. We are very sorry about what happened.'

I look down at the money. It's an extraordinary amount for them, and I'm not used to the idea of one person's crime psychically injuring everyone in the community. I remember last night when they sang to Rob and me. I remember the catfish dinner and the hospitality. Now it feels as if, in one night, Kanduanum 2 has lost its innocence forever. I almost feel responsible. These villagers probably assume I'm wealthy, at least by PNG standards – and I suppose I *am* wealthy here, even if I always lived below the poverty level back home. If I hadn't come to the village yesterday, bringing my money and Western goods, none of this would have happened. The thief wouldn't have been tempted, and the villagers wouldn't be feeling so ashamed.

I look again at the chief's money. I can't accept such an offering; it's too generous, too huge. I'm sure they need it more than I do.

'*Em i nais tumas*,' I say in Pidgin to everyone, telling them how nice the gift is. '*Tenkyu*.' Thank you. But as the chief passes the money to me, I hand it back, explaining I can't take it, that he should give it back to everyone who contributed.

The chief nods and puts the money in his pocket. He smiles apologetically at Rob and me.

'Let's just go,' Rob says. 'There's nothing more to be done.'

'Okay.'

We get on the raft. I start to bail our canoes, while Rob paddles us into the river. The villagers of Kanduanum 2 line up on the shore to watch us leave. Some yell goodbye; others just stare at us silently.

Angoram marks the final stop of our rafting trip. Only a couple more days of paddling, and we'll be there. The river is becoming more and more populated now. Women in canoes come out to greet us, trading watermelons and catfish for my fishhooks. Rob and I can't eat the watermelon fast enough; we have so many that our raft is starting to sink.

The current picks up. Waves splash into our canoes, and I stop paddling to frantically bail. The eddies keep spinning our raft back into the frothy waves, and Rob paddles desperately for the shoreline where the water is calmer. By the time he gets us over there, our canoes are nearly full of water and our raft is starting to sink.

It looks hopeless. We're about to put our things on shore and let the raft sink, but we see two men in dugout canoes approaching from the village across the river. They're balanced perfectly in the middle of their tiny crafts, paddling dexterously across the river's rapids. They look as if they are magically skimming the top of the water, and they wave and smile at us. When they reach us, they help us bail and plug up holes with clay they've brought.

Thanks to them, our raft stays afloat. Rob and I are ready to try to navigate the river again. Our new friends accompany us as we hit the worst of the rapids. They stand with the grace of ballet dancers or high-wire artists in their tipping, jolting canoes, and help keep our raft on coarse through the many eddies until we reach calm water. Neither Rob nor I know what to say to let them know how grateful we are. We offer some watermelons and catfish, and they bashfully accept them.

'*Lukim yu*,' I say in Pidgin. Good-bye.

As we paddle off toward Angoram and the end of our trip, they remain in the river – distant, silhouetted figures watching for our safety. I'm not bothered anymore about the money that got stolen from me earlier this morning. I just keep seeing them in my mind, these two strangers who helped me and Rob get this far. I know that while the world may disappoint me at times, it will also astound me with its grace.

Rob and I sold our raft in Angoram for a pittance. It had been hard to give up. To me, that raft represented a rare sort of peace that I feared would be hard to find again. I had wanted our trip to last longer, and I began to wish that we hadn't actually traveled on a river, because rivers go places. Their current delivers everything to some kind of end.

Now it is Wewak, a large town on the northern coast of PNG. Suddenly there are too many people, too much going on. Rob and I are staying in a youth hostel run by a German expatriate named Ralf Stüttgen, a Papua New Guinean legend. He's in his late 50's, with blond hair, a beard and a red face carved with the deep, telltale wrinkles of a white man who's spent most of his life in the tropics. All backpackers touring the island know of him. His guest house in the mountains outside of Wewak, though inconveniently far from town, is a popular destination. Ralf's place offers what few guest houses in PNG can: a sense of the familiar. People stay in his place, in one of his hot, stinky bunks, because he doesn't put on any airs. In a country based on an exhausting system of niceties and quid pro quos, Ralf charges you for absolutely everything and will tell you point blank to shut up if you're talking too loud.

Ralf's life story would make a good book. Born in the aftermath of World War II, he became a priest and headed to PNG to join the missionary ranks, but he grew disillusioned and left the priesthood, marrying a local woman from, coincidentally, Kanduanum 1. She died while giving birth to their daughter. That girl, now thirteen, subjects the hostel's inhabitants to the blasted pop tunes of *Roxette's Greatest Hits*.

Ralf tells me that a woman hasn't stayed in his hostel for months. Even Roxette sounds surprised: '*Well, she's a miracle . . . yeah, yeah . . .*'

I ask who else is staying here, and Ralf says that in addition to the two Israelis who are now sitting at the other end of the table, there's a man named Chris who sleeps in 'the closet.'

'The closet?'

He points to a small door at the far end of the room. 'There's one bed in there. Usually, no one sleeps in there, you know. You can't stretch your legs. But he wants his own room.'

'The man in there is crazy,' one of the Israelis tells me, tapping his head.

Ralf shrugs and orders his daughter to get out her math homework.

'He never leaves,' the Israeli says. 'Two weeks I'm here, and I never see him leave that room.'

'Is the bloke alive?' Rob asks. 'Any rotting smells?'

Ralf puts a large ledger book down in front of us. 'I don't think either of you have something better to do, so please sign my guest book.'

I open it up and glance at the years of entries. Most are in German, French, English. There are a couple lonely ones in Japanese. Pages and pages are filled with scribbled advice for future travelers: where there's good food in Wewak, or good diving, or 'primitive tribes.' I've seen these books in youth hostels all over the world, nearly every country being conveniently reduced to its must-see attractions and hygiene problems. And here before me now: someone making a recommendation about where one can find native women who don't cover their breasts.

I take out my pen and begin my own entry.

To Whom It May Concern –
Only four words of advice: it can be done.

As I pass the book to Rob, the closet door opens. A man with a striking resemblance to Beethoven steps out. The name 'Chris' registers in my mind. Chris!

He's thinner than he was in Cairns, but he still has the same wild blond hair that flies up from his temples. Everyone in the room except for Ralf is gaping at his wondrous appearance, but he sees no one as he shuffles outside to the toilet.

'I know him,' I say to Rob.

'That bloke?'

'I met him in Cairns, right before I left for PNG.'

The Israelis get up and go to the closet, peering inside as if it were a troll's lair. Rob and I join them at the doorway. We're not greeted by anything too exotic, just a sweaty, musky smell and lots of clothes strewn about the floor.

Ralf is still sitting at the table, reviewing his daughter's math homework. 'If Chris wants to sleep in the closet, you know, I let him sleep in the closet. Why not? It's not my business.'

His daughter stares at us peering into the tiny room. 'He's been here three weeks,' she says and looks back at her homework.

'Is he your boyfriend?' one of the Israelis ask her, walking over to ruffle her hair and turn down her music. 'Your music is terrible, do you know this?'

She turns it up again. 'You don't know good music,' she says, smiling. 'So shut up.'

We all sit back down again. Chris returns. He closes the door and eyes all of us shyly – I don't think he recognizes me yet. To our incredible surprise, he joins us at the table. He takes out a journal, which he has almost completely filled with writing, and begins to write. His hand doesn't falter for a moment. He doesn't look at anyone. If it's possible for a human being to disappear before one's eyes, then Chris has just disappeared.

With my own journal to write in and pages of text I must get down, I join him. We're like marathon writers, Chris and I, competing with each other as the evening hours pass. He must have had a childhood like mine, his notebook acting as best friend and confidant, always clutched under an arm like a favorite teddy bear. I imagine a closet in his house back home in – Germany, was it? Palm Beach? – filled with journal after journal, the childhood block letters giving way to the longings of adult cursive. I wonder if he also writes because he must, because to stop for even a day would be to risk insanity.

Across the room, Rob is annoying the young Israeli men by recounting tales of our trip down the Sepik. They're not interested. They don't need his advice; they will figure it out for themselves, maybe do an even better job. Rob is too kind-hearted and oblivious to notice their annoyance, though; it's his gift – a man who understands and forgives people before he even knows why. He wants to help them out, give them suggestions though they keep cutting him off. He returns again and again to details of our journey to find the Apowasi witch doctor and our subsequent raft trip, his friendly, melodic voice like a balm. I settle down to the familiar refrains as I write.

Exhausted, I stop writing and look up at Chris, still pulling his pen across the paper. For a man who has spent the past three weeks in the closet of Ralf's hostel, I wonder what he could possibly have to say. Yet, the pages are tumbling over with words. His long forehead creased in concentration, his thin hair hanging limply over his shoulders, he holds his pen so tightly that I can see the whites of his knuckles.

'Chris,' I say.

He still writes.

'Chris. Hey.'

The pen stops and he looks at me. His eyes seem clouded.

'Do you remember me? We met that one time in Cairns. Remember?'

'In Cairns?' He looks puzzled and slightly embarrassed.

'You were looking for a woman . . . you'd asked me for suggestions. I think you said you wanted to find someone who wouldn't love you for your money.'

He narrows his eyes for a moment. 'Yes,' he says with a tinge of a German accent. 'I remember now.'

'How has it been? Did you find her?'

He smooths a hand across the journal page he was writing on. 'Not yet.'

'PNG's been no good for that?'

He sighs and sits back. His intense blue eyes meet mine. 'I'm still looking,' he says. 'Can you suggest any places here?'

I don't want to tell him about my Fiak to Hotmin Mission hike, how the jungle can so easily kill a person. And he shouldn't know about the Blackwater refugee camp and all those people who saw their family members killed, their daughters gang-raped. There must be some pleasant place I can tell him about.

I suggest he head to the Apowasi tribe off of the Wogamush River, where it was amazingly beautiful, and where the women didn't seem to have any need of money.

Chris's eyes study a corner of his notebook. His fingers keep turning the pen round and round.

Rob's curiosity has peaked, and he leaves the Israelis to come talk to the strange man who's been living for weeks in Ralf's closet.

'Where are you from, Mate?' he asks, pulling up a chair.

Chris's hands are clenched. 'Florida,' he says.

'I've never been there. What do you do back home, then, Chrisy?'

'I travel,' he says.

'Yeah, but your job, Mate?'

His face is turning red. 'I travel.'

'Your job is traveling?'

'No.' He glares at Rob. 'I don't have a job – I don't need a job. I travel.'

Rob leans back and smiles broadly. 'How do you manage that? Did you win a contest?'

Chris winces. 'My parents,' he says. 'Money is not a problem. Money isn't the issue.' He puts his pen down and centers his gaze on Rob. 'I'm looking for a country where there are women who won't love me for my money. I want them to love me for myself.'

Rob looks over at Ralf, but he's helping his daughter with her math homework. He looks at the two Israelis crouched over a detailed map of the Sepik River. He looks at me, finally, and I bite my lip, saying nothing.

Rob guffaws. His laughter fills the room and causes Ralf's daughter, though weak from a recent bout of malaria, to glance over in curiosity and delight. The Israelis are shushing Rob, but he's laughing so hard that he can't hear them. Tears fill his eyes and stream down his cheeks.

He manages to contain himself. 'It's hopeless, Mate,' he says. 'The kind of woman you want doesn't exist.'

Chris's face is turning nearly as red as Rob's now.

'They don't exist,' Rob squeals out, wiping his eyes. 'Believe me – I *know*.'

'I'll find out for myself,' Chris says.

'All women *want* is a man's money, Chrisy.'

I hit Rob but he winks at me.

Leaning back in his chair, Rob cracks his fingers. 'It's hopeless, Mate. What I would recommend for you is a life as a monk. Join the cloister. Take your vows and devote yourself to a life of celibacy.'

'Do *not* do that,' Ralf's voice booms out from across the room.

Rob has run out of patience, and gets up. Stretching, he points at Chris. 'The cloister for you, Mate.' He gets himself some coffee in the kitchen.

'But the country must be safe,' Chris whispers to me, leaning forward. 'I can't look in a country that's not safe. This country is not so safe, you know? It's dangerous here.'

I nod. He's right.

'Wewak is very dangerous,' he says.

'Have you gone there a lot?'

'One time. It's too dangerous. I have to leave this place.' Tears are coming to his eyes.

'It's not dangerous everywhere,' I tell him. 'If you go to some remote place . . .' But I'm not convincing even myself. PNG *is* dangerous. Almost too dangerous. In a way, we're all mad for being here – Ralf included, a former priest who merely shrugs off a recent armed robbery at his place.

Chris is sitting here looking at me, desperate.

I hear Rob chuckling as he stands by the stove. The Israelis are busy planning their foray into the Chambri Lake region. Chris is probably incomprehensible to all of them, but I think I can understand him. Sort of. He probably compares his life to everyone else's all the time. He probably sees all the happy couples out there, and perhaps it annoys him that their happiness and genuine love seemed to have come so capriciously, so effortlessly.

Maybe they met each other in a class, at a party, at work. That easy. Yet he must search the *world* for someone.

Should I tell him to just go home already? But then I would have to tell myself the same thing. And it's too soon to go home. I haven't found what I'm looking for, either.

I tell Chris to keep looking. I hope the tone of my voice sounds encouraging. He nods his head. Smoothing down the page of his journal, he picks up his pen and starts writing again.

It's the next morning. The closet door is open, the tiny room deserted. Chris has left. Ralf says he's not sure where Chris is headed. All he knows is that he wanted to get out of Wewak as soon as possible, so he left at dawn.

I take a PMV with Rob into Wewak for the lunch he's promised me at the Windjammer Hotel. Wewak sits right on the sea, its oceanfront streets lined with neglected palm trees that leave a legacy of rotting coconuts on dusty esplanades. One senses that Wewak *could* be special if only someone got mobilized. Instead, everyone seems to be wandering the streets without discernible purpose or destination. Wewak, harmless and lethargic, rests like a drunken relative left to himself in a back room. The Windjammer itself, posh and well-guarded, remains an incongruous oasis of Western luxury and convenience in the midst of this town of corrugated iron shacks and poverty.

In the Windjammer's dining room, we order everything we'd been craving during our raft trip. For me, french fries with lots of ketchup. Rob orders steak and a Fosters – and two glasses of red wine. As our food starts to come, Rob is quiet. He wants to know if he'll ever see me again.

I look off through the plate-glass windows at the ocean. Gray waves tumble across the beach. Seagulls hover and dive at scraps as the waves recede. All I have to do is say yes. And what would happen then? Rob would book a room for us. I would have a hot shower, air-conditioning.

We would have clean sheets and an entire night before us.

I hear a voice I haven't heard in a long time, the voice of that Tahitian man, Coco, back in Papeete, *Tu as peur, non? I think I scare you.* Rob takes my hand from across the table. His fingers press into mine. *Tu as peur.*

'Do you mind if I hold your hand?' Rob asks.

'No.'

He pats my hand, half-lovingly, half-paternally, and sighs. 'Your type,' he says, 'the independent, crazy types going off into the world – they always think they need to be alone.' He smiles softly. 'Am I right?'

I shake my head.

'Then spend the night with me,' he whispers.

But I haven't traveled far enough yet. Just a little further. I'm not who I want to be yet – the past still catches me. I'm still that little girl who must single-handedly prove herself to the world. But now Rob would like to burst in, disrupt it all, guide me out. That would be too safe. Too easy.

'Will you spend the night?' he asks me.

Outside, the ocean surges and breaks against the sand. I remember the image I'd had of Chris back in Cairns as he walked away down the street, continuing his search. I can't explain any of my feelings to Rob. They would make no sense. He wouldn't understand.

'I can't,' I say. 'I'm sorry.'

He pats my hand. 'No worries.'

'I can't.'

CHAPTER THIRTEEN

Time Travel

It is Madang now. The town sits on the eastern coast of PNG, and had been so heavily bombed by the Japanese during World War II that barely a building was left standing. Now, fifty years later, the expatriates sentimentalize the place, calling it 'a tropical paradise,' PNG's 'nicest town.' It rests on a peninsula that juts out into a calm, azure sea famous for reefs and getaway islands. Madang looks as if it's never seen a war; only the wrecks of bombers littering its harbors and beaches recall the Pacific struggle in which some 15,000 local people lost their lives while assisting the Allied forces. It's amazing how much can happen in so few years – at the turn of the twentieth century, Madang was nothing but a tiny outpost founded by German colonists, nearly a fourth of whom died from malaria and dengue fever. The Australians took control in 1920, flourishing here for two decades until the start of World War II. Suddenly the Australian presence provoked Japanese attacks, and the local indigenous people, expert seamen who piloted large, impressive canoes, were initiated into the modern world of air wars and bombing raids.

It's still hard to believe that such a war could have had the audacity to disturb Madang's turquoise waters and bougainvillea, its palm trees arching toward thick blue skies. Yet World War II was far-reaching, and sent Australian civilians fleeing as far inland as May River and the central Highlands. It saw Port Moresby threatened and Wewak leveled.

There seems to be no way to get away from modern times. I'm still caught up by the idea of finding the 'untouched' Papua New Guinea that hasn't been defiled. Such a place would be my idea of paradise. No air wars or bombing raids. No intrusion of technology. I equate such a place with peace – true peace. That simplicity of existence. Maybe it's too late? Maybe the missionaries and mapmakers, the gold hunters and explorers, have done their job too well, forcing every last corner of New Guinea into modern times? The Apowasi people were the most remote of the tribes I visited, yet they knew enough to ask for money and to want T-shirts. I'm starting to think that the New Guinea of my imagination can't possibly exist, that it would take nothing short of time travel to find that unmolested world.

I don't think I can leave this country, end this journey, without seeing the images that inspired this trip in the first place. I remember looking through all those issues of *National Geographic* as a kid, studying the artists' renderings of towns in the Andes or Fertile Crescent, cutting out photos of the broken statues of gods resting in the dirt and decay of aeons – sublime, incomprehensible faces staring up from desert graves. Such mysterious wisdom in those images. Such hope.

I've been told about a place called Tari, and it will become my very last destination. It's one of the final stops on the long Highlands Highway, a road that meanders west, hitting most of the major towns until it gives way to a dirt track and scattered villages. Tari has legendary status in Madang; supposedly the people haven't changed since the audacious gold-hunting Aussie Mick Leahy first stumbled into them in the Highlands in 1933. They still wear traditional dress, still engage in tribal warfare, distrusting outsiders of any kind, particularly whites. To go to Tari, I'm told, is to actually go back in time.

As is typical for PNG, however, getting to a place like

Tari by road is like playing a game of Russian roulette. This is what I know: tomorrow there are a couple of PMVs that will be making the eleven-hour journey up to the Highlands town of Mt Hagen, and from there, to Tari. But tomorrow also marks the biweekly payday weekend when people drink away their wages, gangs of rascals go on the prowl and most violent crime occurs. I consider when I should leave. Common sense tells me to wait until after the weekend and see if any more PMVs plan to make the long trip. But I don't feel like listening to my common sense. I'm too eager to keep moving, to leave Madang, to see Tari. I feel as if all my decisions are in the throes of some force beyond me that dictates my every move, as if I were trying to catch up with my own wandering spirit.

If one *must* leave on this day, then the strategy is to leave as early as possible and to arrive at one's destination before dark, when most of the paychecks have been distributed and the rascal gangs get out of control.

Road travel in PNG is very sensitive to the rascal problem. The more experienced, savvy PMV driver will have an arbitrary formula in his mind to decide whether he should make a trip. He'll add up such factors as the time it takes for rascals to get drunk, steal money, carjack a car, decide to set up an ambush on an outlying road. He will add in other variables, such as the weather discouraging or encouraging them; he will consider how many ambushes have recently occurred along a given stretch of road and what the likelihood of another could be. The conclusion he comes to will determine whether or not he'll go. In many cases, he'll decide to chance it – after all, the paycheck is good, the PMV isn't his, and the fares paid by the passengers belong to the boss; it's not his problem if the rascals beat people up, rape them, steal personal possessions. Just as long as *he*'s not beaten up, raped, robbed.

I must decide whether I'll take a PMV to Mt Hagen tomorrow, on payday. My stomach does leaps. I'm getting sick of having to make these kinds of decisions. Could such a drive be any riskier than what I've already been through? I know only one thing: the world will do what it wants with me, regardless of the choices I make.

Walking back from downtown Madang, I stop for a minute and sit down on the side of the road. I know I'm getting sick with something. A strange lethargy. Dizzy spells. My whole body aching.

I get up and head over to the office of the Lutheran guest house where I'm staying. The Canadian caretaker eyes me suspiciously when I ask her if there's a doctor in town.

'What's wrong with you?' she asks. A stern woman with her hair in a bun, she sits beneath a crucifix of a Jesus with weeping eyes.

'I don't know.'

'There's lots of tropical things a person can catch.'

I feel like a sick animal that's wandered into her fold, one she doesn't want to have to deal with. 'When I turn my head, my neck hurts,' I say. 'And I've been getting really faint.'

'Could be anything. I can't make a diagnosis.'

'I'm just wondering—'

'When we really need to see a doctor, we go to Australia.'

I nod. Australia.

'There's a clinic nearby,' she adds, writing down directions and quickly slipping the paper across the desktop as if I were a leper.

I keep expecting the missionaries I meet in PNG to be in some way the exemplars of humanity, people who should make me feel unworthy and humble by comparison. After all, they're here to save souls, to bring people living in 'darkness and sin' to the grace of redemption. The truth, though, is that they're like anyone else. Tired half the time. Not in the mood.

I head over to the clinic. It's an open-air building with dirty, whitewashed walls covered with a few yellowing posters recommending abstinence and encouraging the health of children. Along two walls are benches filled with people. Local women in *laplaps*, holding crying babies, stare at me as I enter. Young women, feverish and quivering, pull weighted eyes up to glance at me. I see an examination table at the other end of the room, and an Indian doctor pressing a stethoscope to the chest of a screaming child. There are a few scattered boxes of medical supplies on a shelf by the examination table. Gauze, bottles of antiseptic cleaner. I don't see much in the way of actual medicine.

One doctor for all of these people. A nurse comes up to me and says that the wait is very long. She wants to know what's wrong with me, if it's urgent. I glance at everyone else, at the children delirious with malaria, the jaundiced men, lying on their sides and clutching their stomachs. I wonder what they would consider 'urgent' here.

'No, it's not urgent,' I mumble.

I return to the Lutheran guest house, going to my room to try to sleep.

I wake up in the middle of the night. The heat covers me like a second skin, sweat soaking my clothes and the sheets. My head pounds from a bad dream. The usual: people coming after me in some vaguely recognizable world. I quickly turn on the lamp and look out the window, convinced that I'm back in Tabubil again, a man staring at me from a corner of the window.

Nothing.

You're in Madang, I remind myself. *You're in Madang*.

Still, I look for his eye in the blackness, in the very corner. There's nothing but the thick, thorny bushes covering the window.

I get up and pull on a skirt. I douse my face with cool water from the sink, my hands shaking. Slowly, I unlock the door and open it. No one outside. The dark hallway is completely empty. There's a lounge area at the end of the corridor, and I go there, flicking on the fluorescent lights. Insects flock to the hissing bulbs, circling and crashing into them. A clock says 3:15 A.M. I sit down on a chair, refusing to go back to my room as if the nightmare still lingered there. When my dreams frighten me, there is nothing else I can do but rest my head on my knees with a light on and wait out the dawn.

The office door suddenly opens and a night watchman peers fearfully inside. He sees it's only me and smiles.

'I thought you were a rascal, Miss,' he says.

'No.' I put my head back on my knees.

'You okay?'

'Okay,' I say, but I can't look up.

'You need help?'

'I'll be all right in a minute.'

'I am outside. If you need help—'

'Thanks.'

He leaves. I wait for my heart to calm, my breathing to quiet. At last I raise my head. I see a reflection of myself in the glass window across the room. The night behind it frames me. I stare at myself: drab, flower-patterned skirt, blonde hair over a gray T-shirt, tired face.

'You should be going home now,' the reflection says to me.

I stare at the dark eyes.

'You can end this,' it says.

But the nightmares still come. And the panic. I had hoped, at least, to defeat them. To find a place where I can stop, get better. Change.

The reflection looks at me solemnly and I can't greet its gaze anymore. I get up and walk over to the guest house's shelves of books, pulling out a poetry anthology. Leafing through it, my eyes settle on a poem by Gerard Manley Hopkins called 'In the Valley of the Elwy.' I'm caught by the last three lines, which seem more like prayer than poetry. I sit down to mouth them over and over again. The tears come, and I can't do anything about them.

> *God, lover of souls, swaying considerate scales,*
> *Complete thy creature dear O where it fails,*
> *Being mighty a master, being a father and fond.*

If it's Russian roulette to get up into the Highlands by PMV on a Friday payday, then I'm ready to play, to see what life will do with me. I want to get to Tari and see New Guinea as it used to be. I'll go as far as I can today – and, I hope, all the way to the town of Mt Hagen.

My head and neck throbbing painfully, I leave the guest house after breakfast and walk down deserted streets to downtown Madang's PMV stop. I find out that all the earlier PMVs to the Highlands have left already, meaning that I've already increased my chances of being ambushed as I'll end up in the Highlands during the risky hours of the late afternoon. I buy a seat in a rickety vehicle and wait for twelve more passengers to come along to fill it up.

A man sitting next to me, Martin, works for the national airlines and speaks excellent English. He says he's only going as far as the Highlands town of Goroka because it's too dangerous to go as far as Hagen on a payday evening. What about me? What's my destination?

I put yet another bullet in my imaginary revolver. 'Mt Hagen,' I say.

A middle-aged woman in a ragged T-shirt and skirt approaches our van. She looks through the window at me and babbles in Pidgin.

'Just ignore her. She's mentally affected,' Martin says. 'Many people in Madang are mentally affected. I get sick of this place.'

'What's she saying to me?' I ask him.

'She wants to know where you put her pig.'

'Where I put her *pig*?'

'She says you are hiding her pig and she wants it back,' Martin says.

'Well, tell her that I'm sorry, but I don't have it.'

He yells this out the window to her, and she shouts something in reply.

'She says she wants it back.' He shrugs.

'I think she's mentally affected,' I say.

The crazy woman continues demanding her pig back even as our van finally fills up and we're ready to head toward the highway. She runs after us as we pull away, hitting her hand against the bumper. When I look back at her, I see that she's glaring at me and furiously mouthing words.

'The people in Hagen are worse than her,' Martin assures me.

I nod. 'Something to look forward to,' I say.

We cruise along the coast for a while, then abruptly head west, into the foothills of the Highlands. This will be a trip from sea level all the way to Mt Hagen at nearly 13,000 feet, which means a tediously long uphill trip. I soon start to understand why we're so susceptible to rascal attacks and ambushes – we're now groaning along at ten miles an hour up a steep, muddy road with thick jungle bordering on both sides. The other passengers look nervously out the window, their eyes trained on the forest. Every few minutes, someone points out a spot along the road where he or a friend or family member has been ambushed; the rest of the passengers, losing their fear to morbid curiosity, crane their necks to get a good look at the spot. Inevitably, the violence stories ensue.

I'm starting to see a pattern in these former ambush spots, noting that they're all on particularly steep, unruly patches of muddy road, usually right before a curve. Understanding this, I'm starting to see choice spots all over. Music blasts from our car stereo – Bon Jovi wailing at over eighty decibels – as if to tempt hiding rascals to a feeding frenzy. My headache pounding to the beat of the music, I rest my machete in my lap and close my eyes, remembering being in Mozambique on its Bone Yard Stretch. I've learned this much since then: if someone's coming to get me, there's not a hell of a lot I can do about it.

At last our PMV groans up what appears to be the last of the uphill climbs, rascal ambushes much less a threat. Luck, I see, has been on my side. The road curls around a mountainside, and I look down at a vast valley full of cropland and villages. This is the valley the gold-hunting brothers Mick and Dan Leahy must have seen for the first time in 1933, which they captured on film. Now, more than sixty years later, the valley remains an overwhelming testament to the agricultural sophistication of the New Guinea tribes whom many anthropologists believe were planting and harvesting their own vegetables long before the rest of the world. Before the Leahy brothers had made their discovery, Westerners couldn't believe that the rugged inland mountains of PNG leveled off anywhere, and that such a series of fertile valleys could exist at over 10,000 feet, feeding a population of at least a million people.

The population has grown dramatically since then, tribes now uncomfortably close to each other as they thrive on the rich agricultural land, lack of mosquitoes, and cool climate. I no longer see a landscape that in any way resembles the coastal areas of PNG. The highest parts of the Highlands have no jungle; instead there are grassy plains, even pine trees. I try to get used to the odd juxtaposition of banana plants under conifers. Mt Wilhelm, the highest peak in PNG, rises to nearly 15,000 feet and occasionally sees snow – hard to believe, considering the suffocating heat and humidity of the lowland jungles.

The people themselves look quite different from Lowlanders, and are reputed to be much fiercer. Most have very wide noses and sharply protruding brows and cheekbones. The men grow large, bushy beards and wear hand-woven Highlands caps, which sport fuzzy cuscus fur. The women, many with tattooed faces, carry long, colorful *billums* on their backs, the carrying strap going around their foreheads. Nearly everyone is remarkably short here, most of the men not even nearing my height of 5'7". Some Western scientists theorize that the Highlanders' short stature is due to inadequate protein in their high-starch diets. Could be, but these are also the most powerful-looking people I've ever seen.

Beside the road, I watch men playing darts or selling rolls of housing material woven from *pitpit* stalks, the muscles in their arms and legs bulging like a weight lifter's. The Highlands Highway has become their lifeline, breathing modernity into a place that has only existed to the outside world for some sixty years. They seem to cling to the road's asphalt borders in much the same way a tribe settles by a major river. This highway brings in goods, offers convenient transportation and a means of meeting others. Yet perhaps more importantly, this road *leads* somewhere, can actually be followed all the way to the sea – which is no small matter, considering that the sea is their connection to the rest of the world.

We drive through village after village, mountains rising in the distance, their tops basking in the clouds. No one worries about rascal ambushes anymore. We've now reached the land of tribal fighting and blood feuds, of paybacks and retribution. Martin tells me that few pay attention to the law out here, and that it's not uncommon for two warring clansmen to start hacking each other on the streets of Hagen. Whether or not he's telling the truth (and I wouldn't be surprised if he was), different rules seem to apply here. An all-pervasive feeling of instability fills me, as if a single rock thrown too hard in one direction will send any semblance of Moresby-style law-and-order running for its life under a torrent of spears and arrows. For me to understand the Papua New Guinean Highlands, I know I'll have to start all over again in my thinking.

Whenever our PMV stops to unload or take on passengers, I notice the women on the streets, silently watching the crowds of men greeting our PMV. When our van pulls out, they continue trudging barefoot along the asphalt road with their heavily loaded *billums*, backs bent forward under the weight, the strap around their foreheads preventing them from turning their heads. As our PMV passes, they gaze at me with expressionless faces.

A Highlands woman, Regina, is now sitting next to me, and she greets me in perfect English, telling me that she works in a missionary craft center.

'What are the lives of women like in the Highlands?' I ask her.

She tells me that women are considered less important

than men. Sometimes they're sold for a few pigs; if they're unable to have any babies, they're often ostracized or discarded by the husband or tribe. Her face tightens. Rape and domestic violence against women are not only widespread, she explains, but sanctioned. If a woman oversteps her marital boundaries in some way, the husband has no qualms about hitting her. Polygamy is common – she herself was one of three wives, though she recently divorced her abusive husband and now lives in the missionary settlement where she works with battered women.

'Do any of these women ever fight back?' I ask her.

She smiles and looks at her lap. 'No,' she says. As if she'd told me something embarrassing. I can tell she hasn't had an easy time.

We approach Mt Hagen. Assorted shops line its busy roads, advertising car services and Western products. Crowds of rowdy young men are gathered along the highway for no discernible reason: 'Payday,' Regina explains. We turn into a parking area where herds of PMVs breathe out clouds of diesel exhaust into crowds bartering for seats. Women in floral skirts, wearing ballooning *meri blouses* with large *billums* hanging down their backs, stare at me as I step out of the van. They don't seem to know what to make of me, as though I were some exotic animal a magician had just conjured. PMV drivers ask me where I'm heading, following up their queries with more juicy questions: Am I married? Where is my husband? When I tell them that I'm not married, that I'm traveling alone, they shake their heads in disbelief and tell their friends. I become the focus of a large crowd, and Regina comes to the rescue, offering me a ride to the downtown in her friend's waiting car.

She drops me off at a hotel where I phone a popular, affordable guest house, the Haus Poroman Lodge, for free pickup. This lodge is located several kilometers outside of Hagen, on the top of a small mountain, where it escapes the violent reputation of Hagen's streets. Before long a van comes to greet me. The driver, a slight man with a warm smile, introduces himself as Pint (pronounced 'Peent'). He loads my pack into the vehicle, and we leave the chaos of Hagen for the peaceful countryside, where wide valleys end before long trains of mountains. This land could inspire even the most discerning of the Romantic poets as the setting sun gently highlights fields of grass and wildflowers, bees flitting in the orange rays.

'Where did you come from, Miss?' Pint asks me.

'Madang.'

'By plane?'

'PMV.'

He tssks and shakes his head. 'Did you have trouble with rascal boys?'

'No,' I say. And add: 'Maybe next time.'

Lying on the seat beside me is a magazine out of Australia, *New Idea*. I pick it up and gaze at the bold print on its cover that reads, 'IS YOUR DOG NEUROTIC?' Crazy First World worries.

My sickness is getting worse, but I must get to Tari. I must see that other world. Early in the morning, I board a PMV heading to the town of Mendi, the next major stop on the Highlands Highway. I'm told it's normally a dangerous stretch of road, rife with tribal fighting, but today – my luck! – it's Sunday and they're having a respite from the violence. My stomach stops doing the usual nervous flips, and I allow my machete to take a rest inside my backpack.

We pass through the grassy landscape of the central Highlands without incident, reaching Mendi by noon. It's a small, comfortable town bordering an airstrip, the last stop on the Highlands Highway before the asphalt road turns into a neglected dirt track creeping westward toward Tari. The trip to Tari takes at least seven hours, and as there's no way I can get there today, it's Mendi for the night.

Downtown Mendi consists of a main drag with a couple of banks, various all-purpose stores and the Muruk Hotel's popular bar and restaurant. The local expatriate population of Chevron workers and Australian soldiers seem to have taken over the town, many of them glancing at me with curiosity as I pass them on the streets.

Changing a traveler's check at a local bank, I'm befriended by an Australian couple, Pat and Janine Walker. They're both teachers at Mendi's International School, and Janine, wanting to hear about my travels, invites me to a party this evening called 'Calcutta Night' at the local Australian Army Club. Usually this club is the private sanctum of the soldiers, but tonight civilians – particularly female civilians – are encouraged to share in the festivities. Janine promises plates of chicken wings and endless beer, and I find it an easy offer to accept.

For the first time since I attended church with Ursula back in Moresby, I find myself concerned with my appearance. And such a strange place to be concerned with it! As I step out of the compound of the Pentecostal guest house where I'm staying, tattooed people in *meri blouses* or ripped T-shirts glance curiously at me in my dress pants and clean pullover – clothes I had to dig out from the bottom of my mildew-reeking backpack. I actually managed to get a brush through my tangled hair tonight. The skin on my arms glows red from the thorough scrubbing I gave myself. For once, I'm clean and pressed, almost presentable.

I meet Janine in front of the gates of the Officers' Club and a watchman ushers us inside. We enter a rustic-looking room filled with a raucous crowd of soldiers and civilians. I feel disoriented, and not just because of the fever I have and all the Tylenol I've taken to try to combat it. I can't make up my mind which world I'm in now – the world of Mendi I left behind at the guarded gate to the compound, or the world I'm now entering, posh and comfortable, filled with people from a similar culture. It occurs to me that during my entire time in PNG, I haven't met a single expatriate who has lived as the local people do, hanging out among them exclusively.

No one seems willing to completely abandon where they've come from. Every expat, from the Larsons on May River to these soldiers stationed in Mendi, create microcosmic worlds for themselves within the larger world of PNG, and I wonder if they ever get a certain panicked feeling as they ponder for a moment where they are and how they got there?

Janine leads me into a large lounge area with a television up on the wall, and I feel nothing but the crowds of eyes upon me. I smell the acrid bite of beer, see the uniformed men inspecting me. Who am I? Where did Janine find me? I'm uncomfortable in crowds and quickly accept a beer. Once again, I feel that familiar anxiety to please, to seek approval from strangers I'll never see again in a few hours. But I don't want to play that game anymore. I've been too long without such a burden, reveling in the freedom of dirt on my face and tangles in my hair, and the knowledge that I needn't concern myself with fears of the past.

The whole gathering, I discover, centers around Australia's celebrated Melbourne Cup horse race. At one end of the room is a large board on which the soldiers have written their bets, which are constantly reconsidered and revised. Janine hands me a sheet of paper with a list of the names of the twenty-three horses due to run, including their histories and odds of winning. I glance at the list though I'm unable to bet because I'm a guest (and a guest with low finances, at that). The odds are daunting, yet these soldiers' average bets are in the hundreds, even thousands, of dollars. Perhaps that's why I don't see any PNG nationals in the room – many of the soldiers' bets are much more than a local person can expect to make in a year. I imagine one of the tattooed women I saw on the street, witnessing someone nonchalantly betting away the equivalent of her yearly income. It would probably seem unconscionable to her.

But this is a different world, I remind myself. I'm not in Mendi anymore, or, for that matter, PNG; the value of money mysteriously changed as soon as I passed through the guarded front gate. A few hundred dollars here is negligible, like spare change.

I finish my beer and a tall man, a general manager of one of the banks in town, immediately goes to get me another one. He's an attractive Aussie named Danny, a thirty-five-year-old who has lived in Mendi for a few years.

'What brings you to this town?' he asks as he hands me a new bottle.

'I'm just passing through,' I say.

'And what do you think of PNG?' His soft brown eyes stare out at me from a face that seems creased with exhaustion.

I consider his question, but it's too hard. Too enormous. It's one of those questions that can only elicit a pat answer, so I tell him, 'It's a pretty amazing place.'

He nods, swigs down the last of the whiskey in his glass, and gets up for another. When he returns, he clears his throat.

'You traveling alone, then?'

'Yeah.'

'Aren't you scared? There are lots of places I try not to go to in this country. Hagen, for instance.'

'It's been difficult,' I say. I'm starting to feel dizzy.

He looks at me and sips his whiskey. For being a large man, easily over six feet high, he seems shy, like a schoolboy. 'When do you go home?'

Home. I haven't even thought about it in any serious way. I refunded my return ticket back when I was in Port Moresby. 'I need to see Tari first,' I tell him.

' "Need" to?'

'I hear it's like going back in time.'

He rolls the whiskey in his glass, smiling slightly. 'That's one way of putting it.'

A soldier stands up to make an announcement about the race, and Danny quickly turns his attention to the betting list. I finish my beer and go to get another one. It could be the fact that I'm feverish, or that the Tylenol and beer combination are doing strange things to my head, but I suddenly feel detached from life, like a kind of phantom. I stare at the giant betting board with a soldier standing in front, making amendments. The people in the room seem ghostlike, obscure.

I return to my seat beside the Walkers, and glance at the betting sheet. It blurs before my eyes. Suddenly, I know who will win. I'm absolutely certain. My finger stops at a name on the first page. *This one.* I read horse number six: Doreimus.

I like the Walkers and want them to make some money, so I tell them that Doreimus will win. They should bet all their money on number six. They smile at me and say that while his odds are pretty good, so are the odds of several other horses. They've already placed their bets and they won't be changing them.

'But Doreimus will win,' I say. I feel the same sense of awe that I did right after the Apowasi witch doctor had made rain for us. I'm absolutely certain, would bet my life on Doreimus winning it.

I turn to Danny, who is still glumly gazing at his betting sheet, and tell him to bet all his money on Doreimus. He blushes. 'I've already bet,' he apologizes.

'Change your bet. Doreimus will win. Trust me.'

He looks at me with concern. I've slumped in my chair. The world is in swirls around me and goes black for a moment. Suddenly Janine is guiding me back to the other world of Mendi, to my closet of a room in the Pentecostal guest house. 'Do you know you have a fever?' she's saying to me, touching my forehead. 'The poor girl has a fever,' she tells the night watchman, who opens the door to my room and helps me inside, onto the bed.

'Put your money on Doreimus,' I tell her.

'I'll take you to our doctor tomorrow,' she says.

I wake up at dawn. The headache is still around, as always, but now my throat is so sore that it hurts to swallow. I eat a few cookies until the pain isn't worth the sustenance. Still, I can get up, function. I take a few Tylenols, determined to get to Tari.

I sneak out of the guest house before the night watchman can see me and ask how I am. I don't want to be told that I'm sick, even delirious, and that I ought not to be going anywhere. I just want to be going. Moving. I want to find this place. The early morning streets of Mendi are deserted. A few hens peck at the dew-covered road, a gaggle of chicks following behind them, peeping. A lone man, old and hunched over, stops his walk along the side of the road to watch me pass. When I look over my shoulder at him, he's still standing there, staring at me. Assessing.

I head to the street in front of the airfield where the PMVs to Tari are supposed to arrive. No vehicle has come yet, so I sit down on the side of the road. I pull out my machete and rest it beside me, leaning against my backpack to wait. As the sun starts to spread cool yellow rays across the dirty pavement, the first vans arrive. People with bundles join me, and some drivers usher us to the proper PMV. I put my backpack under the seat and sit down with my head against the cool window, machete sticking out of my day pack. Slowly, the van acquires passengers.

From across the street, two men get out of another PMV and carry a small girl between them, her entire upper body in a cast. They drop her in the aisle of the PMV, and she gazes up at me from the floor with scared eyes. The girl's mother raises her as if she were a mannequin, depositing a piece of banana into her mouth. She chews slowly, watching me as the van pulls out and we're on our jostling way to Tari. I smile at her, but she just keeps chewing and watching. It feels as if the entire world is watching me. I rub my temples. My head pounds, my vision dulls from the intense pain.

Our PMV slowly climbs higher and higher. We leave sight of all villages, cross a river and greet a stark, rocky landscape. The air is getting thin and cold, and I'm glad for the relief from the fever burning in me. A soft, freezing rain starts to fall, and my breaths come out misty. I clutch my arms together inside my pullover. The little boy sitting next to me leans against my side, enjoying the added warmth until his father accosts him, telling him to get off the *wait meri*. The girl in the cast remains immobile in the aisle of the PMV like a giant papier-mâché doll, her face expressionless, her eyes studying me. Always studying me, as if she were a statue come to life.

We're so high up that the peaks of nearby mountains look low, as if they were merely hills. Strange, sharp-pointed plants resembling joshua trees rest in nooks in the rocky plain. I see very few trees, the landscape having the appearance of a high desert where only the most hearty species can survive. I can barely recall the stifling heat of the jungles of the Sepik region. My forehead throbs with piercing regularity, and I lean down to avoid fainting. I'm unable to turn my head, the pain in my neck is so excruciating, and I imagine myself back in one of my childhood adventures. There were a lot of them like this, me incapacitated, dying from thirst on some deserted island, only to be rescued at the last moment by some sort of wizard or fairy godmother with a glass full of some kind of rejuvenating elixir. The imaginary character would always help me up and raise my chin, pouring the magical drink down my throat. Saved. That easy. Like some kind of miracle.

The little girl in the cast stares at me from the floor – our faces are a few inches away from each other. She mumbles *wait meri*, smiling softly.

At last the dirt road is curling out of the featureless, uninhabited high plains of nearly 11,000 feet. We head downhill, and the pine trees return. The sun peeks out of the cloudy sky and warms the land. Outside I start to see groups of people walking along the road in bark-string skirts, their faces painted. No more Western clothing. We gape at each other as the PMV passes, and I wonder if I've taken too much Tylenol. More people like that now! Men bedecked in huge, plumed headdresses, their faces painted red.

I look around to see if there's some special occasion, a reason for the spectacular dress, but I don't see any tourists anywhere. No one with camcorders or Nikons. These local people, dressed entirely in traditional clothing, are looking exactly how they've *always* looked. This must be their everyday dress.

Our PMV takes a rest stop near the outskirts of Tari, in this grassy, barren country of the upper Highlands. I get out of the van to look around. I must be having a hallucination: the impressively dressed characters out of my youth's imaginary adventures are now crowding around me, as surprised by the sight of me as I am of them. Little boys, dressed just like the men in bark breechcloths with tanket leaves hanging over their buttocks, come up to me to touch my pullover and feel my skin. Women with their faces painted red, yellow and white, wearing bark-string skirts, *meri blouses* and brightly colored handwoven scarves and *billums*, feel my hair and mumble exclamations to each other. Black dots start to take over my vision and I lean down. The women tssk and hold me up. Little girls stroke my arms.

A woman with a bright yellow face steps forward to hand me my water bottle: the magic elixir! I take it greedily, but my throat hurts too badly. I can barely swallow.

Several men wave the women away and inspect me. They wear an assortment of bead and shell necklaces, have quills or bone through the septa of their noses and enormous headdresses of feathers and beads billowing out from either side of their heads like fantastic Napoleon hats. I can tell how much they value ornamentation as I see no man without a headdress and body paint. The headdresses themselves probably differ as much as the men's personalities do. Some men decorate them with ferns, bright red bird-of-paradise feathers, mountain flowers. One young man, the most innovative of the group, wears a beautiful headdress fashioned from a deflated soccer ball. Other men adorn themselves with attractive remnants from the Western world: frilly balls of plastic wrap, aluminum foil armbands, scraps of bright cloth. Bubble wrap, by far, seems the most coveted material, many men sporting necklaces and headdresses made from it.

The time travel feels complete as I stare at these people dressed in their tribal clothing, carrying bows and arrows. I start to walk among them, and they pat my head, stroke my hair. I can see the buildings and houses of Tari far down the road, but they look too much like the beginnings of a typical PNG town. I turn the other way instead, admiring the dress of the people around me and the vastness of the landscape. I sit on a rock by the road, certain I will never pull myself back up again. This place is perfect and complete. There is nowhere else to go.

A great wave of dizziness overtakes me. The woman with the yellow face once again pushes the water bottle toward my mouth. I try to drink, but all the imaginary lands from my childhood rush back. I feel as if I'm in that spot in the desert Southwest again, standing on the Four Corners, only this time anything seems possible. I'm no longer trapped in a single world – I'm finally able to be in several different places all at once. I can go anywhere and do anything. I have unlimited power! I want to tell them all about this power, explain the extraordinary changes occurring in me, but my throat hurts too much to speak. Maybe I'm experiencing magic. *Their* magic? I have finally found the one place in the world where magic truly exists.

Everyone is moving away from me, and the kindly expressions on their faces have changed. I want to ask them where they're going, but they're too far away now. I see a ferocious-looking man in the distance running toward me. He carries a machete, his eyes glaring white through the thick red paint on his face. My body petrifies. I can't even breathe.

He waves his machete wildly and calls to me, and I'm sure he wants to kill me. I have no doubt about it. I am about to die. I manage to move my legs and run. But where? How to escape? I head toward the familiarity of the PMV, struggling to open the door and get inside. The crazy man has come too fast, though, and he grabs my arm just as I'm about to squeeze inside.

'Miss!' he says. He catches his breath. 'Look, Miss!'

I'm shaking, waiting for the final blow. The black dots try to take over my sight.

Instead, he shoves a newspaper in my face. Yitzhak Rabin has been assassinated! he wants me to know. He points at the front-page story, which tells me that somewhere far away from the thick jungles and 14,000 foot Highlands of PNG, in a place called Israel, Rabin has been shot dead . . .

I look at the man, at the bright red face and the pig tusk through the septum of his nose. He smiles in apology for having scared me, and puts his machete under an arm in order to shake my hand. The hand is warm and strong in mine. He leaves me with the PNG *Post-Courier*, and I watch him walk away, the tanket leaves rustling over his buttocks. I know now what I have refused to believe for most of my life: there is only one world to be found – this one I'm in. A world where some men wear headdresses, and where others, like Rabin, are shot dead. If there is a truly 'untouched' place, then it exists only in my imagination. Paradises are a state of mind; they don't actually exist, sitting just out of view like a finish line to be reached – a salvation. This whole trip appears before me like a terrible mistake, an act of incredible naiveté. I sit down, dizzy, exhausted. I must erase all the file-box stories of my youth, all those imaginary worlds promising an ultimate peace and transformation if only I travel long enough, go far enough. There had been so much hope sustaining me, and now it all feels gone. I don't know what I'll do without it.

I glance down at the paper to see that Doreimus has won.

CHAPTER FOURTEEN

Hands and Feet

'The Koogka and Opoka are at war with each other now,'
the driver, Willy, wants me to know. He leans casually
against the dented white PMV van. 'They leave each
other's hands and feet on the side of the road.'

It occurs to me that Willy waits, smirking, because he's
expecting me to show surprise or disgust – to show
something – and not want to make the trip from Mendi
back to Mt Hagen. But I've just come all the way from
Tari, and nothing in this world surprises or scares me
anymore. I lean down to adjust a strap on my backpack.
If there's violence, better I don't know about it. Better
not to know anything.

Feverish, I wipe the sweat from my face and lean
against the van as a bout of dizziness comes on. All
around me, the Highlands town of Mendi nonchalantly
goes about its business. Women wearing colorful *laplaps*
around their waists head to market balancing baskets on
their heads. Men in holey shorts loiter on the street
corners, their black skin gray from the dust of the streets.
With my eyes, I follow the main road of town as it skirts
the airstrip and heads off into the murky distance toward
Hagen. I try to convince myself that the Koogka and
Opoka are at war with *each other*, not me. Their fighting
is none of my business, and so maybe they won't bother
me with it.

Willy still waits, determined to prevent me from going.
I again try to get in the van and he blocks me with his

hand. 'It is very dangerous,' he says, as if I've missed the point.

But what Willy doesn't know is that I am now incapable of being astonished by much of anything. Rather, I'm smiling. Hands and feet on the road. God, what next? The other people waiting in the PMV smile back because violence – as long as it's happening to someone else – is a hysterical subject for most PNG nationals. Humor is how they cope, and the cheer volume of violence stories complete with bizarre twists (someone getting his ears cut off during a robbery, say) tests one's capacity to believe. But you must believe, because suddenly Mr Galo walks down the road without any ears! And everyone knows why.

I want to tell Willy that according to the laws of probability, I'm not due for another robbery or assault for at least a few weeks, as my money was so recently stolen in Kanduanum 2. Of course this incident is barely worth mentioning at all except to say that surely my odds are slightly better in the case of armed robbery.

But I sense that none of this would matter to him. He is determined not to let me go. He keeps running a smooth black hand up to pat his hair, trying to delay me for as long as he can so my seat will be taken. And because I'm used to being delayed, am conscious of being a strange sort of phenomenon as a lone white woman traveling around for no discernible reason, I'm patient with him.

I ask again, calmly, if I can get into the van.

Willy clucks his tongue. 'But, Miss, it is very bad. You are tourist, too. No good. They will see you.'

A 'tourist'? I stopped being a tourist the minute I set foot in a country where they like leaving hands and feet on the sides of roads. I can't help thinking that Willy *wants* the combatants to see me. Having a violence story to tell about a white woman caught in a Highlands battle could be the stuff of legend. Anyone seeing Willy could ask him for that juicy tale about a young American woman falling prey to warring tribes. Violence stories involving tourists are notorious – which probably explains why tourism is essentially nonexistent in PNG.

I remember one particular story. The Swiss Couple Story. An Australian expatriate had eagerly shared it with me when I was staying at Ralf's place up in Wewak. A man and woman from Switzerland had decided to come to Papua New Guinea to hike the famous Kokoda Trail through the jungle. They were newlyweds, and that was their dream, hiking the very trail the Japanese made during World War II to try to defeat Australia's stronghold in the Pacific.

They almost made it across. Almost. It was one hell of a trail. Downpours, heat, leeches. Toward the end, they camped out a bit too late into the morning and some rascals found them. The couple woke up to a gun in the face. Of course, they were robbed. (At this point, my Australian storyteller gasped and shook his head.)

'One of 'em was raped. Guess which one?' he said.

I shook my head.

'Guess!'

I told him I'd rather not guess.

'The *man*! The bloke was raped!'

I don't know why, but the tale of the Swiss couple stays with me. Perhaps because of the Australian man's reaction, his obvious shock that, with a young Swiss woman right there, they had the audacity to rape the man instead. I was reluctant to admit that I rather liked the fact that PNG violence doesn't discriminate.

Willy is telling me again that it is not the place for a white woman inside this PMV. Where is my husband? I'm alone? But the Koogka and Opoka are at war with each other, he wants me to know. The route we are taking, the only road there is, takes us through the fighting.

What Willy doesn't realize is that I've been seriously sick for a week, a fact that leaves me both stubborn and strangely irrational. I *will* get in the van. I *will* get to Mt Hagen, to the Haus Poroman Lodge, which is the only place in PNG that knows how to make chips. I swear to God, all I care about is having a big plate of french fries with ketchup. I'm dizzy, my head pounds, I can't turn my neck without excruciating pain, yet my appetite is mercifully intact. I will risk my life for those chips.

I pull out my foot-and-a-half-long machete from my daypack and show it to Willy. 'I'm armed,' I say.

Which reminds me that owning and wielding a machete is an extraordinary thing: suddenly, quite unexpectedly, I feel a part of the PNG fraternity of self-defense. Interestingly, no one yet has regarded it as surprising that a young white woman should walk around the towns and villages of their country with a large bush knife in her hand.

Willy, I see, is on the verge of relenting. He fingers the dirty blade and hands it back.

'Okay, yes,' he says. 'Get in.' And because I do start to get in: 'Oh . . . they are fighting, Miss.'

The Papua New Guinea Highlands are perhaps among the last places in the world where tribes still regularly fight. The idea still strikes me as preposterously unreal, but then again I've had trouble defining reality ever since yesterday in Tari, when I almost got mauled by a man wanting to deliver breaking news.

I climb inside the van, stuffing my backpack under the front seats. There is only one woman passenger inside, and for her presence I'm grateful. I can talk easily to the women in PNG, while my small talk with men is often misinterpreted as flirtation. She moves over to let me sit beside her, extending a tiny hand to help me get in. She is barely an adult and her *meri blouse* is pulled down to accommodate a baby at her breast. We smile at each other and she introduces herself as Deomi, because in the Papua New Guinea Highlands everyone is polite. Everyone introduces himself or herself, calls you 'brata' or 'sista' unless you're at war, in which case – as is my understanding now – your hands and feet are chopped off and left on the side of the road.

'And they take the stomachs, too,' Willy now adds, practicing his school-learned English. His voice is loud: he is proud of his English. 'They will cut off everything, you know.'

This comment, once translated into Pidgin, sends squeals of laughter throughout the van. I realize I've missed something, haven't been paying atention. *They cut off everything.* Everything . . . oh, yeah. I get it.

'You've seen this?' I ask, incredulous, tired of the bravado. His ever growing list of body parts makes me suspicious.

Both Willy and the man beside him nod.

I rub my pounding temples, and use a sleeve of my T-shirt to wipe the sweat from my face. 'When did you last see this?'

Willy tells me he sees it often. The latest time was just last week. This war, Willy says, has been going on since the early 1980s. He thinks it was started because a Koogka man killed two of an Opoka man's pigs and never offered any payback.

I sit back, anxious for the feeling of motion to begin. Our van finally pulls away to the familiar asphalt road that heads east to Hagen.

'You will see the battlefield,' Willy says, his voice too loud, even with the engine going. It occurs to me that I'm a novelty now, entertainment for him and the van's passengers.

'We're going to pass a battlefield?' I ask.

'Yes, it is by the highway.'

'We're going to see these people fighting each other?'

'Of course. They make their own guns now.'

Our entire conversation is translated. Someone makes the suggestion that I should crouch down in my seat whenever we approach any of the combatants. A general wave of nodding heads agrees: if there is trouble, the fighting men could, at the very least, rob me of my backpack if they see that I'm white.

'Crouch down,' I repeat.

'*Sindaun*,' the man beside Willy says in Pidgin, as if I didn't understand the English.

I'm reminded of the cheap Westerns I used to watch as a kid. *Heading into Injun country. Don't light no fires.*

'If they stop us,' I ask Willy, 'will they kill us?'

He laughs then translates my comment into Pidgin for the rest of the passengers in the van. Almost everyone laughs.

'They just look for enemies in the car.' He points to the woman breast-feeding her baby: Deomi. 'Like her. Her wantoks are Koogka.'

'*Ah, em i meri. Wait meri,*' the man beside Willy says of me.

'He says that you're a woman, though. A white woman—'

'I know what he said,' I snap. I know what he means.

Our van shudders as it hits higher speeds. The road looks new, the yellow dashes bright. I wonder if the road builders with their asphalt and steamrollers were delayed by skirmishes.

We speed along at sixty mph, the grassy hills of the central Highlands careening past. I'm still surprised by the look of the Highlands, by its grassy fields and pine trees, after having trudged through the lowland jungles and swamps for so much of my stay in PNG.

Deomi tells me that she is from Mt Hagen. She has wantoks in the Koogka tribe. She knows that, if caught by the Opoka, they'd kill both her and her child, but there is only one road to Mt Hagen and her father is dying.

Strangely, Deomi doesn't seem nervous. In Western countries violence is a reason for fear and outrage, but in PNG it is as common and accepted as natural disaster – *is* a form of natural disaster, is just as cruel and capricious. Deomi sits silently and pats her baby, perhaps trying to divine the turn of the weather outside.

The little Toyota van rattles at seventy mph. We stream by burnt villages, by groups of men carrying machetes and axes, dressed only in breechcloths of red cloth and what's called 'ass-grass': a few thick tanket leaves hanging down their buttocks. This is, Willy explains in his best English, voice raised as always, their 'battle dress.'

He smiles and points to an empty stretch of yellow grassland: the traditional battleground. He's excited to show it to me because the fighting is none of his personal

concern. Most of the people in the PMV help point to it –
a carload of tour guides save for Deomi and one other
man. The eyes of these two, like mine, are fixed on the
scene in front of the van.

Because a group of the young men are now standing
in the middle of the highway, not moving. I crouch low in
my seat. The PMV slows, our momentum fizzling. More
men in ass-grass materialize from behind a tree and
congregate around a telephone pole, machetes raised.
Deomi reaches over me and locks the van door. She
shelters her baby's head with the palm of her hand.

Some of the older combatants have quills or pig tusks
through their noses. They stand barefoot in battle wear
on the newly paved and painted asphalt road, over the
yellow lines that tell a driver not to pass.

'Opoka,' Willy says, as if he were a safari guide pointing out a new species of animal. He's still smiling in
excitement. 'Do not worry.'

I crouch lower in my seat. Deomi's baby doesn't make
a sound. Willy applies the brakes in a series of jolts. Our
motion is almost gone. The adrenaline rushes into my
limbs, washing away the sickness and oblivion. It makes
all of my senses acute, has a strange way of making me
conscious of each breath. I forget, for once, my unrelenting headache and fever. Being sick is trivial. I eye
my machete, but it has become worthless. It rests in my
bag as a useless talisman, a trinket meant only to ward off
fear. I'd be a lunatic to use it now against several fully
armed men. My hands are violently shaking. Maybe this
is it – the end to all of my searching? I've been too lucky
up to now, and the laws of probability are finally catching
up with me. Getting out of Mozambique was supposed to
have taught me to value my life, yet here I am again,
risking it. I shouldn't even *be* here in this country, in this
tiny little corner of the world, yet I'm here and it's too
late to change anything. Much too late.

Willy rolls down the window. Knowing he possesses at
least three lives, he addresses the men in a very loud,
pompous voice.

'*Yupela stap gut?*' he asks, wanting to know how they are.

And how would men be in the middle of a war? They mumble some rough responses.

Willy isn't discouraged. '*Mi laik baim wanpela tair,*' he says.

Smiles. Happiness from the men. Have I heard Willy right? One young man races off. We watch his form getting smaller as he cuts across the battleground into a clump of bushes. I am still crouched, along with Deomi, in my seat. My heart has a will of its own and is pounding desperately. The men outside are peering in and my title, *wait meri*, is exchanged. Me, I'm used to sticking out everywhere, but do they recognize Deomi and her baby as one of the enemy? Apparently they know, can tell either from recognition or the subtle differences in tribal appearance.

The young man returns holding a tire on top of his head. Further to his left, a number of ass-grassed warriors charge an unseen party, engaged in what seems to be the proper business. We all wait. The sound of a gun goes off and a wisp of gray smoke rises above some distant trees. Willy negotiates the price of the tire. Every time a man starts to look into a window of the van, Willy becomes irate and puts the car in first gear. Forty kina are exchanged and the tire is slipped into the vehicle beside my backpack.

We pull away.

The van shudders again at sixty mph. Some ass-grassed warriors further down charge us as we speed past. One of their machetes hits our van with a heavy *clunk*. The people inside cheer at the failed attempt, looking back at the attackers. Willy, I notice, is adjusting his rearview mirror. He shakes his head.

'Close, those men,' he says, smiling and clucking his tongue.

My fellow passengers are mimicking the warrior's charge with the knife, trying to capture the essence of the attack, to master the movements. It is important that they get it right for future retelling, so there is a lot of correction and practice. Deomi, I see, has her head against her baby's chest and is silent. I peek out the window for signs of hands and feet on the side of the road. Nothing. Only the grassy fields of the Highlands encroaching upon the road, threatening to overtake the new asphalt.

I try to stay calm as the van rattles and drones. I can't figure out why I've been spared again, why those men, who could have easily stolen my things and pulled me out of the van, didn't. What am I being taught? Surely there's a lesson in the fact that I'm still alive.

As we finally approach Mt Hagen, I ask Willy why they didn't pull me or the Koogka people out of the car. Didn't they recognize their enemy? Of course they saw I was white – and a woman, I growl.

'Oh, yes. They knew.' We swing into the dusty spread of cinder-block and corrugated-iron dwellings that compose much of Hagen. Barefoot, half-dressed tribesmen curiously surround our van and stare at me as always, at the lone *wait meri*. Willy explains that he'd recognized those Opoka men, that they were friends of his and he'd needed to buy a tire from them.

'With us in the car?!'

Willy smiles as if at a small child, as if to tell me that I haven't learned the rules yet. And he's right. I haven't. I am hopelessly bewildered.

He talks slowly, patiently. 'They know if they take someone I don't give them forty kina for the tire.'

Of course. I nod. Only where they can wear ass-grass on asphalt. I wonder what might have happened if Willy hadn't been interested in any business deals, but to wonder such a thing is craziness. Wondering about anything in PNG is to create fear, and fear – not violence – is the real enemy. A person can become immobilized by fear. An entire country can shut down from it. Better to smile and count blessings over the changing of the storm. Better still: don't count anything at all.

Getting out of the van, I become aware again that I'm

sick. Too sick for all this traveling business, for hands and feet on the sides of roads and adrenaline-rush highs.

Deomi greets an older man. Her father? She smiles and waves good-bye to me, polite to the end. She says it was nice meeting me.

I tell her, good luck.

I sit down on a curb in downtown Hagen and watch the rush of people pass. I'm unable to move, and I don't care if people stare at me. My body tries futilely to sweat away its sickness, failing. My clothes are soaked. The haze of my fever gives a shiftiness to everything, as if the scenes before me were being pulled and tugged. I watch fetid dogs nuzzle the ground, pawing at scraps. They glance at me and sniff at my backpack before moving on, tails wagging restlessly. They are as enigmatic as the people walking by, women with tattooed faces and colorful *billums* hanging down their backs, men frowning as they carry machetes and walk barefoot down the road. Do any of them care about hands and feet on the side of the road? Should they care?

The world is giving me no answers. I kick at the dirt below my feet, watching plumes of it rise and be carried away in the aftermath of speeding cars. I want to know why I made it back here safely. If some god kept me alive for some reason, then I'd like to know what the plan is. I think it's my right. I can't go on like this forever. Going through tribal fighting and war zones, through jungles that would kill me. I told myself that this trip wouldn't be a repeat of Mozambique, yet I realize now that it is. I just took another huge risk with my life. But I haven't been miraculously transformed into someone 'better.' I am the same as I always was. Which makes me wonder what was wrong with me in the first place.

I look around, as if the passersby could answer my question. And now it comes: there hadn't been anything wrong with me. Didn't I know that?

The knowledge descends upon me. I feel amazement coupled with a growing anger. Anger toward the people in my childhood who never had faith in me, but a seething anger toward myself. For believing their dismissals. It is so easy, as a kid, to believe the people around you. And that belief, once ingested into the mind, holds stubbornly.

An old man missing one of his legs limps by on crutches. A couple of young girls in sundresses, hands clinging to their mother's skirt, study me as they pass. I am kicking my hiking boots again and again into the dirt of the road, sweat rolling off my forehead and marking the dust. Such fury now. I've never experienced this kind of anger, and I don't know what to do with it, how to get rid of it.

I put my machete inside my backpack. Pausing until a feeling of faintness goes away, I get up and head toward the worst area of town. My head and neck throb, and my throat is so swollen that even breathing pains it now. Good. I walk slowly, with calculated steps. Young men standing in front of buildings taunt me as I pass, and I slow down even more, glaring at them. I will give them plenty of time, a perfect opportunity: here I am. I could take them on.

Nothing.

I enter a grassy park I was specifically warned not to go near. I see people in tattered clothing wandering about, muttering to themselves. I see gangs of crouching young men glancing and pointing at me with sardonic grins. In the distance, a man in grimy clothes starts heading in my direction as if he knew me, as if we were old friends. Here it is. I'm not scared, am being consumed by this strange, liberating feeling of anger. I walk straight toward him.

Now he's in front of me, stopping me with his hand. He's middle-aged, has graying hair blooming on each temple. I look down at his bare feet, at the torn black T-shirt and dingy brown pants he wears. I wipe the film of sweat from my face and wait expectantly for him to try to hurt me.

The man smiles. He waves his hand in greeting.

I do nothing but wait.

'Hello, Miss. Are you lost?' he asks.

I try to answer, to tell him that I know exactly where I am, but my voice won't come out through my swollen throat.

'You are lost, I think,' he says. 'It is dangerous here, Miss.'

I nod. I know.

'Please,' he says, his brown eyes connecting with mine through the dizzying, feverish haze. 'Please follow me.'

His cool hand touches mine and I jerk it away from him. Now he rests his hand gently about my wrist, and I don't do anything. I can feel my anger fading, stranding me. *To have come all this way . . .* I look around me. I see the rascal gangs, and notice that I'm very far from the safe area of town.

'It is dangerous here, Miss,' the man says. 'Come with me.'

This time I don't refuse. I follow him, surprised that it takes no effort. The man guides me as if I were a sick child not to be left unattended, his voice cooing to me. I have no idea where we're going, but suddenly it doesn't matter. I'm not concerned. I remember the Apowasi witch doctor promising me that the gods would hear my prayers, and that they would help me. And here it is, the end they promised. For the first time, I'm prepared to just let the current take me.

EPILOGUE

I left Papua New Guinea for Cairns, Australia. I was too sick to even walk. My throat felt on fire, I couldn't eat anything and I wondered what horrific jungle malady I had caught. My illness turned out to be a bad case of tonsillitis, a child's ailment. I had expected more, some kind of insidious disease meant to keep me in Papua New Guinea indefinitely. Instead, a doctor in Cairns cured me with penicillin and sent me on my way. I could go home now.

I wasn't sure where or what 'home' was, though. My childhood town? My parents' house where I'd grown up? My country of nationality? I couldn't definitively describe what I meant by the word, yet mysteriously, I knew I was returning to it all the same. I was going Home. The Chief back in Apowasi Village had made sure that the gods answered my prayers; he had ended my searching.

As soon as I got off the plane in Chicago, I knew that I'd broken my own rules. I was supposed to return as someone entirely 'new,' with an almost superhuman strength and confidence, or I wasn't supposed to return at all. I'd actually been prepared to sacrifice myself. Yet there I was back in Chicago, having deserted the entire challenge. I had given up. It was as if I were embracing the very weakness that I'd always been taught to loathe.

That's one thing we're never taught – giving up. These days, everything seems to be about competition and reward. Being better than the next person. Being admired.

Being worthy. I had spent most of my life thinking that elusive self-acceptance was something that could also be won. Yet in the end, it only came when I was willing to stop and look within. The irony was that I didn't need to *go* anywhere in the first place to find it. Yet women, in particular, seem to be taught that self-worth exists beyond them. They look for it in the makeup they wear, the men they date, the applause they receive. They must always please and be pleasing. Regardless of how intelligent, courageous or talented they might actually be, they learn to evaluate their lives based on others' accolades.

It's a hard cycle to break. For a long time, I was telling people only one version of my trip. This was the tough, 'Amelia Earhart' version, in which I stubbornly followed my childhood dream of being a lone woman, crossing the island of New Guinea. I braved whatever obstacles came my way. I endured the mosquitoes and mud and sweat of the jungle, crossed through crocodile-infested waters and scaled high mountains until – finally – I reached my goal: crossing the island. All my fears conquered. All tests met. Blissful success.

In truth, of course, it didn't really happen that way, which made for an embarrassing admission; better to say I went on an Amelia Earhart voyage of self-determination than a journey bred from years of desperation. But I was too scared of sounding like a failure by admitting the truth, and it took me a while to be satisfied with the fact that, regardless of the motivation for my trip, I had still accomplished something for myself. I *had* made it safely through New Guinea, and no one could ever take that away from me.

In the end, I see that there are many kinds of journeys, and one isn't necessarily any better than another – just different. Travel itself will always seem suspect to me; it is, after all, one of the most obvious forms of escapism. There is some other, better reality that we think we need, so we travel to find it. And maybe we do find it, or we don't, but the endless searches continue so that entire economies are fueled by our insatiable need for

Something More. I don't mean to criticize. I am as drugged by the idea as everyone else, and as stubborn about preserving it. Tahiti would have never been called Paradise were it not for a certain belief that a specific combination of ingredients – palm trees, welcoming smiles, sun and surf and tropical flowers – provides everything that we need. We forgive the delusion because it sustains us. We do feel better in these places, we reason, and they do make it hard to return to whatever was left behind.

But of course we must always return.

I ended up going back to graduate school at the University of Arizona to finish my master's degree in creative writing. Home became Tucson now, and Tucson meant seeing James again. He told me over the phone that he'd been waiting for me. It turned out that while I was gone, he'd been inspired to take a backpacking trip to Mexico. It was his first trip of this kind, and he returned after only a couple of weeks. The traveling life didn't agree with him; for one thing, it was too uncomfortable and sweaty. He couldn't stand the cheap bus rides through villages, crammed in with goats and chickens for hours on end, motion-sick kids vomiting on the seat beside him. On top of that, he'd missed his family and friends too much. He'd missed *me*.

I wasn't really used to being missed. I was used to my family's usual shrug: Kira will do what she has to do; I'm sure she'll be all right. But with James, who used to bring me to his Norman Rockwell family holidays, mistletoe Christmases with presents stacked to the living room ceiling, there was always a reason for him to return home. In fact, the returning was what it was all about.

I couldn't wait to see him again. He used to accuse me of being too reticent about my life, so now I was determined to tell him the truth about my trip (not the Amelia Earhart version of it), and to let him know how scared and lonely I'd been at times, and how I'd needed him. But, more than anything, I wanted to tell him that

I'd come back from it all, changed. It was as if I had peeled away the years of self-doubt and regret, and now only happiness remained, mysteriously playing out in all aspects of my life. I found myself more confident around people and less shy. I found myself more impervious to the opinions of others. But most importantly, I'd found the courage that would enable me finally to give myself over to another, and to take the risk of loving someone for the first time.

Once I got settled in Tucson, I called him and we made plans to go out. After months of wearing raggedy clothes through the jungles of PNG, of being covered in the sweat and dirt of the tropics, I was grateful for the chance to dress provocatively again. I wore a miniskirt, recalling the way James's eyes used to light up whenever he'd see me in it. We'd always had that energy between us, that passion and communion of gazes.

Yet, when he came to my apartment at last, I immediately knew that I'd gotten dressed up for a stranger. He wasn't the same. It was in his eyes. Something was gone.

Superficially, he looked as he always had. Brown hair neatly cut and swept back. A grand, almost ostentatious smile. Confident and content almost to a fault. As if life never scared him and never would. I had always envied that about him – the control he seemed to have over everything. I had once thought that maybe it could rub off on me, or that it was something he could parcel out, like a gift.

Awkwardly, we hugged. He still smelled subtly of expensive cologne – a scent that would linger in my hair and on my skin, reminding me of him. I tried to forget that something had seemed off in his eyes, and that there had been a distance I couldn't explain. A hesitation. I thought that maybe he was angry at me for breaking up with him and leaving him behind, so I told him I was sorry and that I'd missed him.

'I missed you too,' he said, still standing in my doorway as if afraid to come in.

'I thought about you when I was there.' I brushed his

hair back from his face, and he shut his eyes for a moment.

'Really?' he said.

'Yeah.'

'But you always could take care of yourself,' he said. 'You've got balls bigger than this room.'

It hadn't sounded like a compliment. He'd sounded annoyed. I was reminded of when Rob had said a similar thing, back when we'd first met in Ambunti. Only Rob had been impressed because I did the same kinds of crazy things that he did. With James, I had always known that he wouldn't be my 'Indiana Jones man-of-the-world,' gladly running off with me to Bangladesh. I'd convinced myself that that was what I liked about him. James didn't *need* to go to Bangladesh, even if he could have. He liked to stay put, and there was safety in that. Yet I also suspected that traveling scared him. Too many ifs. Too many ways for things to go wrong. I remembered how he used to cling to the routine of his life with a tenacity that had always fascinated me. In my own life, I distrusted any kind of normalcy, seeing it as the harbinger of bad times.

We ended up going to a local pub. As soon as we walked in, he put his hand around my waist and smoothed back my hair. The other customers looked fondly at us as if we were newlyweds. I wondered what it would be like to be a newlywed; surely there was nothing better . . . except, maybe, for a chopper ride over the jungles of New Guinea. Whenever I was nervous or scared I clung to that memory of Jim Mead, the chopper pilot. I found myself missing the world he had shown me. The dimness of the bar burst into the light of a New Guinea day, and I could almost feel the sun on my cheeks again, and Jim's voice exclaiming at the incredible beauty all around us. I saw the uninterrupted jungle flowing to the very edge of the horizon. I saw the glistening marshes, and the herds of rusa deer charging below us, reeds streaming from their antlers. I wondered how Jim was doing, and whether he still remembered me.

'You still do it,' a voice said.

'What?'

It was James. He was smirking at me. 'You drift away.'

I didn't apologize as I once might have. I wished I could somehow describe to him the world I'd seen. I thought he'd like it.

We chose a table. James spent a long time reading the snack menu, his eyes flitting anxiously at me. He wouldn't say anything, wouldn't ask me about my trip. After we finally ordered and the waiter left, I pulled my chair in closer to him.

'Is something wrong?' I asked. 'Are you angry at me for something?'

He acted surprised by my question.

'Tell me what's wrong,' I said.

'There's nothing wrong. Don't worry about it.'

But I worried. He didn't talk, and we ended up drinking our beers in silence. I soon noticed him taking me in – all of me – with his eyes. There was a strange, unabashed hunger in them I'd never seen before; it scared me.

'I really want to kiss you right now,' he said bluntly. 'I won't catch malaria or anything, will I?'

I smiled. 'You can't catch malaria from kissing a person, no.'

He motioned me toward him but I didn't move: he was too much like a stranger.

I asked him again what had happened, and now he started to tell me things in quick and vague terms. Something about his not getting into graduate school. How he felt like a perpetual student because he was twenty-eight years old. How he'd lost all 'perspective' in his life and was now on Prozac. He couldn't just run off to some New Guinea jungle to escape his problems, unlike some of the rest of us. ('Thank you,' I said.) He didn't know what the hell he wanted and didn't think anyone can ever really know.

'I think people know,' I said, 'but they won't listen to themselves or believe in themselves.'

'Oh, yeah?'

'I mean, for the first time in my life, I think I know what I want.'

'Well, you princess,' he said, glaring at me.

I sat back. Why this anger? Was he *jealous* of me? It had been an unspoken 'fact' of our earlier relationship that James was the one who was 'farther along on the road.' We'd even fallen into certain kinds of roles. I became the person in need of help, and James was the savior. But now – here I was sitting before him, having the audacity to offer advice. I could sense his resentment. He had not found whatever it was that he had wanted. And ironically, I had. Perhaps this galled him more than anything.

I saw James only a few more times after that. Though part of me didn't want to give up what was left of our relationship, he remained inexplicably impatient and belligerent and I soon admitted to myself that it couldn't work out between us. So much for the fairy-tale ending I had imagined with him.

We tend to love people who give us what we need. I realize that now. We tend to love those who go out of their way to help us or listen to us or make us feel safe. James had once tried to do all of those things for me, yet I wasn't sure if it had ever been genuine. Perhaps I had idealized him, like some fantasy character from my child-hood stories. I started to see that I had been attracted to him for the same reason I'd been attracted to Papua New Guinea: I was being offered some promise of salvation. But what I was looking for – what we all look for – can only start from within. All the happiness and love we crave. The self-acceptance. The contentment. Papua New Guinea taught me this.

I still receive an occasional letter from little Mastina in Blackwater Camp. I have a photograph of her hanging on my wall: she is smiling fantastically, her face covered with swirling white paint. I regularly send her and her sisters candy and chocolate. I send her parents US dollars, so they can send Mastina and the others to school. When there was a major drought, and the Fly River nearly dried up, I sent them packages of food. I wished there was more that I could do.

I haven't heard from Pastor Carl Waromi, but I'm told he's well. I still feel guilty when I think of him. I wish I could have brought him a camera crew or some newspaper coverage. When I got back to the States, I queried magazines and sent out photos, but to no avail. One editor told me that 'too much of this thing is going on all over the world.' And so Carl's 'silent war' is further silenced. When *Time* International did a brief piece on the OPM, I studied the photo of the guerrilla soldiers, looking for the men I'd met in Blackwater, men with whom I'd shaken hands, whose children had sat upon my lap.

Not long ago, I sent a camera and film to Mastina's parents. They take pictures now, sending me the rolls of film to be developed. Mastina is growing into a beautiful young woman in the photos, and she has a new baby sister: Kira.

I also have a photo of Mastina's little brother, who looks to be about six years old. He wears camouflage fatigues that are much too big for him, the pants legs rolled up several times. He holds his father's rifle with an expressionless face. Hanging on the wall behind him are two pictures his father painted: a giant white cross rising from a dark jungle, and a framed picture of Jesus wearing a crown of thorns, looking out with sad eyes.

I ended up graduating and moving from Tucson. Now I sit in an English doctoral program, doing what I've always loved to do: writing. I still travel, but I don't go to the really dangerous places anymore because I'm no longer in the game of proving anything to anyone. No more war zones or countries in the middle of coups. No more hanging out with guerrilla soldiers. My experience in Tari reminds me that there are no other 'better' worlds to be found beyond the one I'm already in. Knowing this with certainty gives me a great sense of relief, but also a feeling of increased responsibility. I want to learn all I can about the people and places I *do* visit now – though in the process being careful not to put others or myself in danger. Often, I go on easy trips with friends, or I opt for solo trips to unpopular destinations like Cambodia or Mongolia, which are 'safe' in my book, if not entirely comfortable. I'm hooked on the adventure and surprises of these distant places, and on the liberation of knowing that I can will my own life. I say I will go somewhere, and I do it. That simple. I've discovered that no one will ever be able to predict my life if I do exactly what I *say* I'll be doing. Why is it that we have so little faith in each other?

Which reminds me of a lunch I had with a feminist writer who had wanted to hear about Papua New Guinea. When she'd later asked me what I had planned for my summer, I told her about a three-week camping trip in the Montana Rockies.

'By yourself?!' she'd said.

'Yeah.'

'Aren't you scared?'

It struck me as an odd question. 'No.'

'Aren't you scared of the wild animals?'

Again, I was miffed by her question. Of course I would take some basic precautions with food, et cetera, but was I scared? 'No,' I said honestly.

'Aren't you worried about the other campers? You'll be out there by yourself.'

I was starting to understand why I never encountered any other woman travelers during my time in Papua New Guinea, and why the lone woman traveler is still seen as such an anomaly. When are little girls taught to fear camping by themselves? To fear wild animals or insects or mud? Or traveling on their own? They must be *taught* all of this, at some point, but I don't know when. Me, I was raised the same way my brother was, which is to say, I was raised like a boy. Be tough. Don't show emotion. Don't acknowledge pain. Nothing to fear when you know you can kick someone's ass. I was the little girl in pigtails who could fire a .44 Magnum by the time she was twelve. And though I hadn't found this a very ideal way to grow up, I think it did give me a different outlook on life. Among other things, I rarely caught myself thinking that I ought to be afraid to do something because I was a woman.

Which isn't to say that I don't get scared, or that I don't feel helpless. And I will certainly never forget Mozambique and what it taught me about the brutal reality that exists out there. But if I fear anything now, it's what I might be missing by not taking any chances and limiting the experiences of my life. By being scared of all the lions, tigers and bears that my lunch acquaintance had been worried about.

But when I get sick of thinking about all these things – and inevitably I do – I find myself remembering Mr Glen, sitting in his boat in the lagoon near the village of Suki. All he needed was a stash of warm beer and ramen noodles, and fish that would keep on biting. We talk of simplicity in the West, but I'm not sure we know what it means. For Mr Glen, it was the redemption of one day gliding peacefully into the next. Nowhere to go. Everything within view.

I will probably always envy him.

TAKE ME WITH YOU
A Round-the-World Journey to Invite a Stranger Home
by Brad Newsham

Shortlisted for WH Smith's Travel Book of the Year 2003

'For everyone who believes that travel is mostly about kindness and an open heart . . . Newsham brings back treasures that every wanderer might envy'
Pico Iyer

Someday, when I am rich, I am going to invite someone from my travels to visit me in America.

Brad Newsham was a twenty-one-year-old travelling through Afghanistan when he wrote this in his journal. Fourteen years later, he's a Yellow Taxi driver working in San Francisco. He's not rich, but he has never forgotten his vow.

Take Me With You is the compelling account of his three-month journey through the Philippines, India, Egypt, Kenya, Tanzania, Zimbabwe and South Africa as he searches for the right person – someone who couldn't afford to leave their own country, let alone holiday in the West. Newsham's story will change the way you think about your life and the lives of those you meet when you travel.

Who does he invite home? Read *Take Me With You* and find out . . .

'A terrific travelogue. He is a wonderful guide: observant, curious, witty without being clownish, open-minded without being gullible . . . Newsham offers an abundance of colour and telling detail'
San Francisco Examiner & Chronicle

A Bantam Paperback
0 553 81448 6

KITE STRINGS OF THE SOUTHERN CROSS:
Tales from the South Pacific
by Laurie Gough

'A travelogue tracing a life-changing journey across the globe
. . . Gough's experiences are never less than inspirational and
should encourage the would-be traveller to finally throw off
the shackles of the sofa and take flight around the world'
Wallpaper

Drinking the hallucinogen kava around a campfire, sleeping
in a California redwood or rolled up in a rug, hitchhiking
with an Austrian goatherd, fighting off a cab driver in Kuala
Lumpur, living in a Hare Krishna temple, taking an illicit dip in
Sylvester Stallone's pool . . . From a remote beach in the South
Pacific, Laurie Gough recalls her award-winning journey across
the globe.

On the Fijian island of Taveuni, she falls in love, but discovers
that even paradise has a darker side. In the Moroccan walled
city of Fez, she takes a trip on a magic carpet of a different
kind, on the back of a fanatical souvenir hunter's motorbike
she races across America and in Malaysia she is pursued by the
devil himself.

Lauded by *Time* magazine as one of the new generation of
intrepid young female travel writers, Laurie never shrinks from
the lessons of the open road. Funny, insightful and inspiring,
Kite Strings of the Southern Cross will appeal to free spirits and
armchair travellers alike – and to anyone who has ever dreamt
of trying to find heaven on earth.

'Gough is an enchanting guide . . . Passionate and poetic'
San Francisco Examiner

A Bantam paperback
0 553 81424 9

THE WRONG WAY HOME
by Peter Moore

When Peter Moore announced he was going to travel home from London to Sydney without stepping on to an aeroplane he was met with a resounding Why? The answer was a severe case of hippie envy: hippies had the best music, the best drugs, the best sex. But most of all, they had the best trips.

Knowing that his funds were woefully inadequate and that his chances of actually making it through such notorious hot-spots as the Balkans, Iran and Afghanistan were, in a word, slim, Peter was never one to err on the side of caution and over the next eight months (and twenty-five countries) he followed the trail overland to the East. It would prove to be a journey of exhilarating highs and, on occasions, frustrating lows, of diverse experiences – including the world's most expensive disco (in Albania), the bombed-out villages of Croatia, the opium fields of Laos, student riots in Jakarta, an all-night beach rave on a small island in Thailand – and memorable encounters with a wonderful cast of often eccentric, at times exasperating and, once in a while, overly amorous characters.

Funny, irreverent and acutely observed. *The Wrong Way Home* will strike a chord with anyone who has ventured on such a life-enhancing Grand Tour. It will also entertain (and perhaps alarm) all of those who love to read about such adventures but would never be fool enough to grab their rucksack and go.

'Inspirational stuff'
FHM

'Moore's a sharp observer of the bizarre . . . read, enjoy, escape'
Maxim

'Just don't read it in public if you'd prefer not to be caught laughing out loud'
Lonely Planet newsletter

A Bantam Paperback
0 553 81238 6

A SELECTED LIST OF TRAVEL WRITING AVAILABLE FROM TRANSWORLD

81341 2	**LIFE IN A POSTCARD**	Rosemary Bailey	£7.99
99600 9	**NOTES FROM A SMALL ISLAND**	Bill Bryson	£7.99
99786 2	**NOTES FROM A BIG COUNTRY**	Bill Bryson	£7.99
99702 1	**A WALK IN THE WOODS**	Bill Bryson	£7.99
99808 7	**THE LOST CONTINENT**	Bill Bryson	£7.99
99805 2	**MADE IN AMERICA**	Bill Bryson	£7.99
99806 0	**NEITHER HERE NOR THERE**	Bill Bryson	£7.99
99703 X	**DOWN UNDER**	Bill Bryson	£7.99
99858 3	**PERFUME FROM PROVENCE**	Lady Fortescue	£7.99
81424 9	**KITE STRINGS OF THE SOUTHERN CROSS**	Laurie Gough	£6.99
81479 6	**FRENCH SPIRITS**	Jeffrey Greene	£6.99
50552 1	**SPARRING WITH CHARLIE**	Christopher Hunt	£6.99
14681 1	**CASTAWAY**	Lucy Irvine	£6.99
14680 3	**FARAWAY**	Lucy Irvine	£7.99
14595 5	**BETWEEN EXTREMES**	Brian Keenan & John McCarthy	£7.99
81490 7	**BEST FOOT FORWARD**	Susie Kelly	£6.99
99841 9	**NOTES FROM AN ITALIAN GARDEN**	John Marble	£7.99
50667 6	**UNDER THE TUSCAN SUN**	Frances Mayes	£6.99
81250 5	**BELLA TUSCANY**	Frances Mayes	£6.99
81335 8	**THE FULL MONTEZUMA**	Peter Moore	£7.99
81238 6	**THE WRONG WAY HOME**	Peter Moore	£7.99
81451 6	**NO SHITTING IN THE TOILET**	Peter Moore	£6.99
81452 4	**SWAHILI FOR THE BROKEN-HEARTED**	Peter Moore	£6.99
81448 6	**TAKE ME WITH YOU**	Brad Newsham	£6.99
99852 4	**THE ELUSIVE TRUFFLE: Travels in Search of the Legendary Food of France**	Mirabel Osler	£6.99
81356 0	**ON PERSEPHONE'S ISLAND**	Mary Taylor Simeti	£7.99
81465 6	**BITTER ALMONDS**	Mary Taylor Simeti & Maria Grammatico	£6.99
81340 4	**WITHOUT RESERVATIONS: THE TRAVELS OF AN INDEPENDENT WOMAN**	Alice Steinbach	£9.99
99928 8	**INSTRUCTIONS FOR VISITORS**	Helen Stevenson	£6.99
81532 6	**CUBA DIARIES**	Isadora Tattlin	£7.99